D0172449

Taylor's Guides to Gardening

*Rita Buchanan and
Roger Holmes, Editors*

Frances Tenenbaum, Series Editor

HOUGHTON MIFFLIN COMPANY
Boston · New York · London 1992

Taylor's Guide to Gardening in the South

Copyright © 1992 by Houghton Mifflin Company

All rights reserved

For information about permission to reproduce selections from
this book, write to Permissions, Houghton Mifflin Company,
215 Park Avenue South, New York, New York 10003.

Based on *Taylor's Encyclopedia of Gardening,* Fourth Edition,
copyright © 1961. *Taylor's Guide* is a registered trademark
of Houghton Mifflin Company.

Library of Congress Cataloging-in-Publication Data

Taylor's guide to gardening in the South / Rita Buchanan, editor.
    p.   cm. — (Taylor's guides to gardening)
  Based on: Taylor's encyclopedia of gardening. 4th ed. 1961.
  Includes bibliographical references and index.
  ISBN 0-395-59681-5
  1. Landscape gardening — Southern States.   2. Plants,
Ornamental — Southern States.   I. Buchanan, Rita.   II. Series.
SB473.T38   1992   91-36756
712'.6'0975 — dc20   CIP

Printed in Japan

DNP 10 9 8 7 6 5 4 3 2 1

Drawings by Steve Buchanan

Contents

Contributors

Steve Bender. One of the South's best-known garden writers, Steve Bender is associate garden editor of *Southern Living* magazine and has written for *Southern Accents, Horticulture, American Nurseryman,* and *American Horticulturist.* A frequent lecturer at garden symposia, he serves as chairman of the Beautification Board in his hometown, Homewood, Alabama. He wrote the essays on lawn care and pests and diseases, contributed to the garden design essay, and served as consultant for the plant encyclopedia.

Rita Buchanan. With training that combines botany and horticulture, Rita Buchanan has worked and gardened in Texas, Colorado, Virginia, Connecticut, England, and Costa Rica. She was a founding editor of *Fine Gardening* magazine and now writes and edits for *The Herb Companion* and other publications. As a gardener, she specializes in herbs, fragrant plants, and flowers for cutting to make fresh and dried arrangements. She was a general editor for this book.

Steve Buchanan. An illustrator specializing in natural history subjects, Steve Buchanan does black-and-white drawings and color paintings of plants, gardens, birds, insects, and outdoor scenes. His work has appeared in *Horticulture, Garden Design, Fine Gardening, Scientific American, Organic Gardening,* the *New York Times,* and the *Herb Companion* and in several books. He illustrated this volume.

Roger Holmes. Currently a free-lance writer and editor, Roger Holmes was the founding editor of *Fine Gardening* magazine. He was the editorial consultant for *Taylor's Guide to Gardening Techniques* and acted as one of the general editors for this book.

Sam and Carleen Jones. A professor of botany at the University of Georgia from 1967 to 1991, Sam Jones has done extensive research and writing on the native plants of the southeastern United States. He is the coauthor, with the late Len Foote, of *Native Shrubs and Woody Vines of the Southeast* (Timber Press, 1989) and *Gardening With Native Wild Flowers* (Timber Press, 1991). Sam and his wife, Carleen, are the owners of a perennial plant nursery, Piccadilly Farm, at Bishop, Georgia, which specializes in hostas, Lenten roses, and other perennials. They have a large display garden at the nursery, and frequently write and lecture on gardening with perennials and using native plants in the landscape. They wrote the essay on gardening with native plants and served as consultants for the plant encyclopedia.

Sandra Ladendorf. A garden writer for more than twenty years, Sandra Ladendorf won a Garden Writers Association of America award for her book *Successful Southern Gardening: A Practical Guide to Year-Round Beauty* (University of North Carolina Press, 1989). She writes a monthly gardening column for *First* magazine and has published articles in *Horticulture, Fine Gardening, American Nurseryman,* and other magazines. She is currently president of the American Rock Garden Society and is also an avid grower of primroses, gesneriads, and orchids. She wrote the essay on the gardening year and contributed to the essay on garden design.

Glenn Morris. Trained in landscape architecture at North Carolina State University, Glenn Morris has worked as landscape design editor for *Southern Living* magazine and coordinated the editing of *Southern Living Gardening: Trees, Shrubs, and Ground Covers* (Oxmoor House, 1980). He is now a landscape designer and consultant in Greensboro, North Carolina, and continues to write about gardening in the South. He wrote the introductory essay for this book and contributed to the essay on garden design.

Felder Rushing. A seventh-generation Mississippian, Felder Rushing writes a twice-weekly garden column for his state's leading newspaper and has written for several magazines. He hosts both a live, call-in radio program and a television program and gives as many as two hundred garden talks a year all over the South. His first book, *Gardening, Southern Style,* won him the Mississippi Author of the Year award in 1988. He and his family have a cottage-style garden of mostly heirloom perennials and wildflowers in Jackson. He wrote the essay on old standbys and regional favorites.

Preface

Southern gardening has its roots deep in the past. You see the old traditions at Monticello, Salem, Williamsburg, Mount Vernon, and other historic sites. But southern gardening is changing fast. In the past decade or so, dozens of new nurseries have introduced an ever-expanding variety of perennials, shrubs, and other plants. Major cities and universities have created botanic gardens with beautiful demonstration plots. Garden clubs and plant societies now hold annual conferences at which hundreds of enthusiasts gather to share plants and information. Today's gardeners can choose from a stimulating diversity of plants and ideas. More than ever before, the South is a wonderful place to make a garden.

This book acknowledges the past but celebrates the present opportunity. Whether you were raised in the South or have moved to the region, it will help you choose plants that grow well and create a garden that compliments your home and provides year-round interest.

You'll want to try some of the native plants that add regional charm and character to a garden. Spring-flowering redbud and dogwood trees, sweet-scented wild azaleas and red-berried hollies, colorful Caroline jessamine and trumpet honeysuckle vines, easy-to-grow purple coneflower and Stokes' aster are just a sampling of the popular native plants featured in this book.

Rediscover the "old-fashioned" perennials and shrubs — the kinds of plants your grandmother grew. Old-fashioned plants such as shrub roses, fragrant winter honeysuckle, cheerful spring jonquils, and long-lived peonies are welcome in today's gardens.

Find a place in your garden for some modern introductions. Every year we see more kinds of hostas and daylilies and other perennials. Woody plants are making the news, too. Look for the latest hybrid crape myrtles, viburnums, and witch hazels. Compared to the parent species, many of the new introductions have larger flowers over a longer season, better growth form, and increased vigor and hardiness.

Plant shade trees for a cool retreat, and think about a vine-covered patio or arbor where you could hide away on a hot summer day. Use hedges to create private outdoor "rooms."

Instead of mowing a big lawn, substitute low-maintenance ground covers for grass on difficult slopes and banks and underneath groups of trees. This book recommends plants for all these situations.

There are many fine plants to consider, and many creative ways to arrange them. Let this book introduce you to the possibilities of southern gardening today. It can lead you to a lifetime of discovery and satisfaction.

How to Use This Guide

Planning ahead and choosing reliable plants are the keys to successful gardening. Whether you are starting a new garden or renovating an older property, this book can help you. It covers the basic principles of garden design and plant selection and presents a collection of outstanding landscape plants. You will find practical tips on how to grow healthy plants and inspiring suggestions for making your garden more beautiful.

Why a Regional Guide?

Unlike books that treat the United States as a whole, this volume addresses the special opportunities and challenges of gardening in the South. The contributors are all experienced horticulturists with firsthand experience of southern conditions. Of course, there are differences within the region, from north to south and from the coast to the mountains; we acknowledge those differences and explain how they affect gardens and plants. But in general, we feel that gardeners in Richmond, Atlanta, and Memphis have more in common with one another than they do with gardeners in other parts of the country.

How This Book Is Organized

There are three main parts to this book. The first part covers important aspects of gardening in a series of six essays. The center part presents 275 of the region's best garden and landscape plants. A section of color plates of the plants is followed by an encyclopedia of written descriptions, including information on use and cultivation. Several appendices make up the last part of the book.

The Essays

The introduction presents an overview of the South and its geography and discusses the climatic and historic influences that affect gardening in the region. The essay on garden design guides you through the process of evaluating your site and planning a garden that will meet your needs and express your personality. "Old Standbys and Regional Favorites" talks about reliable and popular plants that offer much pleasure in response for little care. The essay on native plants discusses the principles and practices of gardening with these plants and recommends a selection of outstanding natives. The lawn essay tells how to create and maintain a healthy carpet of green, and the final essay cycles through the gardening year, identifying the rewards of and tasks for each season.

The Plants

There isn't room in one book to present all the excellent plants that can be grown in southern gardens. In making choices, we selected plants with more than one noteworthy characteristic (nice foliage as well as flowers) that add interest to the garden in more than one season (flowers in summer, berries in fall). We looked for plants that tolerate difficult weather, require little maintenance, and are relatively free of pest and diseases. A majority of the plants are commonly stocked at major local nurseries; others are available through mail-order suppliers.

Most of the featured plants can be grown throughout the South. The encyclopedia entries indicate plants with limited tolerance for cold, heat, drought, or humidity. Following the system used by many southern garden writers, this book divides the region into four climate zones: the Upper, Middle, Lower, and Gulf or Coastal South.

Color plates

It is difficult to choose plants if you don't know what they look like. The color plates will give you a good idea of a plant's foliage, its flowers, and sometimes its growth habit. The plates are arranged by plant type: trees, shrubs, perennials, ground covers, and ferns and grasses. The short description that accompanies each plate includes the plant's botanical and common names, its height or spread, its bloom season (if appropriate), a comment on its uses or culture, and the page number of its encyclopedia entry.

Plant encyclopedia

If you are captivated by a color plate of a plant that is new to you, or if you need some basic information about a familiar plant, you will find it in this section. The encyclopedia contains descriptions of each plant shown in the plates as well as a number of additional cultivars or related species. The listings are arranged alphabetically by genus. If you do not know the botanical name, consult the index, where botanical and common names are cross-referenced.

Under each genus, you will find a general description of plants within the genus and comments on how to grow them. Descriptions of selected species and cultivars follow, including information about foliage and flowers, landscape and garden uses, the plant's origin, and any restrictions on where it can be grown. Many entries are accompanied by a drawing that illustrates a noteworthy characteristic of the plant.

Appendices

Dealing with pests and diseases is part of gardening. The appendix on controlling pests and diseases identifies common problems and discusses how to prevent or solve them.

The other appendices introduce some of the many excellent resources for gardeners in the region. "Sources of Seeds and Plants" lists a variety of regional suppliers. The public gardens appendix lists large and small gardens in several states. There is no better way to learn about plants and approaches to landscaping and gardening than to see them in person. The references appendix lists several books on southern plants and gardens.

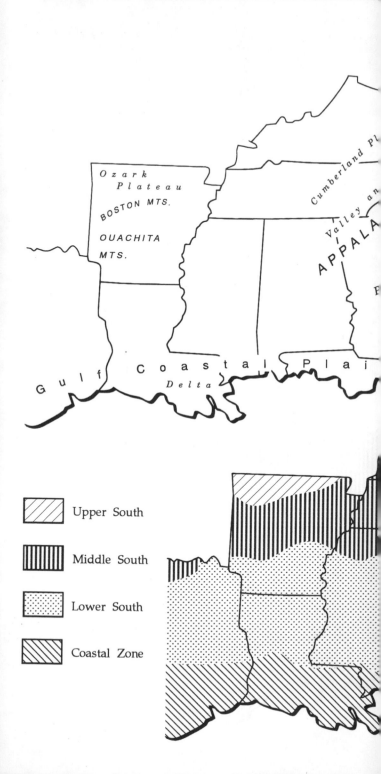

Ozark Plateau

BOSTON MTS.

OUACHITA MTS.

Cumberland Pl

Valley an

APPALA

P

G u l f   C o a s t a l   P l a i

Delta

Upper South

Middle South

Lower South

Coastal Zone

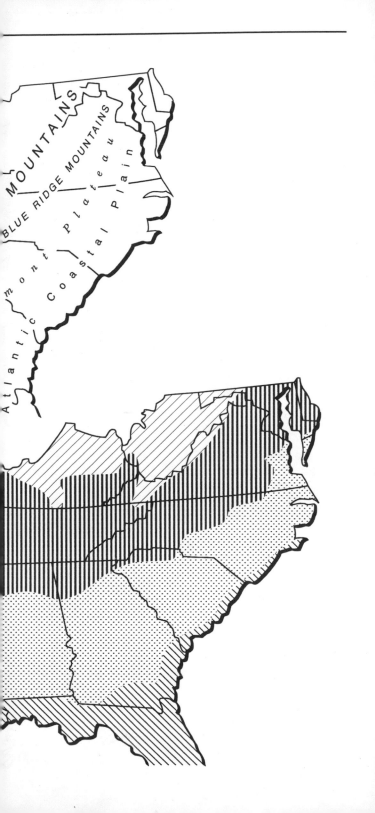

Introduction

The southern call to garden first sounds in childhood. It's kindled by days outdoors in the long barefoot season and evenings awash with the sweet scent of gardenias, the musky fragrance of bruised grass, or the dank odor of turned earth. Cherishing is part of it — tending an heirloom plant, such as a boxwood or camellia, which represents continuity with a fondly remembered person or place. The realization quietly impressed into the subconscious of youth, to be fully appreciated only later, is that you must make your place on the earth and honor it with your attention.

The South is inherently agrarian; agriculture is the historical basis of its economy. The region was farming long before settlement pushed into the heartland of this country. This tradition stamps southerners with an itch to grow things, and most native southerners are too recently removed from a rural setting — often no more than two generations — to be comfortable in a completely urban environment.

Granted, this inherent feeling for growing things doesn't manifest itself equally and universally, but something of it lurks in every resident. Perhaps the calling is no different here than in other parts of the country. As a practical matter, however, it has a broader effect because of the long growing season and the availability of land.

The Natural Richness of the South

The first person to write about the future of gardening in the South was Richard Barlowe. In 1584 he stated in a report to Sir Walter Raleigh that the soil of what would be North Carolina was "the most plentifull, sweete fruitful and wholsome of all the world," containing the "highest and reddest Cedars of the world." Barlowe came from England, where the timber had been cut long ago and every inch of land possible had been cultivated. From his perspective, the seemingly boundless mature forest of the New World — Carolina and Virginia — was a lush, untapped treasure.

There's little doubt that early explorers like Barlowe felt delivered into a botanical wonderland. In the 1500s, virtually the entire Southeast sprawled beneath a continuous canopy of trees. You could travel by horseback from the Atlantic Ocean to the Mississippi River and rarely see the sky except at river crossings or natural burnoffs.

In only a few places today can one experience the type of forest seen by the initial European settlers. There are a few swamps along the coast where cypress trees more than 1,200 years old have escaped cutting. Near Pensacola, the Naval Live Oak Preserve is a forest of these magnificent trees set aside to ensure a plentiful supply of live oak for shipbuilding. The need has long passed, but the forest exists much as it did nearly two centuries ago, a remnant spared from both axes and condominiums. Joyce Kilmer Memorial Forest, near Robbinsville, North Carolina, appears never to have served a sawmill. It holds tulip trees and Canadian hemlock of astonishing circumference and height — not just one, but many of them — a standing mature forest.

In the 400 years since settlement began, people have cleaned the southern landscape of all but vestiges of its original soil layers and forest cover. In this respect all regions of the South, no matter how you define them, are equal — they have been under the ax or plow. But the land regenerates quickly: fallow ground seems to sprout trees, and old farms and forests cycle back to productivity.

The South Is Really Many Places

Local conditions of the native landscape greatly influence gardening. It's all southern, but it has a lot of local flavor. To fully understand gardening in the South, you must not only distinguish the region from the rest of the country but also acknowledge differences between the several states, even within each state.

You notice that the landscape changes as you drive on the interstates, but you can really see the variation if you travel on the blue highways, the historical routes of commerce in the region. Whether you go from east to west or north to south, the topography and vegetation change considerably within a day's travel. The character and mood of the countryside vary as well, sometimes subtly, sometimes with a jarring, dramatic contrast to the landscapes just behind. The South is not one place but many.

The Ups and Downs of the South

If you were to start in Manteo, North Carolina, and follow U.S. 64 across the Tar Heel State, then cross Tennessee to Memphis, you would pass through the major geological provinces of the South. They are, from east to west, the Coastal Plain, the Piedmont, the Blue Ridge and southern Appalachian mountains, the Valley and Ridge, the Appalachian Plateau, the Mississippi River Basin and Delta, and the mountains of Arkansas.

These geological provinces present particular gardening challenges and opportunities. And even though local conditions — right in your own backyard — will determine virtually all of your major garden decisions, a grasp of the bigger picture can help you garden and travel with a more knowledgeable eye.

The Coastal Plain

The Coastal Plain curves along the Gulf and Atlantic coasts. The land is flat, the rivers are wide and winding, the native undergrowth is a broadleafed thicket. The major cities are ports, and the historic settlement pattern is one of large plantations.

From Biloxi north to Wilmington, the Coastal Plain is probably the most uniform horticultural province in the South. North of Wilmington and southwest of Biloxi, the landform is still the Coastal Plain, but with the shift in latitude you see more hardy plants in Norfolk and the eastern shore and more tender plants in Louisiana and Texas. In Texas, the temperature and rain patterns also affect the landscape. Houston is very much a Coastal Plain city, but Dallas belongs to the arid plains.

Coastal Plain gardeners (except those on the barrier island beaches) find the soil fertile and friable, the water table high but drainage good, the summer humidity suffocating, and the winter temperature very mild. The live oaks and magnolias are breathtakingly magnificent, and the southern indica hybrid azaleas capture the essence of Deep South perfume and opulence. Gardenias, too, are guaranteed.

This is where garden romance blooms strongest. The coastal South was the South first settled, where the oldest homes still stand, where the hold of the old South tugs unrepentantly. There is grandeur in both home and garden, and there is style as well, even in the smallest Charleston or Savannah courtyard.

The Piedmont

Inland and uphill from the Coastal Plain is the Piedmont — the name translates as "foot of the mountains." Heading upstream from the Coastal Plain, the Piedmont begins at a rise known as the fall line, the place where easy river navigation ceased because of rapids and waterfalls, and extends continuously from Alabama through Virginia. Its western boundary is the escarpment of the Blue Ridge Mountains.

The many rivers that cross the region provided sources of power early in its settlement, so the Piedmont became the industrial heart of the southern economy, eventually supplanting the agricultural Coastal Plain as the center of commerce and culture after the Civil War. Today the Piedmont cities of Richmond, Raleigh, Charlotte, Columbia, Greenville, and Atlanta make up the population center of the Southeast.

Once blessed with free-flowing rivers and hardwood forests, the Piedmont is in various stages of rejuvenation from constant use and abuse. One sad truth about the entire region is that the topsoil is gone. What's left has an extraordinarily high clay content, so it takes too long to get wet and too long to dry out. However, if you incorporate an organic amendment such as finely ground pine bark, well-rotted sawdust, or peat moss into the clay soil, you can create an excellent growing medium. It's also a good idea in most Piedmont soils to set plants at least 2 inches above the existing grade in an amended soil mixture. The heavy soils drain poorly, a condition conducive to rot, so planting high guards against drowning.

There's a great deal of opportunity to experiment with "marginal" plants in the Piedmont. For example, white pine does quite well in Richmond but becomes testy in Charlotte and shaky in Atlanta. In North Carolina, white pine is very dependable in Winston-Salem, but 25 miles east, in Greensboro, you shouldn't rely on it for long-term plantings.

Happily for gardeners, the topography of the Piedmont creates different microclimates. A north-facing site may be planted with shade-loving mountain plants; a sunny, south-facing site will support only the toughest sun-resistant species. Planting trees to create shade dramatically increases the number of species you can include in a Piedmont garden.

The Mountains

The Blue Ridge and southern Appalachians, two distinct but seemingly intertwined mountain ranges, are the central geologic features of the Southeast. Stretching from Alabama through Virginia, they reach their highest elevation along the North Carolina–Tennessee border, where several peaks surpass 6,000 feet.

The mountain climate can be severe. Winds can exceed 100 miles per hour, subzero temperatures regularly lock up rivers and roadways, and ice storms can be brutal. But the seasons are punctual, the soil is good, the rainfall is usually dependable, and drainage, predictably, is excellent.

Elevation affects both climate and plant associations. Climbing mountains is like driving north. Gardening in the mountains is like gardening in Pennsylvania or New Jersey. In fact, as long as your plants are cold tolerant, it is easier to establish a successful garden in the mountains than elsewhere in the South.

The Valley and Ridge

The geologic collision that lifted the southern Appalachians skyward rumpled the country west of it like corrugated board. The result is a series of parallel valleys and ridges that run from northeast to southwest. Knoxville sits in the Valley and Ridge province, as do Chattanooga and Birmingham. Rock is never very far below the surface here. The higher and steeper the site, the thinner the soil layers. Continual erosion has scoured the slopes, carrying the nutrient-rich particles to the valleys, which are lush; the mountaintops and hillsides are wooded in a gnarly kind of way.

In Virginia, Tennessee, and Kentucky, midwestern weather patterns pound the Valley and Ridge with severe cold. The dry, arctic winter air desiccates many broadleaf evergreens (rhododendron leaves curl up like cigars), and such southern favorites as the magnolia cannot thrive without protection and winter water — they freeze dry and winter burn terribly. However, the sweet soil and cooler air allow perennial bluegrass to thrive, the white oaks and American ash to tower, and crabapples to bloom dependably each year.

Farther south, in Alabama, the winter winds are blunted. Magnolias thrive and warm-season grasses such as zoysia and bermuda are chosen for lawns. Gardeners combine plants that wouldn't grow together elsewhere, such as bearded iris in a bed of mondo grass, lily of the nile and cinnamon fern, or boxwood and ardisia.

The Southern Appalachian Plateau

West of the Valley and Ridge, the land ascends to the southern Appalachian Plateau (called the Cumberland Plateau in Tennessee and Kentucky), a vast, sandstone-capped, water-carved "table" that comprises central Kentucky, Tennessee, and Alabama. Water has eroded the sandstone cap rock, dissolving the softer limestone beneath to create incredible waterfalls and spectacular river gorges. The limestone-sweetened soil of this region is superb for growing trees. The climate favors tree farming as well, and some of the nation's largest wholesale nursery tree farmers can be found on the Cumberland Plateau near McMinnville, Tennessee.

The Mississippi Delta

The Mississippi Delta is a wide floodplain that extends to varying widths east and west of the river's channel. Indisputably agricultural land, it is intensely farmed. Louisiana is nearly all delta. The river is the source of life for this area, having laid down the fertile soil layers and, until recent years, replenished them with periodic flooding.

The eastern bank of the Mississippi, at Memphis, Vicksburg, and Natchez, is a bluff of wind-driven soil accrued during the glacial epochs. The soil is fine and erodes easily. At the Vicksburg National Military Park, visitors are surprised to see the dramatic bluffs; they upset any preconceived notion of flatlands beside the river.

South of Natchez, the Coastal Plain and Delta begin to mix and the landscape starts to look like the low country of South Carolina. Indeed, from Baton Rouge west into Texas you drive through coastal swamp vegetation augmented by humidity that would choke moss.

Gardeners here and in New Orleans are limited by a high water table, summer heat, and humidity. Bulbs require special attention to prevent rotting. The mild temperatures extend the growing season for annuals by nearly two months, but fall color is subtle or nonexistent (compared with other regions). Live oaks are the preferred shade trees, but virtually any shrub can grow into a tree-size specimen. The southern indica hybrid azaleas can become huge living fences, exquisite with their habit of loose, informal growth.

The Ouachita and Boston Mountains
and the Ozark Plateau

Geographically, Arkansas is nearly a mirror of Tennessee, with the land rising higher as you move away from the Mississippi. The peculiar thing about Arkansas is the orientation of the mountain ranges, which trend east to west. The mountains, however, share the same rolling parallel valley arrangement found elsewhere in the South, and the rock formations are similar as well.

The soil of the valleys is plentiful and friable, the vegetation dominated by trees such as hickories and oaks. The vegetation on the mountains scratches existence from soil thinned by erosion, but it includes a mixture of trees nearly as diverse as that of the southern Appalachian Mountains.

Gardeners in Arkansas are challenged by drought. Although rainfall is evenly distributed throughout the year, the summer sun is hot. These factors, combined with the thin soil and rocky outcrops, make plant selection an exacting task. If you establish shade and are attentive to watering, you can grow essentially the same plants that grow in Birmingham. If reduced maintenance is a concern, however, it's best to choose drought-tolerant plants.

Learn What Grows Where

Knowing what grows around you is essential to gardening in the South. If you are a newcomer, please don't carry on as though you've just moved from across town. Take the time to watch the Romans and do as they do — in the garden. Lifelong residents know the area's horticultural legacy.

The three major, unalterable factors affecting gardening in the South are geology, latitude, and compass orientation of the site. Geology is where you stand — Coastal Plain or Mountains, Piedmont or Ridge and Valley. Latitude is how far south or north you are. Compass orientation is which way the land faces or what side of the hill you are on. You have to recognize these factors and the limits they impose on gardening choices. Almost everything else that affects plant selection and growth — water, soil, drainage, shade, sun, nutrients, and even slope — can be modified or enhanced as needed. But if you try to make Dallas be like Richmond, a gently intrusive neighbor may remark about your gardening intentions, "That won't do here."

Latitude

Latitude is the distance from the equator and is measured in degrees. This book covers approximately 10 degrees of latitude, a distance of about 720 miles from south to north. Latitude affects the length of the day, the length of the growing season, and average temperatures. For example, weather records show that Richmond has an average annual frost-free season of 218 days, Birmingham, 240 days, and New Orleans, 292 days. The average January temperatures for these three cities are 39, 46, and 53 degrees, respectively; the average July temperatures are 78, 80, and 80 degrees.

Obviously, the farther south you are, the longer the gardening season. Sun warms the soil both earlier and later in the year. However, the farther north you go, the longer the sun shines on summer days. On the longest day in summer, northern Virginia receives an hour more daylight than Florida does. This difference compensates for the shorter growing season.

The intensity of sunlight at different latitudes has a noticeable effect on plants. For example, if you plant a flowering dogwood in full sun in northern Virginia, it will grow dependably and develop its characteristic spreading branch structure. In Montgomery, a dogwood planted in full sun is not doomed, but it's certainly wasted. It will either burn up or grow huddled and misshapen as it battles the direct summer sun.

Hardiness zones

Garden books and catalogs often refer to hardiness zones, which are based on average annual minimum temperatures. Hardiness ratings measure the winter tolerance of plants — their ability to survive cold temperatures. The system may seem like a good way of choosing plants for different locations, but it's too simple to be very useful.

Long-needle or long-leaf pine provides a good example of the persnickety nature of plant tolerance and the imprecision of hardiness zones. Although it's listed as hardy in zone 7 (winter lows from 0 to 10 degrees F), this native of the Coastal Plain doesn't occur there naturally. In fact, long-needle pines are only rarely seen in zone 7, and then only in gardens. Ice, not cold, is the major factor restricting the tree's distribution. Ice storms, a common phenomenon in zone 7, deposit so much ice on the long needles of the pine that its branches snap. The tree's evolutionary adaptation to this climatic fact is to remain just south of the predictable ice-storm line.

The major problem with hardiness zone ratings, however, is their emphasis on winter cold. The southern climate demands hardiness to the other extremes of the year, summer heat and humidity. Many "hardy" plants that can survive southern winters just can't take the summer sun.

A number of southern garden writers divide the region into four climatic zones — the Upper South, Middle South, Lower South, and Gulf South (see map) — and rate plants according to their tolerance of heat as well as cold. This system is followed in this book's plant encyclopedia.

Local Influences Shape Garden Expression

The gardens of Virginia and Arkansas have little in common, even though they lie in the same hardiness zones and can include many of the same plants. Gardeners grow what the soil, climate, and topography permit. But community or cultural traditions also influence garden design. These traditions, understood by all residents, are tacitly preferred patterns of planting and palettes of plants.

The more you travel through comparable neighborhoods in the South, the more evident the differences in garden tradition and style become. The public and private gardens in city parks and around private homes look distinct and varied because they rely on different plants to serve similar design purposes. The Norway spruce that watches over a park in Washington, D.C., is replaced by a deodar cedar in Charlotte, a holly in Birmingham, or a southern magnolia in New Orleans. When you want privacy in Asheville, you plant a screen of white pines; in Charleston, you'd use Carolina cherry laurel, anise tree, or a camellia. In South Georgia or Florida, you may hide behind sweetbay magnolia or Japanese garden yew.

Charlotte has a tradition of planting large trees next to or in public rights-of-way. The folks there appreciate understory trees, but they realize that only canopy trees make the city distinctive. A Charlottean won't hesitate to plant one willow oak tree 30 feet away from another. Rows of these majestic trees line the city's streets like the pickets of a fence, and entire neighborhoods nestle beneath the high shade of closely planted large trees.

Macon, on the other hand, has (primarily through the perseverance of one individual) made the Yoshino cherry the talk of the town. Mobile is celebrated for its azaleas, which certainly do thrive there. Imagine how the landscape feels in these cities: in Charlotte, the foliage forms a high film; in Macon, the foliage is at eye level and doesn't necessarily provide shade; in Mobile, soft living walls of azaleas spread beneath the live oaks. Such garden traditions shape not only a city's appearance but the aesthetics of its gardeners as well.

Historic Influences on Garden Design

Courtyard gardens. The coastal towns of Charleston, Savannah, and New Orleans created courtyard gardens because of their architectural eccentricities and limited space. Charleston's houses were set sideways to take in prevailing breezes, Savannah was a thoroughly planned city, and New Orleans was the historic cultural melting pot of the South. The density of these cities, as well as that of Portsmouth, Norfolk, and Alexandria, left little room for a garden, so the garden became another room. These were the first townhouse gardens.

The garden as a symbol of civilization. In colonial times, gardens served as havens of order and discipline. Remember that there was little order beyond the courtyard walls of these port towns, and pigs, sheep, cows, horses, and chickens once roamed freely in the streets. The garden was a place of control and dominion, when the domain was very small indeed and the outside world very threatening.

Reconstructed villages such as Williamsburg and Old Salem are excellent laboratories for garden study. The garden at the Colonial Governor's Palace in Williamsburg was designed in a rigid, geometric style, symbolizing the authority of man over the savage new world; there is little doubt over who was in charge. Similar attitudes existed along the Mississippi Delta; again, the houses and gardens were expressions of civilization in a hostile environment.

Grand gardens. The grand historical gardens in Virginia and the low country of South Carolina illustrate magnificently the principles of formal design: symmetry, balance, and rhythm. These gardens are worth studying, to copy or adapt their ideas elsewhere. Following a style blindly, however, risks skewing the proportion, scale, or another element that made the original successful. Gardens need a context or setting, the frame that complements the garden picture; it may be the city of origin or the house to which the garden belongs. To look right, the garden has to fit its setting — a unity of garden, house, and environment that makes a statement.

Any successful garden, old or new, grand or small, has to be created with a particular vision for a particular place, time, and personality. Recreate just a portion of it and you may miss the unifying element. Unquestioning reproduction also begs the question of the gardener's original vision: When was the boxwood intended to be mature — when it reached 6 feet or 12? Perhaps the greatest garden visionaries in the South planted the live oaks at Boone Hall near Charleston and Oak Alley in Louisiana. What did a man who planted live oaks 100 feet apart see in his lifetime? What did he see in his mind?

From the Past to the Present

Today's gardeners, increasingly removed from the colonial heritage of garden design, respond more freely to the cues of the land and to personal preference. Their gardens may hint at historic styles or themes suggested by the environment and architecture, but they reject the rigid conformity of previous decades and explore possibilities borrowed from other locations, sometimes outside the region.

Most new gardeners start with practical concerns: to provide shade, to ensure privacy, and to create a sense of space. Once these requirements are met, you can start to choose plants and to carry on the southern garden trust. Plants and gardens create living ties between individuals and generations, a part of home you can take with you when you leave. Or leave with others when you go.

Garden Design

This book features many wonderful plants, but gardening involves more than choosing and growing plants. In fact, choosing plants isn't even the first step in making a successful home garden or landscape. Good landscaping starts with a plan designed to make the best use of the site and to meet the needs of the people who live there. After addressing these practical concerns, you can have fun selecting which plants to grow and how to arrange them.

Start with the Practical Concerns

A good design is the first step to starting or modifying a garden. You can tackle the design yourself or consult with a landscape designer or landscape architect whose work you admire. Working together, you and the designer can develop a master plan for the property. A professional will evaluate the site as a whole, itemize its problems and strengths, and come up with a practical and attractive plan for the site.

One concern in designing a landscape is making the space usable. Can you get to all the parts of the lot? Are there dry paths to walk on? Are there steep slopes that need to be graded or stabilized? Are there low spots that stay wet after a rain?

Is there enough open space, or do you need to remove some trees and shrubs? Ask questions like these as you examine the property and think about how you can use it.

Privacy and security are other concerns. Is there a private place to relax outdoors? Would you like to screen the house from passing traffic? Do you need a safe play area for children?

Parking, storage, and utilities need attention. Is there enough parking space for family and visitors? Do you need to store sports equipment or recreational vehicles? Are the utility meters and connections accessible to servicemen? Where can you put the garbage or recycling containers? Every successful landscape must accommodate these basic needs.

You may want to get help in solving these problems. Look in the Yellow Pages or classified newspaper ads for contractors who specialize in grading or retaining slopes, building fences and desks, laying patios or pathways, removing or planting trees, putting up fences, installing outdoor lighting, or doing other major jobs.

Once you have a master plan, implementing it depends on your time and budget. Chances are, you won't want to create or redo a landscape all at once. It's practical to spread the investment and effort over several seasons. For example, you may install a patio and plant slow-growing trees the first year, replace a worn fence with a mixed-shrub hedge the second year, and plant a flower bed or border the third year.

Do Some Homework Before You Shop for Plants

Plants add pleasing color and texture to the landscape. They also soften the lines and edges of buildings and hard surfaces such as walks, driveways, and patios. They moderate our environment by creating summer shade, wind screens, and noise buffers. Southern gardeners can select from a host of shrubs, trees, perennials, annuals, ground covers, vines, and bulbs. The possibilities are extensive and exciting. By choosing a variety of plants, it's possible here to have a garden that is interesting and floriferous throughout the year.

But there's much more to selecting dependable landscape plants than simply knowing what size, shape, and color they bring to a design. New landscapers often choose plants on a whim, based on their cost or how they look in the garden center. Many plants require special growing conditions. To determine whether a plant will work in your garden, compare its requirements to your conditions. Does it need damp soil or good drainage? Does it tolerate occasional dry spells or need frequent watering? Does it need sun or shade? How big does it grow, and how much room do you have for it? Some plants need special care. Before buying anything that needs regular maintenance, ask yourself how dedicated you are to tending plants. Good intentions alone do not get the job done.

Consult your extension agent

Visiting your extension agent is a good way to begin choosing plants. Every state has a university landscape and horticulture department that sends information and publications to off-campus cooperative extension offices manned by "agriculture agents." Though many agents are not trained in landscaping, the educators have very specific references on selecting landscape plants for your area. They also have printed information on planting and caring for landscape plants, insect and disease control, pruning and propagating, and other aspects of gardening. County or parish agents also have access to diagnostic and soil testing laboratories and to horticultural specialists. When you visit your county extension office, you may be surprised at the information and services that are available, often at no cost.

Identify the exposure of your site

One of the most important factors to consider is the number of hours and the time of day the sun will shine on a planting site. This is called the exposure of the site, and it's determined by compass orientation. Remember that the sun is directly south and overhead at midday.

In the South, a planting site that gets direct summer sun for at least three hours between 11:30 A.M. and 4:30 P.M. is considered a full sun location, regardless of shade earlier or later. If you plant against the south and west foundation walls, you're planting in a reflector oven. Select accordingly — only something as tough as a holly or juniper will do. Of course, you may have a south-facing site that is shaded. If so, it will be much cooler.

If your lot slopes, the compass direction of downhill is the orientation you must be concerned with. A north-facing slope receives the least amount of sun of any landform in this region. It is usually possible to grow plants associated with more northern locations on such sites because the most severely limiting factor — the summer sun — is mitigated by the landform.

Is there an ideal orientation? Perhaps, but usually you have to make do with what you have. There is, however, an ideal to work toward unless you want a full shade garden or full sun for vegetables or perennials. Two to three hours of sunshine daily, unless at high noon, will let you grow the widest variety of plants possible.

Test and prepare your soil

Soil conditions in the South vary from the infertile sands of the Coastal Plain to the eroded, depleted clays of the Piedmont and the rich sweet loams of the Cumberland Plateau. Your extension agent can describe the soils characteristic of your area and give advice on standard soil treatments. The soil on your lot, though, may not be typical of the region. It may be worse than normal if the topsoil has eroded or was stripped away by the developers who built your house; or it may be above average if the site has been favored by nature and human care.

In general, it's a good idea to have your soil tested and apply lime as recommended by the lab. If your soil lacks nutrients, you can choose from a range of synthetic and natural fertilizers and apply them according to label directions. Nearly all soils benefit from the addition of organic matter, such as composted pine bark chips, aged manure, peat moss, or homemade compost. Mix a generous layer — 3 or 4 inches deep — of organic matter into the soil for flower beds and borders. Use a little less for shrub or ground cover plantings and just an inch-deep mulch on the surface where you plant trees.

Porous mulches, such as pine straw, shredded bark, or the new landscape fabrics, layered over the surface of newly prepared soils and around plants will help in many ways. Mulches help keep weed seeds from sprouting, prevent soils from crusting and drying, and make the landscape neat. Perhaps most important, they act as a thermal blanket, keeping the soil from going through rapid fluctuations in temperature. They cool soil in the summer and help prevent root damage when freezes follow sunny days in the winter. Organic mulches are something of a chore to maintain — you have to add extra material every few years. But they are attractive in the landscape and condition the soil as they decay.

Plan for growth

One of the questions to ask when you're considering plants is, How big will this particular plant grow? Unless you've done a lot of homework or seen a mature specimen in a garden or arboretum, it's hard to guess what those cute nursery babies will turn out to be. Every gardener has made an impulse purchase and regretted it later. Know that the neat little honeysuckle you bring home in a gallon can will quickly explode into a shrub 8 feet tall and equally wide. It will also produce suckers around its base. Be sure to plan ahead and space plants far enough away from the house, driveway, patio, paths, and fences. Also, space plants far enough apart from one another so that each can achieve its natural size and form.

Designing with Plants

Use plants to complement the house

Consider the house itself when you're thinking about the garden design. A formal garden will reflect the dignity of a formal house; informal plantings are better suited for a rustic home. Compare the size of the house to the nearby trees and shrubs. Large trees and shrubs can "bury" a small, single-story home; small bushes look silly next to a large two-story house.

Look at the basic landscape plantings around the house. They are not permanent. Most foundation plantings need to be replaced or renovated every 10 to 15 years. Trees grow and change a sunny spot to shade. Attractive shrubs get taller, lose their lowest limbs, and become unattractively leggy. A landscape is always evolving. If Burford hollies are growing over your windows or if once-small junipers by the front door are now 20 feet high, pull them out.

Many landscapers think it's time to replace traditional foundation plantings with some fresh alternatives. Instead of a "green worm" hugging the foundation, consider planting a mixture of evergreen and deciduous shrubs and perennials. Or try using a single specimen plant, chosen for its unusual shape or other outstanding feature, to accent the entryway or front door.

Plan for reduced maintenance

Good design produces a garden that's practical as well as pretty. Plant trees, for example, on the hot, west side of a patio but not near a pool, where leaf litter and shade can cause problems. Where a head-high screen is needed, choose midsize rather than large shrubs to reduce pruning chores. For landscape color, consider long-blooming, disease-resistant shrub roses instead of their fussy cousins that make good flowers for cutting.

Consider year-round interest

Select plants that provide desirable features over a relatively long period of time. Some flowering shrubs, for example, are lovely for a couple of weeks in the spring, but their foliage is uninteresting for the remainder of the growing season. For example, a mass planting of azaleas offer a single short season of color, then become ho-hum lumps of green the rest of the year.

Choose plants that have varying seasons of color to make a display over many months. Try following winter daffodils with spring iris, then daylilies and cannas in summer and asters in fall. With shrubs, let mahonia and early spirea lead into azaleas, then viburnum and roses, hydrangeas, and ornamental grasses in summer. For fall, use *Camellia sasanqua,* overlapped by *Camellia japonica* and witch hazel for winter glory.

Extending the season by selecting early, midseason, and late varieties is an excellent idea, whether you are purchasing dogwoods, camellias, deciduous azaleas, irises, evergreen azaleas, daffodils, primroses, lilies, or a number of other plants. For example, if you plant several pinxterbloom deciduous azaleas, you will have one burst of airy pink and white bloom that lasts a week or two, depending on the temperature at the time. However, if you select among the species and hybrid deciduous azaleas, you can have up to five months of flowers, from *Rhododendron canescens* in late March through the plumleaf azalea, *R. prunifolium,* in July and August.

Add color with flowers

Colorful flowers can be used as accents, in repeated groups, or in massed plantings. In general, annuals provide a longer flowering season, whereas perennials combine a shorter season with more interesting foliage texture. Many gardeners combine annuals and perennials to have both a long season and lower maintenance. Adding a fence, sculpture, birdbath, or other "hard" feature or a showy shrub, such as a dwarf yucca or rose, sustains the appeal of a flowerbed when nothing's in bloom.

Although it's usual to emphasize flowering plants, don't forget the "blenders" — plants that unify a design. The gentle forms and subtle shades of hostas and ferns can be used to calm a clash of color. Both shade-lovers work well in drifts, although each has varieties that also make outstanding specimen plants.

In a sunny garden, grays are effective blenders. A number of artemisias serve well. Low varieties like *Artemisia* 'Silver Mound' are suitable for the front of the border. 'Silver King' is a taller form. Perhaps the best in the South is the still larger and relatively new 'Powis Castle'. Magic in combination with pinks, blues, and mauves, it is both heat- and drought-resistant.

Use hanging baskets, window boxes, and planters to enhance a porch or patio. Remember that in the heat of summer, they will have to be watered once — perhaps even twice — a day. Buy planted containers or create your own. Imaginative combinations of plants are popular today. Pot a sleek hosta with a fluffy fern for the shady side of your deck; it's an attractive combination. But if you make it a variegated green and white hosta and add white impatiens, suddenly the planting is exciting, and it will remain so throughout the growing season.

Fall and winter color

Berries. Colorful berries and fruits, as well as seedpods, add interest to a garden in the fall and winter. Shiny red, blue, or black berries adorn many evergreen and deciduous shrubs and trees, including hollies, nandinas, beautyberries, and mahonias. Most berries are attractive to birds (fascinating landscape visitors in themselves), and many are edible for gardeners as well.

Leaves and bark. Fall foliage adds an important color element to a garden. Oakleaf hydrangea leaves turn a rich wine. Ginkgo tree foliage becomes bright yellow, then the leaves all drop at the same time. Sweet gums, maples, crape myrtles, and a host of other trees, shrubs, and perennials add color to the autumn scene.

As the deciduous trees and shrubs lose their leaves, the intriguing patterns of barks become more important. The mottled, smooth, colorful trunks of mature crape myrtles beg for a caress. The older the tree, the more decorative the bark. Shagbark hickories, green-stemmed kerrias, yellow- or red-stemmed shrub dogwoods, snake-bark maples, leucothoes, and fothergillas all add color and textural interest to a winter garden.

Evergreens. Evergreen plants come in a wide range of greens as well as blues, pinks, reds, yellows, and an astounding array of variegated patterns and combinations. Many evergreens change color from summer to winter, often turning from green to red, purple, or brown as the days get shorter and cooler.

Evergreen forms and textures add beauty to the winter landscape. Look at your garden in December and see where obvious holes could be enhanced by the addition of a dwarf evergreen, a variegated daphne 'Carol Mackie', or a choice pieris. Perhaps the wall above the garage door or an unsightly fence could be improved by training the evergreen *Clematis armandii* over the area. Its glossy, leathery leaves are attractive year-round, enhanced by pink or white flowers in the spring.

Lawns

Lawns occupy such a large proportion of most lots, and tending them can take so much time and effort, that it's worth thinking carefully about how much lawn you need and what you need it for.

The lawn as a design element

From a design standpoint, the lawn's most important function is to serve as a unifier. It links a garden's major elements, such as trees, shrubs, flower borders, walks, and pools. It's also a transporter, both visually and physically, taking you from one area of the property to another. And it can enhance the other plantings by establishing interesting textural and color contrasts. You can juxtapose, for example, the rigid formality of a closely cropped lawn with a naturalistic woodland planting of dogwoods and native azaleas. Or you can play off the light green of a centipede lawn against the rich, dark greens of English ivy, cast-iron plants, or Burford holly.

The size of a lawn

Your lawn's size depends on several factors, not the least of which is your budget. If you're establishing a new lawn, you'll soon learn that laying several thousand square feet of sod can be a pricey proposition; you may opt for a smaller lawn bordered by ground cover or natural areas. The size of your family also affects this decision. Children enjoy playing on spacious lawns, but couples and single adults often find small lawns more appealing. Don't forget that the amount of maintenance is directly proportional to the amount of grass. The larger your lawn, the more time you'll spend mowing, fertilizing, raking, and watering.

The shape of a lawn

Shape is something most people don't connect with a lawn. In fact, in many neighborhoods lawns are essentially shapeless, blending into one another in a continuous strip of green down one side of the street. This is unfortunate, for a well-defined lawn can be a dynamic part of your overall design. One way to define your lawn is to place planting beds between it and the adjacent lawns. Edging your lawn with brick will further emphasize its form.

Keep topography and architecture in mind when deciding on the shape of your lawn. In small Savannah courtyards, for example, where the ground is flat and houses tend to be formal, a rectilinear lawn is appropriate. However, in suburban Atlanta, where rolling hills and huge shade trees foster a more natural, less restrictive atmosphere, an undulating, curvilinear lawn may be a better choice. A curvilinear lawn is more difficult to design, as curves are harder to work with than straight lines. As a result, people often end up with a series of awkward squiggles snaking their way across the ground instead of pleasant, broadly sweeping curves. Try using a garden hose to outline the proposed boundary of the lawn. This way, you can "eyeball" the entire curve and adjust it so that it flows smoothly.

Plan ahead for easier care

A well-thought-out design is more than aesthetic; it also reduces maintenance. If you'd rather spend your weekends sipping lemonade by the pool than raking clippings by the sidewalk, take heed of the following design tips.

• Minimize the number of sharp corners in the lawn so that you can mow the lawn smoothly instead of constantly stopping and backing up.

• Install a brick "mowing edge" level with the lawn along its borders. You can run the mower's wheels on the brick and edge the lawn as you mow.

• Place mailboxes, lampposts, and bird feeders in the middle of planting beds, not the lawn, so that you won't have to mow or edge around them.

• Leave sufficient space between trees in the lawn so that you can easily mow between them. If possible, place trees in a single mulched bed so you don't have to mow between them at all.

• Don't grow grass on steep slopes that are difficult and dangerous to mow. Instead, plant an appropriate, low-maintenance ground cover. For a sunny bank, consider ajuga, Asian jasmine, cotoneaster, juniper, mondo grass, or wintercreeper euonymus. For shady slopes, give English ivy, pachysandra, liriope, mondo grass, or common periwinkle a try.

• Don't plant grass in heavy shade — it won't thrive. Pave or mulch the area or plant a shade-tolerant ground cover instead.

Old Standbys and Regional Favorites

Experienced gardeners know that the easiest way to succeed with plants is to choose ones that are well adapted to the conditions of both your region and your site. To be dependable in the South, plants need to tolerate high temperatures and humidity in the summer, often combined with periods of drought. Then they must survive the wildly fluctuating temperatures of the relatively sunny, wet, mild winters. Other regional characteristics are strong seasonal winds, a lack of protective snow cover, and a range of soil types.

Despite these challenging conditions, hundreds of woody trees and shrubs, vines and ground covers, bulbs and herbaceous perennials, not only thrive in the South but also become more beautiful year after year. It's possible to have a landscape that offers six or more distinct seasons of color and texture, using plants that are perfectly at home in the South and require little or no special care. Many outstanding plants around us have been through the test of time and place. Many tolerate adversity; some can even take outright neglect.

Common plants with problems. Remember that the most common plants are not always the best plants. All too often, the selection of plants at retail garden centers emphasizes those that are easily mass produced, look good in containers, and provide "instant gratification" in the landscape. Researchers estimate that as few as forty plants represent more than 80 percent of sales in urban areas — a far cry from the great diversity of plants that could be available. Some of these so-called top forty plants are almost guaranteed to have problems adjusting to the wide range of conditions in which they are forced to grow. Such popular plants as red-top photinias, hybrid tea roses, azaleas, Bradford ornamental pears, and certain selections of Japanese hollies are quite vulnerable to root problems, winter damage, insect attack, and disfiguring diseases. Before investing money, effort, and time on plants for your garden, make sure they aren't prone to pests or cultural problems and that they have a history of performing well in gardens in your area.

Rediscovering old standbys. Today's gardeners don't have time to nurse marginal plants, so landscapers and plant breeders alike are looking at the survivors, the tried-and-true favorites that have shown great tolerance of our conditions and needs. All around us are older landscapes filled with plants from "grandmother's garden" which are making a strong comeback for their hardiness and easy care. An example is the althea (*Hibiscus syriaca*), an especially hardy drought- and cold-tolerant shrub that offers a long season of bloom (even in the shade), interesting winter seed pods, and nice foliage texture. It is available in a wide range of flower colors, including blue, red, white, pink, and combinations, in both single- and double-flowering forms. Because it is so tough, althea is now the subject of breeding programs to increase the size and number of flowers and to develop several sterile selections that don't self-seed all over the landscape. In short, the attention to old-fashioned favorites has centered on finding the tough ones, then improving them to suit contemporary needs.

These old standbys from southern gardens also have regional appeal — they offer a satisfying feeling of place. Recognizing and using reliable, time-honored plants is part of the widely acclaimed "new American Garden style." New American gardens combine trees and shrubs, ground covers, mulches, flowers, and a reduced turf area and rely on regional plants and materials — both native and well-accepted imports — for lower maintenance, comfort, and style.

Large Trees

Until fairly recently, much of the southeastern United States was a vast forest. Left alone, many contemporary landscapes would quickly be covered by weeds, followed by shrubs and then trees, in what is called natural succession. There's a lesson in this for gardeners who want to have a naturalistic or low-maintenance landscape.

Large trees set the stage for the landscape and should be given top priority early on in planting. Trees can reduce landscape chores by taking up space normally sodded in high-maintenance turfgrass, and established trees can be left alone with little care. Since tree roots have a tough time finding life-giving air in moist or heavy soils, most end up fairly shallow — in the top few inches of soil. For this reason, and because of our predictable summer droughts, it's difficult to grow grass beneath the shade of large trees. Ground covers and natural mulches are more successful. Natural leaf-litter mulches and woodland plants such as ferns, phlox, shade-loving shrubs, and vines can give a mysterious and earthy effect to a wooded lot.

Popular large evergreen trees in southern gardens include pines, cedars, magnolias, live oak in the Lower South, and hemlock farther north. These evergreens cast shade year-round. Deciduous trees, including the many excellent native oaks, drop their leaves in winter, letting in warm sunshine. Their fall colors offer seasonal drama as well as a welcome source of mulch and compost for shrubs and the flower garden. Shade trees with excellent fall colors include the ancient ginkgo, most of the maples, sweetgum (worth growing in spite of its round, spiny seedpods), and the native black gum, which turns a brilliant red. The baldcypress, a deciduous conifer, has ferny foliage that turns a rusty red before shedding neatly in autumn. Although swamps are its native habitat, it grows very well on dry sites.

Small Trees and Large Shrubs

Small-growing trees and large, tree-form shrubs can be planted as accents, in groups, or as a midlevel understory beneath larger trees. They often serve as screens or hedges or, in rows, as see-through baffles. When set close together and mulched, they are much easier to mow around than individual plants are.

Deciduous trees. Small deciduous trees include shade-loving dogwood and buckeye, sun-loving vitex, redbud, silver bells,

Japanese maple, star magnolia, purpleleaf plum, and ornamental flowering fruit trees such as flowering peach and plum, pear, cherry, and crabapple. Large deciduous shrubs often used as small trees include mountain laurel, sumac, fig, crape myrtle, mock orange, the popular old althea, hawthorn, heavy-berried deciduous holly, many viburnums, winter-blooming witch hazel, and the incredibly sweet-smelling winter honeysuckle. It's enough to keep any gardener busy with choices.

Evergreens. In the winter, take a drive through deep woods, where the glossy southern magnolia contrasts with pines and the tan winter foliage of American beech, and notice the native cherry laurel. This large evergreen shrub makes a superb tall hedge in sun or shade and rarely suffers from the leafspot diseases often associated with red-top photenias. Other large native evergreens are the wax myrtle, star anise, and both the yaupon and dahoon hollies.

Some very fine non-native evergreen shrubs, grown to maturity, become handsome specimens, tall hedges, or corner plantings for two-story homes. For shady gardens in the Upper South and higher elevations, few plants can rival the magnificent rhododendrons, while in warmer areas the winter-blooming camellias are excellent choices. Outstanding holly selections include the heavily berried Foster hybrids and Burford holly. Other choices are the beautiful pyracantha, huge Chinese photinia (*Photinia serrulata*), privet, Japanese ligustrum, and the exotic Hollywood juniper.

A tall grass. One of the best and most often grown ornamental grasses is *Arundo donax*. This grass grows as tall as a shrub and plays a similar role in the landscape. Its plumelike flower stems reach 12 feet or more. The new growth in early spring and summer of the popular white-variegated form, commonly called striped cane, is particularly showy. Unlike bamboo, this grass is a moderate spreader, usually staying within a few feet of where it is first set out.

Medium Shrubs

Too often, when a head-high or slightly taller shrub is needed for a hedge or barrier, gardeners set out large shrubs for an instant effect. The result is usually a need for constant pruning. However, there are quite a few perfectly suitable evergreen and deciduous shrubs that, when set out with room to grow, quickly reach just the right size and don't need more than an occasional shaping. Shrubs of medium height are often placed in foundation plantings around corners, either singly or in groups.

Evergreen shrubs. Two of the most popular medium-height

evergreen shrubs, both seen across the entire South, are glossy abelia, with its summer-long flowers that attract humming-birds and butterflies, and the quintessential nandina, a four-season informal plant for spring flowers, summer texture, fall and winter color, and berries. Other evergreen favorites seen throughout the South are dwarf Burford holly, indica azaleas (Lower South) and Glen Dale azaleas (Upper South), rhodo-dendrons, shade-loving acuba, slow-growing common box-wood (*Buxus sempervirens*), and the somewhat cold-sensitive banana shrub (*Michelia figo*).

Flowering deciduous shrubs. Long-popular deciduous shrubs for spring flowers include flowering quince, wiegelia, forsythia, native pinxterbloom azaleas, barberry, sweet shrub (the fragrant, native *Calycanthus*), sweet olive, and both rab-biteye and highbush blueberries. The blueberries also have delicious, pest-free summer fruit and outstanding fall color that holds over into early winter.

Spireas have been mainstays for many years, although they sometimes have sporadic flowering in mild winters and in the Lower South. The earliest spirea is the single-flowered "baby's breath" (*Spirea thunbergii*), followed by Reeves spirea (*S. can-toniensis*), perhaps the most elegant of the spireas, with grace-ful, arching limbs and buttonlike double flowers. Similar to Reeves, only a little larger and later-blooming, is the bridal wreath spirea (*S. × vanhouttei*), whose limbs are more upright and may reach 6 feet tall or more. The white-flowering spireas may be planted by themselves, as specimens or in hedges, or together for a longer flowering effect. They also make excellent companions to azaleas and other spring bloomers.

Medium-height, summer-flowering deciduous shrubs in-clude some of the larger shrub roses, hydrangeas (especially the shade-loving native oakleaf hydrangea), and dwarf crape myrtles. One of the most outstanding shrubs for fall color is the winged euonymus; it is often called burning bush for its brilliance. Another showy shrub for fall color is the native beautyberry, with long stems studded with tight clusters of magenta berries. Though beautyberry is hard to find com-mercially, it is easily rooted from stem cuttings taken in the late winter.

Medium-size grasses. Two ornamental grasses of note can both be used effectively as medium shrubs. Pampas grass, which is perhaps too popular in spite of its being only half hardy in the Middle South, is widely planted for its tall, white, plumelike panicles. A much more dependable grass for all parts of the region is the slightly smaller maiden grass (*Miscanthus sinensis*). Maiden grass turns tan at the first frost but is never damaged by cold. Like pampas grass, it is very tolerant of heat and drought. Instead of plumes, its flowering stems make arching, feathery clouds over the entire upper half of the plant. Zebra grass, a variant of maiden grass with unusual yellow bands across its leaves, is often found in old gardens in rural towns throughout the South.

Small Shrubs

Evergreen and deciduous shrubs under 4 feet tall are perfect for foundation plantings, for traffic control in the landscape, and for bordering larger plants. They also work very well in flower beds, providing out-of-season structure as well as unusual color. Small shrubs come in a large array of shapes, colors, flowering habits, and textures. Some are dwarf forms of larger plants: there are dwarf abelias, dwarf gardenia, and several forms of dwarf nandina, all of which mimic their larger parents. Occasional shearing keeps most small shrubs within bounds. Some get out of scale with age but can be rejuvenated by heavy pruning.

Small evergreen shrubs. Perhaps the most widely sold small shrubs are diminutive Kurume azaleas, which are compact and have small leaves. They are often planted at the base of larger azaleas for contrast. Other evergreen shrubs commonly used as foundation plantings are dwarf yaupon holly, Carissa holly, and the lush green but terribly spiny Chinese holly. You'll see them at nurseries, but think twice before planting the various Japanese hollies. For the most part, they are beautiful but not dependable. When planted in the heavy, compact soil often found around buildings, they get root rot. They then suffer from drought and "brown out" in midsummer.

Sophisticated gardeners are bored with them, but generic green boxwoods, spring-flowering Indian hawthorns, and informal, spreading junipers have traditionally been popular small evergreen shrubs. One of the most astounding shrubs seen in all quarters is the almost garish golden euonymus, an eye-catching plant best used in masses against gray backdrops or kept in the flower bed, where its almost unbearably bright foliage is more at home.

Deciduous shrubs. Small but showy deciduous flowering shrubs include the double pink-flowering almond, crimson pygmy barberry, red 'Anthony Waterer' spirea, and polyantha roses — perhaps the most dependable small flowering plants for the landscape. Polyanthas such as 'The Fairy', 'China Doll', and 'Margo Koster' are disease-free, all-season bloomers that generally stay under 3 feet tall.

Unusual shrubs. Two of the most interesting but misunderstood shrubs, both natives, are the prickly pear cactus (*Opuntia humifusa*) and the compact, soft-tipped forms of yucca (*Yucca gloriosa*). Both contrast in form and texture with the more familiar gumdrop-shaped shrubs; both are hardy in all parts of the South; and both are easily maintained, in sun or shade, in low-maintenance, droughty gardens. The prickly pear, our only native cactus, has large, bright yellow or orange flowers followed by attractive purple fruit. Yucca has tall, branched stalks of fragrant, white, edible flowers that jut skyward from spring until frost. These two plants, long popular in older gardens, deserve more attention in new landscapes.

Vines

A selection of favorite vines can provide exceptional service when trained on arbors, fences, gates, or trellises. Vines soften lines, cover walls, and shade patios from glare and heat. They can be grown in narrow spaces, and their roots can be several feet from where their foliage or flowers are needed. But vines are a mixed group. Some climb by means of clasping or twining aerial tendrils. Others must be tied or trained by hand. Some have tenacious roots that can rot wood or peel paint. Quite a few are invasive and must be contained to be kept within bounds.

Flowering vines. The showiest flowering vines are clematis, wisteria, thornless Lady Banksia and other climbing roses, and several natives, including Carolina jessamine (commonly called yellow jasmine), crossvine, trumpet creeper, and coral honeysuckle. All have their places in the landscape; each has its peculiar needs and habits.

Of the honeysuckles, the most invasive and cursed vine short of kudzu and poison ivy is the evergreen, sweet-smelling Japanese honeysuckle (*Lonicera japonica*), an escapee from cultivation that has overwhelmed the South. Its value as a fantastic ground cover and container plant is overshadowed by its ability to get out of control quickly and take over nearby shrubs and ground covers. Still, when contained, it is handsome, sweet, rugged, and pest-free.

A much better honeysuckle is the native coral or trumpet honeysuckle (*L. sempervirens*), a noninvasive vine with sprays of carmine red tubular flowers. Often in bloom by late February, it is an important early source of nectar for hummingbirds migrating north from South America. Coral honeysuckle is a woodland plant that flowers in moderate shade or full sun. Its yellow fall color adds to any landscape.

Grapes. Self-pollinating varieties of muscadine grapes are natives that have good yellow fall color and bear much more consistent and heavy crops than bunch-type grapes. However, all grapes require heavy annual pruning to produce well. Most gardeners would be wise to plant grapes only on traditional single- or double-wire grape trellises rather than on overhead arbors or fences where pruning is a chore and falling fruit can make a mess.

Evergreen vines. Three excellent evergreen vines are the highly popular English ivy, yellow-flowering Carolina jessamine, and glossy-leaved smilax or greenbriar, which looks so good when trained up and across a wire to cascade over a porch or entrance. Figvine or creeping fig, often planted to climb up brick, is evergreen in the Lower South. In the Upper South, it may freeze to the ground, but it comes back from the roots. Boston ivy and Virginia creeper are excellent deciduous vines with red fall color; both are very dependable in all parts of the South.

Ground Covers

Ground covers make good sense where the shade is too dense for turfgrass and on steep slopes where mowing is impractical. Using ground covers along with organic mulches to replace turf and even shrubs is part of the trend toward low-maintenance landscaping. The two basic categories of ground covers are woody plants and herbaceous perennials. Both groups include plants that are evergreen, spread to fill a wide area, can hold soils on slopes, and generally tolerate adverse growing conditions.

Woody ground covers. Woody ground covers include both vines and prostrate shrubs. Both may take a while to become established; soil preparation and mulches are important in getting them off to a good start. One of the most popular woody ground covers, especially for shady gardens, is English ivy; it is easy to root and spreads quickly. Asiatic jasmine will tolerate full sun or partial shade but remains thin in heavy shade for its first two or three years. Purple wintercreeper and other ground-hugging forms of euonymus may be susceptible to powdery mildew, a disfiguring foliage disease, but are fast and economical to establish. Ground cover junipers are best suited for full sun but tolerate light shade. Cotoneaster is very attractive when covered with berries, but it's too thin to shade out weeds, which you'll need to control with a mulch. One of the most aggressive ground covers, useful where matted roots are important for erosion control on steep slopes, is the weedy Japanese honeysuckle. It works well if you can keep it away from other plantings.

Herbaceous ground covers. Herbaceous ground covers are generally invasive; they spread quickly once established. This group includes violets, wild strawberries, ferns (especially the native southern shield fern), verbenas, ajuga, creeping phlox, dwarf bamboo, and pachysandra (not for the Lower South). *Vinca major* and *Vinca minor* do well in the shade and have large, very attractive lavender flowers in spring.

Two of the most popular herbaceous ground covers are members of the lily family. Mondo grass, or "monkey grass" (*Ophiopogon japonica*), is small, dark green, and invasive and has short stalks of pinkish-white flowers hidden in the foliage. It can be mowed in late spring to make a coarse but believable turf substitute, even in very heavy shade. Liriope, also called lily-turf, is generally available in both spreading (*L. spicata*) and clumping (*L. muscari*) forms. Both have flower spikes held above the foliage in midsummer.

Perennials

Colorful flowering plants are an important element of the new American garden style. Once prominent in many landscapes, herbaceous perennials — plants that "come back" for several years — are being rediscovered for their dependable seasonal effects. Favorite perennials, including many herbs and native wildflowers, have long been exchanged by gardeners and sold through garden centers and mail-order nurseries. Many are treasured as heirloom plants and have proven themselves hardy enough to withstand our weather and climate extremes, often with little care. Others are exciting new discoveries or hybrids and may take several years to prove themselves in southern gardens. However, a good many perennial plants simply do not survive for more than a year or two in our warm, humid climate, just as some of our favorites will not survive for long in colder areas of our huge country. This is a fact that gardeners have to work around.

Perennials are normally rated according to how much cold they will tolerate in the winter. (The USDA hardiness zone maps are based on average winter low temperatures.) However, cold hardiness is just one aspect of survival. In the South, perennials must also endure heavy rains, prolonged droughts, hot nights in the summer, and warm spells in the winter, all of which can weaken tough perennials and cause them to fail.

For this reason, it's best to follow a trial-and-error approach with perennials. Start with common, easy ones like daylilies, cannas, phlox, coneflower, and yarrow. As you gain confidence with these, try others, fitting them into your beds according to size, time of bloom or foliage effect, color, and texture. The main point is, don't be intimidated by what you don't know or by unfamiliar names on a list. And don't plant perennials hand over fist. Read about them one at a time and compare notes with other perennial gardeners, asking what grows best for them. Who knows — along with some advice, you may get a start.

Growing healthy perennials. Soil preparation is usually crucial to long-term success with perennials. Lighten heavy clay soils by adding coarse sand and generous amounts of organic matter such as peat moss, finely ground bark, compost, or old sawdust. Add peat or other organic matter to dry, sandy soil to improve moisture retention. A 2–4-inch layer of organic matter spread over the soil surface and then tilled or dug in can work wonders toward improving almost all garden soils. Porous mulches of pine straw or bark, spread 2–3 inches deep, can help keep roots cool and moist in the summer, reduce weed competition, and insulate the soil from wind and temperature extremes.

It's important to select the right site for a plant. Sun-loving perennials may grow leggy and have few flowers in even a moderately shaded bed; shade-loving plants can easily burn in just a few hours of hot sunshine. And although soils can vary greatly between being wet or dry, many plants simply will not tolerate extremes. Roots die in waterlogged or overly dry soils.

Watering during our typically dry summers is one of the most crucial requirements for success with perennials — they all need water for best growth and performance. Although some can survive a drought, others need a deep soaking every week.

Increasing your collection. Although dozens of perennials have long been shared by gardeners who got their starts from friends or mail-order nurseries, retail garden centers are beginning to offer more hardy perennials. By planting only three or four new types each year, you can quickly build up a showy perennial garden and make divisions to move about or share with other gardeners. Many perennials can be propagated easily by division. Dividing crowns and roots or separating bulbs can be mastered quickly. The rule of thumb is to divide plants during their dormant or "off" season, opposite the flowering period: divide spring bloomers in the fall, fall bloomers in the spring.

Outstanding perennials for southern gardens

Start your perennial garden with these reliable favorites; most should be available at local nurseries and garden centers.

ARTEMISIA (*Artemisia,* many species and cultivars). Ht. 1–3 feet, sun or partial shade, gray foliage blends well with other plants. Tolerate dry soil. Some kinds are rapid spreaders.

ASTER (*Aster,* many species and cultivars). Ht. 2–5 feet, sun or partial shade. Pinch in spring for bushier growth. Masses of purple, lavender, rosy, or white flowers in fall.

BLUE STAR (*Amsonia tabernaemontana*). Ht. 2–3 feet, sun or partial shade. Tolerates wet soil. Hundreds of tiny blue flowers in spring.

BOLTONIA (*Boltonia asteroides*). Ht. 3–4 feet, sun or partial shade. Masses of asterlike white flowers in fall.

CANNA (*Canna × generalis*, many cultivars). Ht. 3–5 feet, sun or partial shade. Coarse foliage often colorful. Showy flowers from spring to fall.

CARDINAL FLOWER (*Lobelia cardinalis*). Ht. 3–5 feet, sun or shade. Tolerates wet soil. Spikes of red flowers in fall.

CHRYSANTHEMUM (*Chrysanthemum × morifolium*). Ht. 1–3 feet, full sun. Blooms fall and spring, good for cutting but needs dividing each year.

COREOPSIS (*Coreopsis*, many species and cultivars). Ht. 1–3 feet, best in sun. Bright yellow flowers in spring and summer.

DAYLILY (*Hemerocallis*, many cultivars). Ht. 1–5 feet, sun or partial shade. New types offer range of colors, bloom spring to fall.

DIANTHUS (*Dianthus*, many species and cultivars). Ht. 6 inches to 2 feet, sun. Fragrant flowers in spring, good for cutting. Attractive foliage year-round. Needs well-drained soil.

FOUR OCLOCKS (*Mirabilis jalapa*). Ht. 3–4 feet, sun or partial shade. Fragrant flowers open in evening, spring to fall. Drought and heat tolerant.

HELIOPSIS (*Heliopsis helianthoides*). Ht. 3–5 feet, sun or partial shade. Blooms like small sunflowers, summer to fall.

HOSTA (*Hosta*, many species and cultivars). Ht. 1–3 feet, shade or partial shade. Excellent foliage plant for shady spots. Some types have lavender or white blooms in summer.

LANTANA (*Lantana camara*). Ht. 3–4 feet, sun or partial shade. Heat and drought tolerant. Bright flowers spring through fall.

LIATRIS (*Liatris*, a few species). Ht. 3–4 feet, sun or partial shade. Tall spikes of flowers in spring and summer, good for cutting. Tolerates wet or dry soils.

LYTHRUM (*Lythrum virgatum*). Ht. 3–6 feet, sun or partial shade. Spikes of purple or rosy blooms spring to fall. Tolerates wet soil. Cultivars are not invasive.

MONARDA (*Monarda didyma*). Ht. 2–3 feet, sun or partial shade. Red, pink, or lavender blooms in summer. Scented foliage. May be invasive.

PEONY (*Paeonia lactiflora*). Ht. 1–3 feet, partial shade. Early blooming, single varieties best in the South. Good for cutting.

PHLOX (*Phlox*, many species and cultivars). Ht. 6 inches to 4 feet, sun or shade. Several species offer wide variety of flower color and long season of bloom.

PHYSOSTEGIA (*Physostegia virginiana*). Ht. 3–4 feet, sun or partial shade. Lavender or white blooms spring to summer. May be invasive.

PURPLE CONEFLOWER (*Echinacea purpurea*). Ht. 3 feet, full sun. Purple daisylike flowers in summer, attractive seedheads last through winter.

RUDBECKIA (*Rudbeckia fulgida*). Ht. 2–3 feet, sun or partial shade. Flowers like black-eyed Susans in spring and summer.

SAPONARIA (*Saponaria officinalis*). Ht. 2 feet. Pale pink flowers are fragrant in evening, blooms spring to fall. May be invasive.

SEDUM 'Autumn Joy' (*Sedum* × *'Autumn Joy'*). Ht. 2 feet. Tough and hardy. Attractive in every season.

SHASTA DAISY (*Chrysanthemum* × *superbum*). Ht. 1–2 feet, sun or partial shade. New cultivars have extended bloom, spring and summer. Good for cutting.

SPIDERWORT (*Tradescantia* × *andersoniana*). Ht. 1–3 feet, sun or shade. Blue, purple, or white flowers in spring. Often invasive.

STOKESIA (*Stokesia laevis*). Ht. 1–2 feet, sun or partial shade. Blue flowers in spring, good for cutting.

SUNDROPS (*Oenothera fruticosa*). Ht. 2–3 feet, sun or partial shade. Bright yellow flowers spring and summer. May be invasive.

VIOLETS (*Viola,* many species). Ht. 6 inches, sun or shade. Spreading ground cover, fragrant blooms winter and spring.

WILD OR HARDY AGERATUM (*Eupatorium coelestinum*). Ht. 2–3 feet, sun or partial shade. Blue flowers in fall. Invasive in good soil.

YARROW (*Achillea,* many species and cultivars). Ht. 2–4 feet, sun or partial shade. White, yellow, pink, or pastel flowers in spring and summer, good for cutting and drying. Some forms invasive.

Annuals

No other group of flowering plants can give as much color as quickly and economically as annuals — plants that sprout, grow, flower, set seed, and die within one growing season. Annuals come in a wide array of colors, heights, and textures. Outstanding in masses of solid or mixed colors, they are also effective in small groups or used to accentuate lines and borders. Many annuals, especially newer, compact varieties, are perfectly at home in containers. Others are large and may be used as specimens or accents or along the back of a flower or shrub border. Still others are vines to grow on fences, arbors, porch rails, or trellises.

Many common and favorite annuals grow well in the South. For specimens or accents try basil, candlestick plant, castor bean, coleus, hollyhocks, and ornamental pepper. Mass plantings are easily accomplished with ageratum, begonia, gloriosa daisy, Johnny-jump-ups, marigold, pansy, petunia, snapdragon, and zinnia. Good flowers for cutting include cornflower, gaillardia, gomphrena, larkspur, Queen Anne's lace, snapdragons, strawflower, and zinnia. Flower breeders have developed varieties of many annuals with increased heat tolerance and disease resistance. Look for varieties that have won the All-America Selection seed trials award.

Growing annuals. Nearly every community has a garden supply outlet stocked each season with dozens of annual flower transplants. Transplants are more expensive than packets of seed, but the instant effect they create is nearly irresistible to most gardeners. With a little planning and a minimal investment of time and supplies, it's fairly easy to grow your own transplants. Some large-seeded, fast-growing annuals can be seeded directly in the garden, and some annuals reseed themselves and reappear in the garden every year.

Selecting the right type of plant is the first step, but annuals also require your gardening skills to perform at their peak in a single growing season. For best results, choose plants that prefer the conditions found in your garden — sun or shade, moist or dry soil. Prepare the soil by adding plenty of organic matter to improve root growth, plant performance, vigor, and pest resistance. Be prepared to water annual plantings during dry spells, and use pine straw, shredded bark, leaves, or other porous mulches to help retain soil moisture and control weeds.

Annuals for hot weather. Most annuals are planted in the spring and killed by frost the following fall. For summer flowers, plant ageratum, bachelor's buttons, balsam, basil, celosia, cleome, coleus, cosmos, cyress vine, impatiens, marigold, morning glory, moss rose, ornamental pepper, periwinkle, salvia, tithonia, and zinnia.

Annuals for cool weather. Other annuals, more tolerant of cold than of heat, are best planted in the fall for late winter, spring, and early summer flowers. This group includes black-eyed Susan, coreopsis, cornflower, dill, feverfew, gaillardia, hollyhocks, Johnny-jump-ups, larkspur, pansy, petunia, phlox, poppy, Queen Anne's lace, and sweet Williams.

Gardening with Native Plants

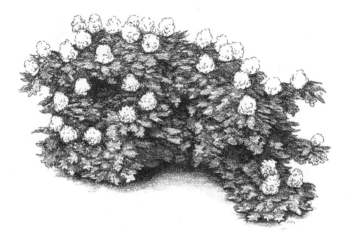

If you believe that variety is the spice of life, you'll find that gardening with native plants is a very palatable experience. The Southeast has a wealth of native plant materials in an astounding array of forms, textures, colors, and sizes. Many native species have showy flowers. Others have attractive foliage throughout the growing season, brilliant color in the fall, or interesting bark and stem features in the winter.

Whether the setting is rural or urban, sunny or shady, wet or dry, there are native trees, shrubs, and perennials that will flourish in your garden. The keys to success are choosing the right plants and providing them with suitable growing conditions. Today, more and more nurseries specialize in the propagation of native plants, and many local garden centers now stock natives that are beautiful and easy to grow.

What Is a Native Plant?

As used here, a native plant is a species that was growing in the Southeast when the first European settlers arrived. Good examples are flowering dogwood and redbud trees. An introduced or "exotic" plant, such as Japanese honeysuckle, is one that was brought into the area through intentional or accidental human activity. Exotics that become established as part of the flora plant life of the region are said to be naturalized.

Why Garden with Natives?

From coast to coast, modern suburban landscapes commonly consist of closely mowed lawns, brightly colored bedding plants, trimmed evergreen shrubs, and identical balloon-shaped trees planted in straight rows. Such gardens look the same, whether in Boston, Washington, or Atlanta. By contrast, visitors will know that they are in the South if your garden features the native plants that are part of your southern heritage.

Landscaping with natives helps integrate your home with the immediate environment and the regional landscape and gives your garden a sense of place. It is also ecologically sound. Native species have evolved adaptations to the climate and soil of their particular habitat. Using adapted species usually means that your garden is easier to maintain and requires less water and fertilizer and fewer pesticides.

As the population of the Southeast continues to grow, a number of plant species are becoming endangered because their natural habitats are being destroyed or modified through urban development, agricultural use, or clear-cutting to harvest timber. You can help conserve endangered species by purchasing nursery-grown plants and maintaining them in your garden. In the future, some Southeastern native species will survive only in gardens. For example, the beautiful franklinia is a species once found in the wild but now known only in cultivation. This shrub was last seen in the wild in 1803, but, fortunately, descendants of earlier collections still thrive in cultivation.

Trees Dominate the Natural Landscape of the South

To understand and appreciate the native plants of the South, it helps to review the history of the area. The landscape those first Europeans saw was unbroken virgin forest. Treeless areas were rare. There were a few naturally barren spots and occasional openings where Native Americans were raising crops, but for the most part the Southeastern landscape was covered with trees — mature pines on the Coastal Plain, mixed hardwoods inland.

The forest was a burden to the settlers, who needed to create fields for agriculture. At first they followed the Native American practice of girdling trees. As the girdled trees died, crops were planted among the standing dead trunks. Later, as their numbers increased, the settlers cut and burned the virgin trees, using the ashes to enrich the soil. The land suited for the agricultural practices of the time was rapidly deforested and occupied. For example, the Native Americans were removed from one county of the lower Piedmont of Georgia around 1824. Some 20 years later, according to old tax records, only 204 acres had not been cleared and planted in cotton.

Today, little if any of the original forest remains. However, much of the South is covered with secondary forest — trees growing on previously cleared land. Trees take over wherever farms have been abandoned, and many areas have been turned into pine plantations that supply trees for paper and other wood products.

Geographic Regions of the South

As described in the introduction, geographers and botanists divide the Southeast into several major regions: the Coastal Plain, the Piedmont, the southern Appalachians, the Ridge and Valley, the Interior Plateaus, and the Arkansas mountains. These areas differ in topography, climate, and soil, and each has its own flora — a characteristic assortment of native plants. Keep this in mind if you want to create a landscape with a clear sense of place. For example, our native palm tree, the cabbage palmetto, occurs along the edge of brackish marshes and in the sandy maritime forest of the Coastal Plain. It looks just right in seashore gardens, but it seems out of place in the rolling red clay hills of the Piedmont.

Where to Get Native Plants

A warning about plants collected from the wild. Avoid removing plants from their natural habitat unless the area is about to be destroyed by a bulldozer. In this case, a rescue mission to dig plants may be organized, but first you must obtain written permission from the landowner.

Some nurseries sell plants collected from the wild. This practice is thoroughly undesirable from a conservation standpoint.

Often these plants are collected illegally from public or private lands, some from populations of species endangered by over-collecting or by habitat destruction. If you encounter native plants that are very inexpensive, they were probably collected from natural areas. In one wholesale nursery journal recently, trilliums were advertised at 35 cents each. It takes 6 years to produce a flowering-size trillium from seed; no nursery can produce plants that cheaply. Those plants were obviously collected.

Buy nursery-propagated plants. Thanks to the conservation movement and the growing interest in native plants, an increasing number of small specialty nurseries as well as several large wholesale growers are offering nursery-propagated native species. Although these plants may seem expensive, their survival rate is much higher than that of collected material. (Some nurseries collect plants from the wild, hold them in a bed for a year or so, then call them nursery grown. This is a devious ploy. Insist upon "nursery-propagated" native plants — that is, plants propagated in a nursery by seeds, cuttings, or division; do not support nurseries guilty of decimating wild populations.)

Another place to acquire native plants is at plant sales run by a nearby native plant society or botanical garden. Some native species multiply rapidly, and, as with puppies and kittens, their owners are eager to find a home for them. Surplus plant sales are ideal places to purchase plants, often at low cost, and at the same time to assist a worthy group. Often such sales feature species that do particularly well in your area. These sales will also make you aware of the many fascinating native species that can be grown in your area as well as bring you into contact with other gardeners interested in native plants.

Understanding Native Plant Performance

To succeed with natives, it's necessary to understand their ecological requirements. Just because a plant is native to a region will not ensure its survival in your garden. Native species require particular growing conditions, just as exotics do. To determine if a native plant is suitable for your garden, compare your conditions to those where it grows in the wild. Does it prefer wet or well-drained soil? Does it grow in sun or shade?

For example, ferns such as cinnamon fern can't thrive on a dry, sunny hillside when their natural habitat is a moist bog or wet woodland. Rhododendrons that grow wild on rocky hillsides will do fine in raised beds, but you can't put a rhododendron in a poorly drained hole where water stands and expect it to live. Natives that normally grow on limestone, such as southern maidenhair fern or Virginia bluebells, need lime added to an acid soil in order to survive.

Properly selected natives are not necessarily hard to grow. Many native species thrive when given proper nutrients, soil preparation, moisture, and light; and natives grown in a favorable garden environment often have better form, foliage, flowers, and fruit than those found in nature. The following examples are southern natives that perform well over a wide range of growing conditions.

Native Trees

Trees are a great place to start with native plants because they fill so many roles in the garden. They can form a background and block unpleasant views, or they can frame a distant scene in a way that increases the apparent size of your garden. Trees also provide shade — always welcome in a southern garden.

Oaks. Oaks are useful, large, long-lived trees, and several species occur in the South. Although they are considered slow growing, oaks grow surprisingly fast under the proper conditions. One excellent for southern gardens is scarlet oak (*Quercus coccinea*), a medium-size, fast-growing, handsome, deciduous shade tree that often reaches 60 to 70 feet tall. The shiny green leaves turn a spectacular scarlet-red in autumn, and it bears large, interesting acorns. Found in nature on dry sites, scarlet oak is drought tolerant, a matter of critical concern in these days of water shortages. Plant it on well-drained sites and fertilize generously each March to promote vigorous growth. If you can't get scarlet oak, substitute pin oak (*Quercus palustris*). In the Gulf and coastal South, the evergreen live oak (*Quercus virginiana*) is often the tree of choice.

Sourwood. Sourwood (*Oxydendrum arboreum*) is a striking, slow-growing, deciduous ornamental tree. It usually reaches 20 to 30 feet in cultivation, although larger specimens can be found in nature. It is easily recognized by the drooping clusters of white flowers that appear in early to mid summer and the greenish fruit sprays that persist into early winter. In the southern Appalachians, sourwood is valued as an important bee tree whose nectar yields an excellent honey. Sourwood is the first tree to show autumn color; its brilliant red foliage contrasts with the showy fruit clusters. Plant sourwood in well-drained, acid soil enriched with plenty of organic matter, and fertilize lightly each year in early spring. It is essentially pest-free and can be grown either in full sun or very light shade.

Sweetbay. Used as a landscape accent for its open form and fragrant white flowers is sweetbay (*Magnolia virginiana*). In nature, sweetbay can grow into a medium-size, semi-evergreen tree up to 50 feet tall, but it often develops as a large, loosely branched, shrub 3 to 20 feet tall. Under cultivation and given adequate space, it forms a bushy tree. Sweetbay flowers are creamy white, 2 to 3 inches in diameter. The fruits are conelike clusters about 2 inches long. The narrow leaves are covered underneath with fine silvery hairs; selected forms of the plant are nearly evergreen. Sweetbay should be grown in full sun, in moist to wet acid soil well supplied with organic matter and nutrients. Undemanding, it requires little care after planting.

Shadbush. Readily available in the nursery trade is shadbush, or serviceberry (*Amelanchier arborea*). Among the first native trees and shrubs to bloom, shadbush announces the arrival of spring. (The name reflects that its bloom coincides with the run of shad, a small fish once abundant in the streams of colonial America.) The showy clusters of pinkish-white flowers open before the leaves expand. In summer, birds are attracted to the soft juicy fruit, and the leaves turn a pretty orange in the fall. Shadbush is a small deciduous tree or large shrub that grows 20 to 30 feet tall. Adaptable to a wide range of conditions, it is best grown on upland sites in well-prepared soil in full sun to light shade. More or less pest-free, shadbush welcomes a light application of a complete fertilizer when it flowers.

Silverbell. Widely used in English gardens but neglected here at home, silverbell (*Halesia carolina*) is now offered by a number of nurseries in the Southeast. A small native tree, 20 to 40 feet in height, it has showy, pendulous, bell-shaped flowers that are pure white or tinged with pink. The flowers and leaves appear simultaneously in earliest spring. In summer the striking, yellowish, four-winged fruit dangles from the branches. Silverbell occurs on moist fertile slopes in the southern Appalachians or along alluvial stream banks in the Piedmont. It's a marvelous small tree for planting along streams or in moist, fertile sites in either full sun or partial shade, and it can be grown throughout the South.

Native Shrubs

Native shrubs bestow many favors on gardeners. Some have attractive foliage, others interesting and colorful flowers or unusual bark features in winter. Shrubs provide years of pleasure with relatively little bother. Use them to form the background or matrix of your garden, to make a visual connection between the trees and the ground-level plantings, to define boundaries, screen unwanted views, and to reduce noise. The diversity of native shrubs allows you to select plants for every condition from dry hillsides to wet bogs.

Florida anise, Ocala anise. Among the more popular and readily available evergreen shrubs are Florida anise (*Illicium floridanum*) and Ocala anise (*I. parviflorum*). These Coastal Plain natives have proven hardy in the Piedmont and northward. The popularity of both species increased a few years back when a record cold spell hit the South and the two species of anise proved to be hardier than many widely planted exotics such as red-tip photinia and Chinese holly. Florida anise is a large shrub, 8 to 20 feet tall, loosely branched in habit, with dark green leaves and dark red flowers that appear in early spring. A white-flowered form is also available. Ocala anise is also a large shrub but more upright in habit, with light green leaves and small yellow flowers. The leaves of both have a spicy odor when crushed. Both grow best in moist, fertile soil in either sun or light shade; they are pest-free and require little maintenance.

Oakleaf hydrangea. Some horticulturists consider oakleaf hydrangea (*Hydrangea quercifolia*) one of the South's best native shrubs. It is medium-size, 5 to 6 feet tall, with a spreading habit. The large, oak-shaped, gray-green deciduous leaves turn a rich red in fall, and the exfoliating bark adds interest in the winter. It bears large oblong clusters of flowers that open snowy white in summer, later drying to a pinkish beige and lasting through the winter. Larger-flowered cultivars are available, but many gardeners prefer the simplicity of the wild types. Although typically found in nature on dry, exposed bluffs, oakleaf hydrangea grows best in gardens in light shade in fertile, moist garden soil.

Virginia willow. Also called Virginia sweetspire (*Itea virginica*), this shrub prefers moist soil but grows equally well in full sun or light shade. It reaches 4 to 6 feet in height and has a loose, open habit of growth. It is pest-free and needs only a bit of careful pruning to maintain the graceful arching effect of its branches. In late spring, it bears small, white, bell-shaped flowers in dense terminal clusters 4–6 inches long. 'Henry's Garnet' is a popular cultivar of Virginia willow, named for the late Mrs. Mary Henry, a noted collector of Southeastern plants. This selection is recommended for the deep garnet red of its autumn foliage.

Ocala leucothoe. Ocala leucothoe (*Agaristra populifolia*, previously known as *Leucothoe populifolia*), is terrific as quick screen in sun or shade. It grows upright at first, then bends gracefully into an arching shape. Its foliage is a dense evergreen mass of small, narrow, bright green leaves, and it bears honey-scented white blossoms in spring. Native to the Coastal Plain,

Ocala leucothoe has proven remarkably hardy in the Piedmont and northward. It grows 10 to 12 feet tall but can be maintained as a large foundation plant with severe pruning. It doesn't seem to be bothered by diseases or insects.

Southern wax myrtle. Common in the piney woods of the Coastal Plain, Southern wax myrtle (*Myrica cerifera*) is an excellent, fast-growing shrub for full sunlight or light shade. Its leaves are aromatic and the fruit, a small, waxy gray berry. You'll delight in using the branches of this shrub in your home at Christmastime, for they fill the air with the fragrance of bayberry candles. Wax myrtle tolerates infertile soils but responds vigorously to good growing conditions; if it gets too big for its space, you can prune it back severely. In cooler regions of the South, plant 'Evergreen' wax myrtle, an unusually hardy cultivar that resisted leaf browning during the record cold winters of 1984 and 1985. (Heavy ice and snow, however, can bend or break its stems.) Coastal forms of wax myrtle show tolerance to salt spray, making it useful for oceanfront gardens.

Sweet pepperbush. Long clusters of fragrant white or pink flowers make sweet pepperbush (*Clethra alnifolia*) a welcome addition to any garden. It has glossy deciduous foliage and grows 4 to 5 feet tall. This summer-blooming shrub is suitable for sun or light shade. Sweet pepperbush is terrific for landscaping a damp area, although it will grow in almost any soil and is relatively pest-free. As a garden plant, it's most effective if planted in clumps at the edge of woods or near water features.

Native Vines

Woody vines can be used to soften structures such as fences, gates, mailboxes, and rock walls or to camouflage unsightly poles, rock piles, or tool sheds. Climbing on trees, arbors, latticework, or trellises, they provide welcome shade with a bonus of flowers. Some vines make excellent ground covers, especially in difficult areas such as dry slopes. Two of the more popular and readily available native vines are Carolina jessamine and cross vine.

Carolina jessamine. The state flower of South Carolina, Carolina jessamine(*Gelsemium sempervirens*), also called Carolina jasmine or yellow jasmine, has bright yellow flowers, 2 inches long, that open in March. It is an evergreen twining vine that can be used either as a low climbing vine or as a ground cover on sunny slopes. It often serves as a "mailbox" plant in the South. In the wild, Carolina jessamine is typically a sparse vine found in poor soil on exposed sites in thin shade.

It's much denser and more attractive when grown in full sun and fertile soil in a garden. A double-flowered form is frequently sold at nurseries, but its blossoms lack the natural beauty of the wild single-flowered form.

Cross vine. The showy flowers and dark evergreen leaves of cross vine (*Bignonia capreolata,* known until recently as *Aniostichus capreolata*) make it an ideal, high-climbing vine for trellises and arbors or even next to a small tree where it is allowed to climb freely. The large, attractive, trumpet-shaped flowers are in clusters of two to five, orange to reddish outside and yellow to red within, and almost 3 inches long. Cross vine grows best in rich moist soil in either sun or light shade. Cutting the stem reveals the appearance of a cross, hence its name.

Native Herbaceous Perennials and Ground Covers

Trees and shrubs frame and give structure to your garden, but herbaceous perennials and ground covers provide special accents and embellish a garden with their lovely colors and textures. Used in groups or drifts, they add rhythm and harmony. An array of perennials and ground covers makes an attractive alternative to traditional grassy lawns — and also reduces expensive lawn maintenance.

The list of native perennials suitable for garden use is extensive, however, and choosing among them can be confusing to a beginning gardener. Try to avoid going through a nursery catalog or visiting a nursery and selecting one of each native perennial offered. One of the basic reasons for using native perennials is to create a natural-looking garden. If you examine plants in nature, you'll see that they grow in groups or drifts of one kind, not in a hodgepodge of single plants. Choose three, five, or seven of each plant and set them in groups as space allows. Select species that suit the character of your space and the physical environment of the site. Listed below are several species selected for their garden value, long seasonal interest, availability at local nurseries, and ease of culture.

Perennials for shade
Wild bleeding heart. Wild bleeding heart (*Dicentra eximia*) is a true jewel for the shade garden, with finely dissected gray-green foliage and nodding, deep pink flowers that continue from April through October or until frost. Plant it in fertile, slightly acid woodland soil enriched with organic matter. It self-sows and over time will form natural drifts in your woodland garden.

Phlox. Several native species of phlox do well in the shade.

One favorite is blue woodland phlox (*Phlox divaricata*), which provides several weeks of heavenly blue color in early spring. Its persistent sub-evergreen foliage can hide the yellowing foliage of interplanted narcissus, and it tolerates some competition from later perennials. It is easily grown in rich, moist woodland soils and forms beautiful natural drifts on wooded slopes — the plants just seem to slide down the hillside through self-sowing.

False Solomon's seal. False Solomon's seal (*Smilacina racemosa*) adds height and structure to the ground layer of a shade garden. Its arching, leafy stems grow 2 to 3 feet tall in good soil. Each stem bears a terminal cluster of small white flowers in late spring, followed by dark, ruby red fruits in late summer. Rich, moist woodland slopes are ideal planting locations.

Crested iris. No shade garden would be complete without a patch of crested iris (*Iris cristata*). This lovely little gem gradually spreads by rhizomes but is not at all aggressive. The deciduous, linear leaves are only 4 to 8 inches tall, so it is best along the front of a bed or beside a path. In the spring, dainty, miniature blue iris blossoms nestle among the leaves. (White-flowering forms are also available.) Crested iris grows best in ordinary, well-drained soil in a lightly shaded woodland garden. Be careful not to overwater or overfertilize it.

Green-and-gold. Green-and-gold (*Chrysogonum virginicum*) is another native that thrives in ordinary, well-drained garden soil. Southern forms of this species typically grow low to the ground; northern forms are more upright in habit. All have rich green hairy leaves and bright yellow, miniature, sunflowerlike flowers. Flowering peaks in the spring, but scattered blossoms can appear throughout the year. A couple of warm days in December often bring forth a few of the golden yellow flowers. Green-and-gold is useful as a ground cover in small areas, especially in light shade. Avoid overwatering or overfertilization.

Columbine. Our native columbine (*Aquilegia canadensis*) does best in ordinary, well-drained woodland soil in light shade. This erect, 18- to 30-inch-tall herb has finely divided leaves that are evergreen in the Piedmont and Coastal Plain. The unusual nodding flowers have five yellow petals with red spurs and five red sepals. Self-seeding produces striking natural drifts, but columbine is easily thinned if too many seedlings appear.

Wild ginger. One of the richest looking native ground covers is the deciduous wild ginger (*Asarum canadense*). Its dark green, heart-shaped leaves look like velvet. Wild ginger is a rapid grower, but it isn't aggressive. It grows best on rich, near-neutral, moist woodland soil.

Ferns. During the hot summers common to most of the South, your garden becomes more inviting if it presents an illusion of coolness. One of the best ways to create this effect is by the use of ferns. Their calm green colors coupled with their light airy textures are truly restful to the eye. Garden writers constantly suggest adding warm, bright colors to a garden, but remember that green is also a color and a desirable one in the South because of its cooling effect.

Many native ferns thrive in southern gardens, but some have very specific requirements, such as wet soil or a limestone substrate. Two evergreen ferns that do well in a variety of conditions over a wide area of the South are Christmas fern (*Polystichum acrostichoides*) and marginal wood fern (*Dryop-· teris marginalis*). Both form clumps of fronds 18 to 24 inches tall. Christmas fern has a coarser texture and is a darker green than wood fern. Both require shade and prefer a loose, slightly acid woodland soil, but they tolerate drier conditions than many ferns. These two form clumps and do not spread aggressively like some ferns.

Perennials for sun

Although many native perennials survive in light shade or partial sun, some require at least 8 to 9 hours of sun each day. Without enough sun, they grow straggly and fail to bloom. The following three plants are good natives for sunny spots.

Purple coneflower. Purple coneflower (*Echinacea purpurea*) is an erect perennial, 3 to 4 feet tall. It bears striking terminal flower heads with drooping pinkish ray flowers and a cone of dark purple disk flowers. The dried cones are outstanding in dried flower arrangements. If you regularly remove the old flower heads, the plant will continue blooming into early fall. The foliage of purple coneflower is a rich, dark green. For the best effect, plant in groups of three to seven about 18 inches apart. In nature, purple coneflowers grow in neutral to basic soil, so add a bit of extra ground limestone to the soil.

Stokes' aster. A widely grown perennial long known to horticulture, Stokes' aster (*Stokesia laevis*) is native to the Coastal Plain from Georgia to Louisiana. It grows about 12 inches tall and has a basal cluster of bright green, lance-shaped leaves that persist throughout the winter in much of the South. Its large and showy flower heads are an attractive sky blue. Stokes' aster makes an effective plant for the front of a perennial border when spaced 12 to 18 inches apart in groups of three or more. Although not a fussy plant, it thrives best in full sun in a slightly acid soil.

Rose verbena. Like the annual verbenas sold as bedding plants, the native perennial rose verbena (*Verbena canadensis*) is a low, spreading plant. It reaches a height of 8 to 12 inches and is excellent for the front of the bed or as a ground cover for sunny places. The finely dissected leaves make a nice contrast to the dense, flat-topped flower spikes. Flower color varies from pink to light blue, purple, or white. The blooming period extends from early spring well into the fall. Plant it in well-drained and slightly acid soil in full sun.

Meadows

Meadow gardening has often been touted as a simple, effortless way to garden or to get rid of unwanted lawn, but, alas, this is not true. A well-made meadow garden of native perennial grasses and wildflowers is a sight to behold, but it requires careful planning and years of work. Don't be discouraged, however; just realize that meadow gardening is not going to be as easy as throwing some seeds out, standing back, and watching them grow.

If you want to establish a meadow planting in the South, consider these desirable native grasses: big bluestem (*Andropogon gerardii*), switch grass (*Panicum virgatum*), and Indian grass (*Sorghastrum nutans*); and these native perennial wildflowers: butterflyweed (*Asclepias tuberosa*), white heath aster (*Aster ericoides*), purple coneflower (*Echinacea purpurea*), hairy sunflower (*Helianthus mollis*), gayfeather (*Liatris spicata*), wild bergamot (*Monarda fistulosa*), black-eyed Susan (*Rudbeckia hirta*), compassplant (*Silphium lacinatum*), and lanceleaf coreopsis (*Coreopsis lanceolata*).

Note that some of the seeds included in so-called wildflower mixes are not native to the Southeast. These non-natives often include tall fescue grass, white yarrow, bachelor's buttons, Shasta daisy, chicory, Chinese houses, cosmos, California poppy, blue flax, lupine, baby blue eyes, Shirley poppy, and bouncing bet. Avoid these plants if you wish to have only natives in your meadow garden.

To be successful, a meadow garden must get 8 to 10 hours of sun daily during the growing season. Don't try to make a meadow in a shady place. Before beginning, eliminate the undesirable weeds on the site. Spray perennial weeds with a recommended herbicide. Annual weeds can be reduced by shallow and frequent cultivation of the area during the previous growing season.

For small areas, it's best to start with plants, not seeds, and set them out in well-drained, ordinary garden soil. Avoid excess fertilization, which encourages the growth of weeds. The meadow area must be weeded by hand regularly and watered during periods of drought until the plants are well established, generally in 2 to 3 years. After that, the meadow can be maintained by mowing it late each winter with the mower blade set high or by burning it in late winter. (Before burning, be sure to (1) obtain the proper permits, (2) clear the matter with your neighbors, and (3) be prepared with the proper equipment and assistance to control the fire.)

Southern Lawns

Southerners take considerable pride in their lawns, but growing grass in the South brings its own special set of rewards and complications. On the plus side, the southern growing season is longer than that in most other areas of the United States. Thus the lawn stays actively growing longer and receives considerably more use. On the other hand, more warm days and nights mean more time for insects, weeds, and diseases to do their dirty work. Mowing the grass, moreover, becomes nearly a year-round task.

Growing a lawn may seem daunting at times. Who among us really has the last word on high-tech fertilizers, organic pest control, and the newest experimental grasses? But the salient point to remember is, *most southerners work much harder on their lawns than they have to*. You don't need a degree in agronomy to grow a lush lawn.

A Guide to Southern Lawn Grasses

Grass	Hardiness*	Texture	Drought Resistance
Bahia	GS, LS	Coarse	Excellent
Common Bermuda	GS, LS, MS	Medium	Excellent
Improved Bermuda	GS, LS, MS	Medium to fine	Medium
Buffalograss	LS, MS, US	Fine	Excellent
Carpetgrass	GS, LS	Coarse	Medium
Centipede	GS, LS	Medium	Medium
Kentucky Bluegrass	US	Medium	Poor
Perennial Ryegrass	US	Medium	Poor
St. Augustine	GS, LS	Coarse	Medium
Tall Fescue	MS, US	Medium to coarse	Medium
Zoysia	GS, LS, MS, US	Medium to fine	Excellent

*GS = Gulf South; US = Upper South; MS = Middle South; LS = Lower South. See map on page xiv.

Picking the Right Grass

Growing a lawn would be a whole lot simpler if everyone could plant the same type of grass. The South, however, is a diverse region, and what grows in one area may not do well in another. The type of grass you select will have a major impact on your lawn's success or failure.

Turf specialists divide lawn grasses into two groups, warm-season (bahia, bermuda, buffalograss, carpetgrass, centipede,

Wear Resistance	Shade Tolerance	Fertilizer Needs	Method of Establishment
Excellent	Poor	Low	Seed
Good	Poor	Medium	Seed, sod, plugs, sprigs
Medium	Poor	High	Seed, sod, plugs, sprigs
Poor	Poor	Low	Seed, sod, plugs
Medium	Medium	Low	Seed, sprigs
Medium	Poor	Low	Seed, sod, plugs, sprigs
Medium	Poor	High	Seed, sod
Medium	Poor	High	Seed
Medium	Good	Medium	Sod, plugs, sprigs
Good	Medium	Medium	Seed, sod
Excellent	Good	Medium	Sod, plugs

St. Augustine, zoysia) and cool-season (Kentucky bluegrass, perennial ryegrass, tall fescue). Warm-season grasses grow rapidly in hot weather and go dormant when it's cool. Cool-season grasses do just the opposite. Although all of these grasses will grow in some portion of the South, the farther south you live, the likelier you are to grow a warm-season grass.

Once you've identified the appropriate group, you then have to consider drought tolerance, shade tolerance, wear resistance, fertilizer requirements, texture, cold hardiness, and method of establishment (see chart above).

Warm-season grasses

Bahia grass. Bahia grass (*Paspalum notatum*) is rarely grown outside Florida. A very coarse, durable grass, it thrives in poor, sandy, dry soils and develops an extensive root system to withstand drought. It's easy to establish from seed, has few pests, and needs little fertilizer. However, prolific seedheads combined with tough leaves and stems make it difficult to mow. 'Argentine' is the preferred selection.

Common bermuda. Common bermuda (*Cynodon dactylon*) is the South's most widely used grass. It establishes quickly and can form a thick lawn from seed within a year. Adapted to both clay and sandy soils, it tolerates drought as well as salt spray, so it's a good choice for seaside lawns. On the other hand, it's not reliably hardy in the Upper South and won't put up with the slightest shade. It also spreads so aggressively that it often invades shrubs and flower beds.

For finer texture and better color, southerners often turn to improved bermuda grasses, such as 'Tifgreen', 'Tifway', and 'Santa Ana', which are used on golf greens. While these selections behave better than common bermuda, they're also a lot fussier, demanding more fertilizing, watering, and mowing to maintain their good looks.

Buffalograss. Buffalograss (*Buchloe dactyloides*) is still being evaluated for widespread use as a lawn grass. Native to the Great Plains, it shows considerable promise for the dry plains of West and North Texas and Oklahoma, and it may eventually be used in the South. This low-growing grass actually prefers low rainfall and fertility. Easily started from seed, plugs, or sod, it forms a fine-textured lawn with a light blue-green color. The main drawbacks of most commercially available selections, such as 'Texoka' and 'Comanche', are lack of wear resistance and an abundance of seedheads. However, a new selection called 'Prairie' promises thicker, tougher turf and fewer seedheads.

Carpetgrass. Carpetgrass (*Axonopus affinis*) is a coarse grass appropriate for lawns where low maintenance is more important than appearance. It performs best in wet, poorly drained, infertile soils. Its wide blades remind some people of St. Augustine grass. However, carpetgrass produces numerous seedheads throughout the growing season, while St. Augustine grass does not.

Centipede. Centipede (*Eremochloa ophiuroides*) is often called lazy man's or poor man's grass because so little is required to keep it growing. It is particularly well adapted to the acid, sandy soils of the Southeast, and it dislikes frequent fertilization, needs mowing less often than other grasses, and forms a thick lawn from seed or sod. However, centipede isn't as drought tolerant as some other grasses and turns yellow from iron deficiency in alkaline soils.

St. Augustine. St. Augustine (*Stenotaphrum secundatum*) is the most popular grass for lawns in Florida and along the Gulf and South Atlantic coasts. This vigorous, wide-bladed grass is the best warm-season grass for growing in light shade or salt spray. It holds its green color longer in fall and greens up earlier in spring than most other warm-season grasses. Lack of cold hardiness is its major disadvantage: St. Augustine isn't reliable north of Birmingham or Atlanta.

Because common St. Augustine often suffers injury from chinch bugs and a virus called St. Augustine decline (SAD), researchers developed improved selections to combat these problems. 'Floratam' and 'Floralawn' resist chinch bugs and SAD, but aren't as cold hardy or shade tolerant as the common type. 'Seville' resists insects and disease and sports a finer texture than the common type, but isn't any hardier. 'Raleigh' resists SAD, is finer textured and hardier than the common type, but doesn't resist chinch bugs.

Zoysia. Zoysia (*Zoysia matrella*) is the South's best all-around grass, growing well in most areas. Exceptionally drought tolerant and wear resistant, it forms a soft, lush carpet that your bare feet will love. Nearly as shade tolerant as St. Augustine but with fewer disease and insect problems, zoysia generally requires little maintenance. But because it's only available as sod or plugs, establishing a zoysia lawn can be expensive. 'Emerald' and 'Meyer' ('Z-52') are the most popular selections. The former is more attractive and has a finer texture; the latter is hardier and more wear resistant. 'Cashmere,' a recent introduction, shows considerable promise. Preliminary reports indicate that it offers low growth, fine texture, and improved cold hardiness and shade tolerance.

Cool-season grasses

Kentucky bluegrass. Kentucky bluegrass (*Poa praetensis*) sets the standard for rich blue-green color, but an attractive lawn is a chore to maintain. Although bluegrass is quick to establish and spreads rapidly, it requires frequent fertilizing, watering, and spraying for pests. For these reasons, only Upper South homeowners should plant bluegrass. Suggested selections include 'Adelphi', 'America', 'Eclipse', and 'Parade'.

Perennial ryegrass. Perennial ryegrass (*Lolium perenne*), like bluegrass, is restricted to the Upper South by its dislike of summer heat and drought. Although it germinates quickly, it doesn't spread by rhizomes, like bluegrass, so it takes longer to produce a thick lawn. Homeowners in the Lower and Gulf South sometimes overseed their warm-season lawns in fall with perennial rye. The ryegrass gives the lawn a bright green color all winter, then dies the next spring when warm temperatures revive the warm-season grass. Improved selections of perennial ryegrass include 'Citation', 'Pennfine', 'Premier', and 'Regal'.

Tall fescue. Tall fescue (*Festuca arundinacea*) is the South's only true "transitional" grass. It does well in areas where winters are too cold for warm-season grasses and summers are too hot for other cool-season grasses. Like bluegrass and ryegrass, tall fescue holds its green color all winter. But it far surpasses them in terms of drought tolerance, wear resistance, and disease and insect resistance. Regardless, tall fescue cannot compete with warm-season grasses in the Lower South. In this area, it needs afternoon shade or it will gradually die out. And it won't do at all in the Gulf South.

Familiar only with the coarse, outdated selection 'Kentucky-31', many people think tall fescue is suited only to athletic fields. However, recent introductions, such as 'Falcon', 'Fine-lawn', 'Houndog', and 'Rebel', offer much finer texture and better color.

Establishing a New Lawn

There are four basic methods for establishing a new lawn: seeding, sodding, plugging, and sprigging. The right one for you depends on a combination of factors, including cost, the amount of time and labor you're willing to invest, how quickly you want a finished lawn, and what kind of grass you choose. But no matter the method or type of grass, your most important step is preparing the soil properly.

Begin by tilling the existing soil to a depth of 6 to 8 inches. If your soil is poor, till in 2 to 3 inches of good topsoil to which you've added generous portions of organic matter, such as sphagnum peat moss. While you're tilling, work in some high-phosphorus seed-and-sod fertilizer, such as 18-24-10, at the rate recommended on the bag. Next, use a steel rake to smooth the soil, remove stones and debris, and establish the lawn's basic contours. Shape the ground so that excess rainwater doesn't collect on the lawn or run toward the foundation of the house.

At this point, the soil will be rather soft and in need of settling. To speed the process, use a roller (basically, a big barrel with handles attached). Fill the barrel one-third to one-half full with water and roll it gently over the soil to smooth and firm it. Then get ready to plant your grass. Don't wait too long — a heavy downpour can wash bare soil away in the wink of an eye.

Seeding

The biggest advantage of seeding is that it costs less than other methods of starting a lawn. For example, you can buy enough fescue seed to sow a 1,000-square-foot area for about $20. To sod that same area may cost between $200 and $500, depending on the kind of sod. So why doesn't everyone use seed? One reason is that sodding gives you an instant lawn, while seeding takes a year or more to produce the same effect. Moreover, the seed of some grasses isn't commercially available.

When you buy your seed, select only quality, certified seed. Check the label on the bag for the name of the seed selection, the weed-seed content, the germination percentage, and the date the seed was tested. High-quality grass seed should have a germination percentage of 80 percent or more and a weed-seed content of less than 1 percent, and it should have been tested within a year of sale.

Sow warm-season grasses in the spring and cool-season grasses in late summer or fall. Use either a drop or broadcast spreader (for seeding rates, refer to the chart below). To ensure that the seed is distributed evenly across the lawn, divide the seed into two equal portions. Distribute the first portion by running the spreader forward and back lengthwise over the lawn. Distribute the second portion by running the spreader back and forth across the width. When you've sowed all the seed, roll the lawn gently once more. Cover the seedbed with a thin layer of weedfree wheat straw to protect the seed from drying out, being washed away, or being eaten by birds.

Water the lawn every rainless day for the first several weeks to keep the seedlings moist. When the new grass is 1 to 2 inches high, reduce watering to every 2 to 3 days. Let the straw rot in place — it won't harm the new grass, but raking it will take a lot of grass with it. Give the new grass its first mowing when it's about ½ inch above the desired summer mowing height for that particular type of grass (see mowing chart, page 58). After you've mowed the grass twice, water the lawn as

Table 1.
Seeding Rates (per 1,000 square feet)

Bahia	6–8 pounds
Bermuda (hulled)	1–2 pounds
Buffalograss	2–4 pounds
Carpetgrass	1–2 pounds
Centipede	½ pound
Kentucky bluegrass	1–2 pounds
Perennial ryegrass	6–8 pounds
Tall fescue	6–8 pounds

frequently as you would an established lawn. Don't apply weedkillers until after the lawn's first growing season.

Sodding

It's just as important to start with good sod as it is with good seed. Select certified sod that's guaranteed to be free of insects, diseases, and weeds. Ask to inspect it before it's delivered. Each piece should be green, moist, and firm, with a thick set of roots. Reject any sod that's sparse, brown, yellow, or flimsy.

Although theoretically you can sod at any time of the year, spring and fall are definitely the best times. Lay the sod as quickly as possible after delivery. If you can't lay it all in one day, store the remainder in a cool, shaded place. Water the lawn area thoroughly the night before sodding so that the soil is moist but not muddy.

Establish a straight edge for the first strip of sod by lining it up against a sidewalk or driveway. If neither of these is available, stretch a line across the middle of the lawn and lay sod on either side. Trim the sod as necessary when you come to an irregular edge. Lay each strip as tightly as possible against the strip next to it. Stagger the joints between pieces as you would the joints between bricks when building a wall. If you need to cover a slope, lay the long side of each strip along the face of the slope.

When you've finished laying the sod, roll it gently to firm it into place. Water it every rainless day for the first two weeks. After that, water as you would an established lawn.

Plugging and sprigging

An alternative to seeding or sodding is plugging or sprigging. The first method involves setting 3-inch cubes of turf, called plugs, into the lawn in a checkerboard pattern. The plugs, which generally take about a year to fill in completely, come in trays, sixteen plugs to a tray. Using a plugging tool, a sort of miniature posthole digger that excavates a 3 x 3 x 3-inch hole, space plugs of most warm-season grasses about 18 inches apart (at this spacing, one tray covers about 50 square feet). The exception is zoysia, which takes longer to spread; space zoysia plugs about 12 inches apart. Plugging costs less than sodding — about 5 cents per square foot versus 15 to 30 cents or more. And, unlike seeding, you can plug almost any time of the year.

Sprigs consist of small sections of stems with roots attached. You can buy them by the bushel or make your own by shredding pieces of sod. There are several ways to plant sprigs. Perhaps the simplest is to distribute them evenly across the lawn, then cover them with ¼ inch of topsoil. Roll the lawn, then water thoroughly.

Waking Up a Tired Lawn

A new lawn may start out nearly perfect, but chances are it won't stay that way. Eventually, factors such as winter cold, summer drought, soil compaction, and thatch buildup will cause the grass to thin. When this happens, you need to renovate the lawn. Spring is the time to renovate warm-season grasses; renovate cool-season lawns in fall.

In the worst situation, winter cold or summer drought has thinned the lawn so seriously that opportunistic weeds such as wild bermuda, crabgrass, and chickweed have taken over. At this point, it's best to start over, because there's no way to kill the weeds without harming the grass. Spray the weeds and remaining grass according to label directions with a nonselective herbicide, such as Roundup L&G. When the entire lawn is dead, rent a power rake and completely remove the dead debris from the lawn. Then seed, sod, plug, or sprig, after preparing the soil as just described.

Usually, the lawn isn't that far gone. It may only be lacking vigor due to a buildup of thatch or soil compaction. Thatch consists of a layer of dead grass stems and other plant debris that accumulates on the surface. It often results from overwatering and overfertilization. Zoysia and St. Augustine lawns are especially susceptible. Actually, a thin layer of thatch can benefit grass by retaining soil moisture and shielding roots from temperature extremes. But thatch thicker than ½ inch makes grass prone to insects, disease, and drought. To remove thatch from a small lawn, use a steel dethatching rake. For large lawns, rent a power dethatcher. Don't use a power dethatcher on St. Augustine turf, however, or you may tear it to pieces.

Years of people walking across a lawn can lead to soil compaction. Compacted soil loses many of the pore spaces needed for the free passage of water and oxygen so essential for vigorous plant growth. You can remedy this by renting a special coring machine that pounds the lawn with hollow tubes that extract small cores of soil. It drops the cores behind it on the ground, so you'll need to rake them up into the compost pile or run a lawn mower over them to pulverize them.

Often the lawn hasn't deteriorated all over. A single patch may be the problem. In this case, take a sharp spade and cut out the thin or dead grass. Use a garden fork to loosen the soil and add any necessary soil amendments, such as topsoil or peat moss. Then seed or sod, using the same type of grass you already have.

Keeping Your Lawn Green

Maintaining a lawn is like caring for a house or automobile — a little attention on a regular basis can prevent major headaches later on. While a lawn doesn't need assistance every day, during the growing season it requires maintenance at least once a week in the form of mowing, watering, fertilizing, liming, or controlling insects, diseases, and weeds. By doing these tasks promptly and properly, you can reduce both the amount of time and amount of money you spend doing them.

The do's and don'ts of fertilizing

When it comes to fertilizing, it's good to remember the old adage about having too much of a good thing. True, most lawns need feeding periodically to stay healthy and green, but many southerners feed their lawns too often and too much. Overfertilization causes a host of troubles, both for the lawn and for the environment. For the lawn, it increases problems with insects, diseases, and thatch; reduces root growth and drought resistance; and makes the grass grow faster, meaning more cutting. The environment also suffers, because excess fertilizer not used by the grass washes into streams, lakes, and groundwater.

Kinds of fertilizers. Clearly, it's important to apply the right kind of fertilizer in the right amount at the right time. Let's begin with the right kind. There are many brands of lawn fertilizer on the market — some, obviously, better than others. Be sure to base your choice on quality, not price. Many inexpensive brands contain nitrogen — the most important grass nutrient — in the form of ammonium nitrate, ammonium sulfate, or pure urea. When contacted by water, the nitrogen in these "quick-release" compounds dissolves almost immediately. If it isn't absorbed by grass roots right away, it either leaches into the groundwater or runs off into storm drains.

Look for fertilizers with the words "slow-release" or "controlled-release" on the bag. At least 25 to 33 percent of the nitrogen in the fertilizer should be in slow-release form; thus it is released gradually, feeding the lawn over a period of weeks. A good slow-release fertilizer for most southern lawns contains nitrogen, phosphorus, and potassium in a roughly 3-1-2 ratio, such as 21-7-14 or 18-6-12. However, you'll find different formulations for individual grasses. For example, a bahia formulation may be 24-6-12, while one for centipede may be 15-0-15.

How much fertilizer should you apply? It's hard to state guidelines because fertilizer requirements depend on many factors — your soil type, the amount of rainfall, whether you rake clippings, the kind of fertilizer, how heavily you use the lawn, and so on. The best you can do is to purchase a name-brand fertilizer recommended for your type of grass and apply it as suggested on the bag.

Feed grass when it's actively growing. Feed warm-season grasses in spring, about three weeks after they turn green, and again in midsummer. You may want to use a weed-and-feed fertilizer for this second application. Feed cool-season grasses in fall and spring. If you've been having disease problems in your cool-season lawn, eliminate the spring feeding or use a fertilizer with a lower nitrogen content than you use in fall.

Spreaders. To distribute fertilizer across the lawn, you'll need a spreader. The two types commonly used are the drop and the rotary spreader. A drop spreader drops a trail of fertilizer behind it as wide as its hopper. A rotary spreader uses a propellerlike device to sling fertilizer out. A drop spreader takes a lot longer to cover the lawn, but it's much more precise than a rotary spreader, which often scatters fertilizer on walks, driveways, ground covers, and flowers.

Liming

Soil pH is a number that compares a soil's acidity to its alkalinity on a scale from 1 to 14, with 7 being neutral. Below 7 is acid; above 7 is alkaline. Most grasses prefer a pH between 6.5 and 7.5. (Centipede is an exception; it likes a pH between 4.5 and 5.5, the same range often recommended for blueberries and azaleas.) If your soil is too acid, you can correct it by spreading ground limestone, using a drop spreader.

Soils east of the Mississippi are generally acid, requiring periodic liming, while those west are alkaline and don't need lime. However, there are always exceptions. Parts of Tennessee and Kentucky, for example, sit on ancient deposits of limestone and have alkaline soil. The only sure way to know the pH of your soil is to test it. Then you will know whether you need to add lime, how much to apply, and the kind of fertilizer to use.

Think before you mow

Most people, believing a closely cropped lawn looks neater, cut their grass purely for appearance's sake. But there's much more at stake here than mere cosmetics. How and when you cut the grass can make the difference between a healthy and an ailing lawn.

If you remember only one thing about mowing, make it this rule: mow your grass often enough to maintain the desired height, but never remove more than one third of top growth in any one cutting. For example, if the grass is 3 inches tall, don't remove more than 1 inch in a single cutting or you will weaken the grass.

The proper mowing height for your lawn depends on the type of grass you have. In general, you can cut warm-season grasses lower than cool-season ones. For specific mowing heights, refer to the following chart.

For many reasons, it's a good idea to maintain your grass at the highest recommended height for that type. A lawn maintained at 2 inches or higher, for example, will contain much less crabgrass and other weeds than one maintained at 1 inch. In addition, taller grass needs less watering and less frequent mowing and has fewer disease and insect problems. During hot, dry weather, mow the grass ½ to 1 inch higher than the recommended mowing height.

Lawn mowers. There are two basic types of lawn mowers, rotary and reel. A rotary power mower cuts grass with a twin-edged, rapidly spinning blade attached to a single shaft. A reel mower, on the other hand, uses whirling blades attached to the wheels to cut with a scissorslike action. Reel mowers are usually the push type, powered only by your legs. They make a cleaner cut than rotary mowers (and don't produce exhaust). However, they're not effective for cutting high, overgrown grass. They also lack a rotary mower's ability to vacuum leaves, clippings, and other debris off the grass.

Clippings. This brings us to the matter of clippings. Most people bag and discard clippings as a matter of course. While there may be an aesthetic reason for doing so, in most cases it benefits the lawn to leave them right where they are. Clippings contain a significant amount of nutrients, which they

Table 2.
Recommended Mowing Heights

Grass	Height
Bahia	2–3 inches
Bermuda, Common	1–1½ inches
Bermuda, Improved	½–1 inch
Buffalograss	1–3 inches
Carpetgrass	1–2 inches
Centipede	1½–2 inches
Kentucky Bluegrass	2–2½ inches
Perennial Ryegrass	1½–2½ inches
St. Augustine	1½–3 inches
Tall Fescue	2–3 inches
Zoysia	1–2 inches

return to the lawn when they decompose. In fact, it's been estimated that 100 pounds of dry clippings from an average lawn may contain 3 to 4 pounds of nitrogen, ½ pound of phosphorus, and 1 to 2 pounds of potassium. By leaving clippings on the lawn, you can reduce its fertilizer requirements by 25 percent. Using less fertilizer not only saves money, it reduces the amount of nutrients leaching into groundwater. (Not bagging or raking clippings may also save your back.)

The primary objection to not removing clippings is that they often form unsightly mats that smother the grass beneath them. You can prevent this from happening by doing two things. First, cut the lawn when it is dry; late afternoon is usually an excellent time. Second, cut the grass regularly; don't let it get more than an inch taller than its recommended mowing height. This will reduce the volume of clippings. On a dry, sunny day, clippings will disintegrate within hours. Should any persist, just scatter them across the lawn with a soft rake. These clippings will not form thatch. Instead, they'll feed the existing grass, helping to keep it green.

The way we water

Most southerners take their water supply for granted, and in a normal year, there's plenty to go around. But when the rain clouds disappear and the well runs dry, it's important to use water efficiently. And that means taking a good look at the way we water lawns.

The sad fact is, a large percentage of the water used on lawns is wasted. Many people, for example, water the lawn during the hottest part of the day. As a result, most of the water evaporates before it ever reaches the grass roots. Another common mistake is leaving the sprinkler on too long. After several hours, the ground becomes saturated and any additional water simply runs off.

How much to water. A good rule of thumb is to give a lawn an inch of water in a single watering per week. (A few grasses, however, such as buffalograss and bahia, need little or no watering.) An easy way to measure the amount is to spread some empty tuna cans beneath the sprinkler. When they're full, you've probably watered enough. If your soil is sandy, however, you'll probably have to water more frequently, as sandy soil dries quickly. In this case, apply ½ inch of water every 4 to 5 days.

When to water. Early morning is the best time to water for two reasons. First, the air is cool, so the water won't evaporate before it gets the job done. Second, the grass blades have time to dry during the day, reducing the chances of fungal attack.

What if you can't water in the morning or local restrictions mandate watering only late at night, when you're usually asleep? The answer in both cases is to purchase a battery-powered water computer, which is available in many hardware stores and mail-order catalogs. You can program it to turn the water on and off at any time of the day or night for up to two weeks at a time. Depending on the model and where you buy it, such a device will cost between $30 and $60.

Inevitably, there will be times when you forget to water and the lawn turns brown. Does this mean the grass is dead? Not usually. Most southern grasses are used to summer droughts. When the soil dries, the grass turns brown and goes dormant. However, the next rainfall or watering quickly revives it, restoring its bright green color.

Weeds, diseases, and pests

The best way to control weeds, diseases, and insects in the lawn is to keep them from getting started in the first place. If you follow the proper procedures for mowing, watering, and fertilizing, serious lawn problems will seldom arise.

Herbicides. The fastest way to control weeds is to use a herbicide. Herbicides can be divided into two categories, pre-emergent and post-emergent. A pre-emergent herbicide prevents weed seeds from germinating. It usually contains either Balan or Dacthal and is used to control grassy weeds, such as crabgrass and annual bluegrass. Apply it in late winter or early spring.

A post-emergent herbicide kills established weeds. It commonly contains either 2,4-D, MCPP, or Dicamba and is used against broadleaf perennial weeds, such as dandelion, clover, and plantain. Apply it in late spring or summer, when the weeds are actively growing. Be sure to follow the label directions carefully; some post-emergents are safe for certain grasses and not others. These products may also damage shrubs, flowers, and trees if improperly used.

Pests and diseases. Most of us find diseases and insect problems nearly impossible to diagnose. The truth is, a brown spot on the lawn may be caused by one of several different things. If you discover a problem area, watch it carefully. If it begins to spread, consider asking a lawn care professional to identify the cause. Many companies offer diagnostic services to their customers. Your county agricultural extension agent may also be able to help.

These procedures may seem complicated, but don't be intimidated. Lawn care isn't that hard. Just do three things correctly — fertilize, mow, and water — and before you know it, you'll be enjoying the green, green grass of home.

The Gardening Year

Gardening is a year-round activity in the South, for a southern garden can offer attractive foliage and flowers in every season. There's always something to do, and there's always something to enjoy.

Winter

By northern standards, there is no winter in the South. Most winter days are above freezing, and many days are shirtsleeve weather, with temperatures in the 60s and 70s. The ground doesn't freeze for more than a day or two. The average low temperature ranges between 0 to 10 degrees in zone 7, 10 to 20 degrees in zone 8, and 20 to 30 degrees in zone 9. Southern gardeners can work outdoors throughout the winter, harvesting lettuce from beneath a plastic cover or planting bulbs in late December, moving trees and shrubs in January, pruning fruit trees and crape myrtles or dividing perennials like astilbes and Shasta daisies in February.

Winter storms in the South are unpredictable and short-lived. Winter can come in the form of a snowstorm that paralyzes Atlanta for a day or a sudden blizzard that closes the airport in Raleigh. More often than snow, the wintery blast is an ice storm that magically coats every branch, twig, and berry with crystal — and causes a huge number of fender-benders on the highways. These storms quickly melt away, but the one or two shocks of winter may come as early as November or as late as March.

In an ideal year, the autumn days would gradually get cooler and cooler. Woody plants would slowly harden off. With the first frost, tender annuals like impatiens and basil would go to the ground. Growing colder yet, the hostas, daylilies, peonies, and other herbaceous perennials would disappear for the winter. Then, sometime after the first of the year, each day would get a little warmer. The first bulbs would appear. Buds would swell on the fruit trees, viburnums, and magnolias. The smooth progression of springtime life would unfold.

Freeze damage

However, the South rarely has that ideal year, that smooth inverted curve on the temperature graph. Rather, the typical graph is jagged. And in the mid-1980s, the entire South was ravaged by two winters of extremes. On Christmas Eve of 1984, it was mild and balmy at noon. The fall weather had been extremely mild. No plants had hardened off. By midnight, it was 10 or more degrees below zero. Old camellias, crape myrtles, and loquats went to the ground or were killed outright. Nurserymen throughout the South lost millions of dollars' worth of container-grown plants sitting with their roots aboveground, vulnerable to the freeze.

Experts said that this wild swing happens only once in a hundred years, so gardeners began to replant, nurserymen reordered. Then the same sort of below-normal, destructive freeze occurred the next year, zapping tender plants that again were not hardened off.

Gardeners, nurserymen, and farmers have always been at the mercy of the weather, and they pay attention to weather reports. Many serious gardeners use a Weatheradio, a small radio tuned to the nearest U.S. Weather Bureau report 24 hours a day. Nevertheless, conditions in your own garden can differ from those at the nearest weather station.

When a severe freeze is forecast, gardeners can help their plants in two ways, with both protection and water. Northern gardens are frequently blanketed with snow, a wonderful protection against frost and wintery winds. In the South, gardeners must create a cover. Depending on the plants, protection can be a layer of mulch, a huge pile of pinestraw or leaves, a frame built around a shrub and filled with leaves, or even a small plastic greenhouse. Professionals, like the citrus growers, go even further, protecting their fields with smudge pots and large fans. Amateurs and professionals alike use water.

Northern gardeners put away their hoses in the winter. You can't do that in the South. If it doesn't rain, you need to water on mild winter days. If a freeze is predicted, take care to soak your garden, paying particular attention to trees and shrubs planted within the past year. (Then detach and drain the hose.) A well-watered azalea or camellia can survive a sudden freeze that would devastate a stressed, thirsty plant.

You can even use water to save azalea flowers threatened by a late frost. Simply start a sprinkler over the azalea bed in the early evening and let it run through the night, coating each blossom with ice. As the freeze passes, the ice melts and the flowers survive.

Winter flowers

But snow and ice are infrequent visitors. You can be out in the garden on most winter days, and you can enjoy some flowers even during the winter months. In December and January, depending on the year, airy blossoms of Japanese apricots (*Prunus mume*) appear on bare branches. While snowdrops and sprays of golden forsythia announce spring in the North during March or April, here in the South, wonderfully fragrant branches of yellow winter jasmine (*Jasminum nudiflorum*) tumble over old rock walls and mark property lines with low, tangled hedges during January.

Unusual winter- or early-spring-blooming shrubs have become more popular in the last decade. Gardeners are now enjoying witch hazel cultivars like 'Arnold Promise' and 'Diana' in addition to the native species. The dangling, small golden flower chains of coryolopsis species are attractive. The fragrant wintersweet (*Chimonanthus praecox*) produces sweet yellow and purple flowers in midwinter.

Spring

In the South, there is no clear-cut division of seasons. Winter and spring overlap, with no heed to the calendar. Which day the trees, shrubs, perennials, and bulbs bloom depends on the year. The normal sequence of flowering is predictable, but the starting date is not. Magnolias may vary as much as 6 weeks, depending on the specific winter. Some years, weather conditions cause the late winter–early spring season to telescope, and plants that would normally flower over a period of several weeks do it all at once.

Most springs, the redbuds lead the dogwoods. In spectacular years, they bloom together along the roadsides and in the understory of the woodlands. In great numbers, the wild dogwoods are glorious. However, do not take a seedling from the woods as a specimen tree. Spend the money instead for a quality named cultivar, like 'Cloud 9' or 'Cherokee Chief', which flower at an earlier age than wild seedlings, and have both larger and more numerous flowers. Today you can purchase choice dogwoods that have red, pink, or white flowers, are dwarf or weeping in form, and carry variegated foliage or even double flowers. To extend your dogwood season, add a Japanese dogwood (*Cornus kousa*), which blooms after the native dogwood has finished.

Spring tasks

As the crocuses and other bulbs poke their leaves through the ground, throw some 10-10-10 or other balanced fertilizer around them. In the South, bulbs should be fed twice a year: in late fall after a true freeze and again when the foliage appears. If you use Holland Bulb Booster, a slow-release formula based on bulb research at North Carolina State University, one application in the fall is enough. It's a tradeoff — Holland Bulb Booster saves time, but it costs more than an ordinary fertilizer.

Check established plants that need early spring care. Some homey signals are handy. For example, give the lawn its dose of crabgrass killer when the first forsythia bud opens in your area. When the first crabapple flowers appear, check the crotches of vulnerable trees for caterpillar webs. These nests appear overnight, it seems, and they need to be eliminated before the caterpillars are large enough to leave and begin to munch on the foliage of the host tree. A primitive but satisfactory method of handling these webs is to remove them from the trees with a long pole and then simply stomp on the wriggly mass. If you prefer to spray, Sevin is effective.

March is the mad month for gardeners in zone 7. (The madness strikes a little earlier the farther south the garden.) Suddenly all of the roses need pruning, garden beds must be raked and neatened, stakes should be placed around the peonies, heavy oak leaves need to be brushed off the anemones, bloodroot, arabis, and primroses on the woodland paths, developing seed pods should be snapped off the spent daffodils, and fertilizer should be spread around all of the trees, shrubs, and perennials.

After the last frost

While the peak of dogwood and azalea bloom can vary by several weeks, typically it comes a week to 10 days before the date of the average last frost in your area. Many gardeners plant their tender annuals and vegetables outdoors after this date. The gamblers plant a week or so before the ALF. The most conservative wait until after the last recorded frost. Unless you are this cautious, listen to the weather report and stand by to cover tender plants during the changeable, tricky days of spring.

With all danger of frost past, the last weeks of spring are delicious. The days are balmy. Mats of campanulas follow the earlier drifts of phlox in the rock garden or at the edge of the perennial bed. Late azaleas, peonies, and clematis continue to come into bloom. It's time to sow annual seeds into the cutting garden, fill spots that need color with bedding plants from the garden center, and plant the most tender vegetable seedlings and seeds.

You don't have to farm the back acre to have a lot of fun with vegetable gardening. Grow what you find tasty, but grow it in reasonable amounts. Only plant huge crops if you have a large family and want to freeze or can the surplus. It is not even necessary to have a vegetable garden per se. Try planting four tall, staked tomatoes at the back of your perennial garden — if that is the sunniest place in your yard. Grow lettuce, carrots, and radishes among the annuals at the front of the border. Use rabbit-eye blueberry shrubs as design elements in your landscape — they are attractive in form and have pretty little bell-like flowers in late spring, followed by a delicious crop of berries in the summer. There are many ways to enjoy an edible landscape.

Just be careful when you use garden chemicals in a mixed planting of ornamentals and edibles. Read the labels and use only as directed. If you prefer not to use pesticides, try the line of Safer products, today's equivalent of the soapy dishwater Grandmother tossed at the aphids on her rosebushes.

Summer

While it's easy to be a springtime gardener in the South, summer gardening is another matter. Summer can mean 10, 12, or 14 weeks of heat and humidity, often combined with drought. To southern gardeners, the heat tolerance of plants is often more important than their cold hardiness. For summer bloom, study the seed and perennial catalogs and look for heat-tolerant and drought-resistant varieties. Many Southeastern native plants, like coreopsis, cone flowers, green-and-gold, gaillardias, and butterfly weed fall into these categories — and move happily into a garden setting.

Roses

With sunshine and reliably warm weather comes the first exuberant flush of roses. In the Triangle of North Carolina, the time is typically mid-May; in Atlanta, early May; and at the American Rose Society's garden in Shrevesport, the display of 20,000 roses begins the last two weeks of April. After their first springtime show, modern roses will bloom on and off during the summer and then put on another grand display in the fall, after the first breath of cooler weather. The last rose of summer here often blooms in late November.

Despite the challenges of growing roses in the hot and humid South, where diseases and insects are rampant, many gardeners are dedicated to raising modern tea roses, multifloras, climbers, miniatures, and grandifloras. To combat blackspot, mildew, aphids, spider mites, and all of the other rose problems, rosarians need to follow a spraying routine that begins in the spring and continues until frost.

If you are a competitive rose grower who wants to win the Queen of the Show in the local rose show, you'll spend long hours disbudding, fertilizing, and spraying. If, however, you simply want beautiful splashes of color in your yard and flowers in your house, you may be happy with a larger number of smaller flowers on foliage that is less than perfect.

Monitor your roses and other plants for insect and disease problems. One pest you will probably notice first on your roses, clematis, and crape myrtles is the Japanese beetle. Some years there is an invasion; at other times the problem is minor. If only a few of these glistening, iridescent bugs are munching on your foliage, you can pick them off by hand or knock them into a can with kerosene at the bottom. If you have vast numbers, you will probably want to resort to chemicals. Check with your county agricultural extension agent for current recommendations.

Many southern gardeners who love roses but do not want to be bothered with extensive care have turned to old roses. Old roses tolerate more shade than the modern hybrids and take much less care. Some, like *Rosa rugosa,* are grown both for their charming single flowers and for the large red hips that decorate the shrubs until frost. Today several nurseries specialize in old roses, and there is a plant society, the Historic Rose Group, dedicated to the growing, study and preservation of old roses.

Summer-blooming perennials

June means daylilies in many gardens, public and private. These tough, floriferous, reliable perennials are essentially problem free. Give them rich, humusy soil, sunshine, and plenty of water and they will bloom abundantly. Even if planted in poor soil and neglected, they will flower generously. They even bloom in partial shade. Hundreds of cultivars are on the market, and more are being introduced every year. Hybridizers are developing dwarf daylilies and tall ones, daylilies with spidery forms and broad petals. They range in color from dark velvety wine to almost white, and some have contrasting throats, spots, or bicolors. 'Stella de Oro', a small golden yellow variety, is an exciting innovation because it blooms again in the fall.

Summertime gardens dance with daisies, from Shasta daisy 'Miss Muffet' in a small mound at the front of the perennial bed to large rudbeckias, coneflowers, and marguerites farther back. For strong verticals amid the daisies, both salvias and veronicas offer a number of choices as well as complementary hues of blue and purple to combine with the whites, yellows, and oranges of the daisies.

Watering

Unless you are developing a xerophytic garden, using only drought-tolerant materials, watering will be a major summertime activity. Dry weather can set in as early as May if the spring rains stop and the temperatures climb. Suddenly you may notice that some leaves are drooping or the lawn is "footprinting" — both signs of stress. One inexpensive, useful garden tool is a rain gauge, available in most garden centers and hardware stores. If your lawn and garden are not getting an inch of rain each week, you'll probably want to water.

Water is becoming a precious commodity in many areas, so gardeners are learning to use it more efficiently. A number of watering systems are on the market. If you have a small orchard or a rose garden, a drip system will use water economically and put it where it is needed. Several types of hoses that leak are available, and you can run them back and forth in the perennial or vegetable garden. However you water, do not sprinkle lightly. Water thoroughly to encourage plant roots to go deep into the ground. And once a decade or so, you will not have to water at all during the summer. Nature will provide.

Along with watering, other summer chores include pinching chrysanthemums and asters, feeding water lilies, dahlias, roses, gentians, and other vigorous plants, and pruning the spring-flowering shrubs, like forsythia, mock orange, and weigela. Most shrubs will be rejuvenated and perform best if one third of the oldest wood is removed each year. Also, cut back perennials that have flowered. Many will bloom again if the first spent flowers are removed.

Making cuttings

Summer is also the time to propagate woody plants. Depending on the number of new plants you want, you can stick cuttings in a pot, flat, or plastic shoe or sweater box. Fill the container with a mixture of moist peat moss and perlite, dip the cuttings in a rooting hormone, stick them in the damp medium, and enclose the pot or flat in plastic. Cover the container with glass or clear plastic and put it in the shade. Many cuttings will begin to produce roots in 3 weeks.

If you want just a cutting or two, try the old-fashioned method of taking a rose or azalea cutting, sticking it in the ground in the shade of the mother plant, and putting a glass jar over it. You can also layer a number of shrubs by nicking the underside of a branch that can reach the ground and then pinning that branch to the ground with a rock. Separate the baby plant from its mother the following year.

Fall

Fall flowers

In the perennial garden, daisylike flowers continue to reign from late summer until frost. A succession of asters can provide mounds of purple, lavender, white, pink, and blue blossoms. Asters come in every size from almost ground-hugging to 6 feet high. You'll find that any of the New York or New England asters thrive here, but *Aster* × *frikartii* is one of the most choice for the South. It makes a sturdy plant that doesn't need staking, and it's covered with clear blue flowers for weeks and weeks.

Japanese anemones provide another daisy form for the fall garden. Like most perennials, it takes about three years for them to reach their full potential. After seeing mature plantings, you will never again be without these anemones. They thrive in all but the hottest parts of the South.

Sedums are a huge genus of more than six hundred different species and cultivars. Many are fine garden plants, but if you have space for just one, make it 'Autumn Joy'. It is considered a "must" perennial because it is beautiful for months, not just days. During the summer, it forms large clumps of sturdy 24-inch stems with succulent foliage. In September, each stem is topped with a large, flat head of pink flowers that gradually age to a lovely russet brown. The dried flower stalks are decorative throughout the winter.

Fall tasks

Early fall is a good time to take a critical look at your entire garden. Is the lawn shabby? Perhaps it's time to renovate it.

(See the chapter "Southern Lawns" for advice.) Have the foundation plantings grown out of bounds? Fall is the best time to plant or move trees and shrubs in the South. They continue to develop root systems throughout the mild winters and are established before they have to cope with the stresses of hot, humid, drought-plagued summers.

Fall is also the time to plant spring bulbs. Don't plant them too early, though — wait until the soil cools off. (Bulbs are liable to rot in warm soil.) Even though bulbs arrive in the garden centers in early September, don't plant daffodils, tulips, scillas, and crocuses until after November 1. You can continue to plant bulbs throughout November and December.

As fall proceeds, clean up the vegetable garden. Don't leave plant debris lying about — it provides a haven for insects and plant diseases. Compost all garden trash. After all the harvesting is over, amend the garden with shredded leaves, compost, manure, or other beneficial materials and till. Fall preparation makes it easy to plant in the spring.

The Color Plates

The color plates and plant encyclopedia feature a variety of plants that grow well in southern gardens. The color plates are grouped according to plant type: trees, shrubs, perennials, ground covers, vines, and ferns and grasses. Within each group, the plants are arranged alphabetically by genus and species. Each plate is accompanied by a short description that includes the plant's botanical and common names, its height or spread, its bloom season (if appropriate), a comment on its uses or culture, and the number of the page on which you will find the encyclopedia entry. Unless otherwise indicated, these plants can be grown throughout the region covered by this book.

A Word about Color

Color, more than many visual attributes, is in the eye of the beholder. What one person describes as blue, another may call lavender or even purple. And it is not just the names that vary. Sun and shade, time of day, and neighboring colors can all affect what we actually see. A leaf that looks rich red in midday sun may be a deep lavender in late-afternoon shade. As you look through the photos on the following pages, remember that the camera, no less than the eye, captures colors as they appear at a certain moment. Add to that the vagaries of the printing process and the natural variation among plants and you'll see why it doesn't pay to count on getting exactly the color that you see in a photograph.

Trees

Acer ginnala

*Amur Maple
Height: to 20 ft.
Fall color*

*Average soil
p. 219*

**Acer palmatum
'Dissectum'**

*Cutleaf Japanese
Maple
Height: to 12 ft.
Fall color*

*Average soil
Slow-growing
p. 219*

Acer rubrum   *Red Maple*   *Fall color*
                 Height: to 70 ft. *p. 219*
                 Showy flowers in
                 spring

Acer saccharum *Sugar Maple*   *Moist, well-*
                  Height: to 100 ft. *drained soil*
                  Fall color   *p. 219*

Amelanchier arborea

Shadbush,
Serviceberry
Height: 20–30 ft.
One of first trees
to flower in spring

Average soil
Does not tolerate
drought
p. 224

Betula nigra

River Birch
Height: 60–80 ft.

Tolerates moist or
wet soil
May drop leaves in
dry weather
p. 231

Cedrus atlantica 'Glauca'

*Blue Atlas Cedar
Height: 40–60 ft.*

*Well-drained soil
For Upper and
Middle South
p. 239*

Cercis canadensis

*Eastern Redbud
Height: to 35 ft.
Flowers in early
spring*

*Prefers sandy,
well-drained soil
Tolerates partial
shade
p. 239*

Chionanthus virginicus

Fringe Tree
Height: to 18 ft.
Fragrant flowers
April to May

Moist, fertile soil
Handsome
specimen plant
p. 242

Cladrastis kentukea

American
Yellowwood
Height: to 35 ft.
Fragrant, showy
flowers in spring

Well-drained soil
Best in Upper
South
p. 245

Cornus florida
*Flowering
Dogwood
Height: to 30 ft.
Fall color*

*Subject to
anthracnose
Native to eastern
U.S.
p. 250*

Cornus kousa
*Kousa Dogwood
Height: to 20 ft.
Flowers later than
native dogwood*

*Fall color
Best in Upper and
Middle South
p. 250*

× **Cupressocyparis** **leylandii**

Leyland Cypress
Height: to 100 ft.
Evergreen

Full sun
Fast-growing
p. 252

Fagus grandifolia

American Beech
Height: to 100 ft.
Fall color
Specimen tree

Best in Upper and
Middle South
p. 259

Fagus sylvatica

European Beech
Height: to 100 ft.
Fall color

Moist, acid soil
Specimen tree
Upper and Middle
South
p. 259

**Gordonia
lasianthus**

Gordonia
Height: 25–40 ft.
Evergreen
Showy flowers in
spring and summer

Moist, acid soil
Not hardy in
Middle and Upper
South
p. 264

Halesia carolina   Silver-bell Tree   Pest-resistant
                       Height: to 40 ft.   Native to South
                       Flowers in spring   p. 264

Ilex × attenuata   Foster's Holly   Evergreen
'Fosteri'   Height: 10–25 ft.   Scarlet berries
                                             p. 272

Ilex
× 'Nellie R. Stevens'

*Nellie R. Stevens
Holly
Height: 15–25 ft.
Evergreen
Profuse red berries*

*Fast-growing
One of best for
South
p. 272*

Ilex opaca

*American Holly
Height: to 50 ft.,
usually 15–30 ft.
Evergreen*

*Prefers acid soil
Native to eastern
U.S.
p. 273*

**Koelreuteria
paniculata**

*Golden-rain Tree
Height: 30–40 ft.
Blooms in summer
Showy flowers in
long clusters*

*Tolerates drought
and heat
p. 278*

**Liriodendron
tulipifera**

*Tulip Tree
Height: to 100 ft.
Fall color*

*Moist, slightly acid
soil
Fast-growing
p. 284*

Magnolia grandiflora

Southern Magnolia
Height: to 80 ft.
Evergreen
Large, fragrant
flowers

Fine specimen tree
p. 289

Magnolia macrophylla

Bigleaf Magnolia
Height: 30–40 ft.
Fragrant flowers
Not good for
windy areas

Native to
southeastern
forests
p. 289

Magnolia × soulangiana

Saucer Magnolia Height: 20–30 ft., equally wide Flowers in early spring

Moist, acid soil Fine specimen tree p. 290

Magnolia stellata

Star Magnolia Height: to 15 ft. Fragrant flowers

Average soil p. 290

Magnolia virginiana

Sweet Bay Magnolia
Height: to 60 ft.
Semi-evergreen
Fragrant flowers

Good for wet places and shade
p. 290

Malus 'Callaway'

Callaway Crabapple
Height: 15–25 ft.
Flowers March to April

Tolerates heat and humidity
One of best crabapples for South
p. 292

Malus floribunda   *Japanese*   *Moist, acid soil*
                        Crabapple   *Dependable*
                        Height: to 25 ft. *p. 292*
                        Red and yellow
                        fruit

Nyssa sylvatica   *Black Gum,*   *Tolerates wet or*
                       Tupelo   *dry soil*
                       Height: to 85 ft. *Good specimen*
                       Scarlet in fall   *tree*
                                            p. 298

Oxydendrum arboreum

*Sourwood
Height: usually
20–30 ft.
Fragrant flowers in
summer*

*Striking fall color
Excellent specimen
tree
p. 302*

Pinus echinata

*Shortleaf Pine
Height: 50–60 ft.
Evergreen*

*Fast-growing
Native to South
p. 311*

Pinus strobus   Eastern White Pine   For Upper and
                       Height: 50–80 ft.   Middle South
                       Evergreen   p. 311
                       Fast-growing

Pinus   Japanese Black   Tolerates wind,
thunbergian ·   Pine   salt spray
                       Height: 20–80 ft.   Useful for coastal
                       Evergreen   areas
                                               p. 311

Pistacia chinensis
Chinese Pistache
Height: to 60 ft.
Fall color

Full sun
Tolerates drought
p. 312

Prunus cerasifera
'**Thundercloud**'
Cherry Plum
Height: 15–30 ft.
Flowers in early
spring

Moist, well-
drained soil
Full sun
p. 315

Prunus mume   *Flowering Apricot*   *Moist, well-*
                       Height: to 20 ft.   *drained soil*
                       Blooms January to   *Full sun*
                       March   *p. 316*

Prunus serrulata   *Oriental Cherry*   *Moist, well-*
'Kwanzan'   *Height: to 30 ft.*   *drained soil*
                       Double flowers in   *Full sun*
                       spring   *p. 316*
                       Fall color

Prunus subhirtella 'Autumnalis'

Higan Cherry Height: 20–40 ft. Flowers late fall to early spring

Good winter specimen tree p. 316

Quercus acutissima

Sawtooth Oak Height: 35–45 ft.

Rich, deep soil Fast-growing p. 318

Quercus alba　　*White Oak*　　　　*Slow-growing*
　　　　　　　　　Height: to 80 ft.　*Largest native oak*
　　　　　　　　　Fall color　　　　　*p. 318*
　　　　　　　　　Prefers heavy,
　　　　　　　　　damp clay soil

Quercus coccinea　*Scarlet Oak*　　　*Tolerates alkaline*
　　　　　　　　　Height: 50–80 ft.　*soil*
　　　　　　　　　Fall color　　　　　*p. 319*

Quercus
laurifolia

Laurel Oak
Height: 40–60 ft.
Semi-evergreen

Fast-growing
Native to coastal
plain
p. 319

Quercus palustris

Pin Oak
Height: to 100 ft.
Fall color
Prefers heavy,
damp clay soil

Tolerates city
conditions
p. 319

Quercus virginiana

*Live Oak
Height: to 70 ft.
Evergreen*

*Best in Lower
South, especially
along coasts
p. 319*

Sophora japonica

*Japanese Pagoda
Tree
Height: 40–70 ft.
Fragrant flowers in
long clusters in
summer*

*Fruit fall to winter
Upper and Middle
South
p. 331*

Styrax japonicus

Japanese Snowbell
Height: 20–30 ft.
Profuse flowers in
late spring

Handsome bark
Not for Coastal
South
p. 335

Taxodium
distichum

Bald Cypress
Height: to 100 ft.
Fall color

Prefers acid soil
Tolerates wet soil
Specimen tree
p. 336

Tsuga canadensis   *Canada Hemlock*   *Well-drained,*
                        Height: to 90 ft.   *moist, acid soil*
                        Evergreen   *Tolerates shade*
                                               p. 340

Ulmus parvifolia   *Chinese Elm*   *Immune to Dutch*
                        Height: to 60 ft.   *elm disease*
                        Attractive bark   *p. 341*
                        Fast-growing

Vitex agnus-castus

Lilac Chaste Tree
Height: to 20 ft.
Fragrant flowers in
long clusters in
summer

p. 347

Zelkova serrata

Japanese Zelkova
Height: to 70 ft.
Fall color
Slow-growing

Tolerates wind and
drought
p. 350

Shrubs

Abelia
× grandiflora

Glossy Abelia
Height: 3–6 ft.
Semi-evergreen
Flowers summer to
fall

Good for mixed
hedges
p. 218

Aesculus
parviflora

Bottlebrush Buckeye
Height: 8–12 ft.
Showy flowers in
early summer

Tolerates light
shade
Native to
Southeast
p. 221

Aesculus pavia Red Buckeye Tolerates moderate
Height: 10–20 ft. shade
Showy flowers in Native to
late spring Southeast
p. 221

Aucuba japonica Japanese Aucuba Shade
Height: to 10 ft. p. 230
Evergreen
Scarlet berries on
female plants

Berberis julianae   Wintergreen   Bluish black
                        Barberry   berries in fall
                        Height: 6–8 ft. Hardy
                        Evergreen   p. 230

Berberis   Japanese Barberry   Many cultivars
thunbergii   Height: 4–6 ft.   available
'Atropurpurea'   Fall color   p. 231

Buddleia davidii   Orange-eye   Blooms summer to
                       Butterfly Bush   fall
                       Height: 6–10 ft.   p. 233
                       Fragrant flowers in
                       clusters

Buxus   Littleleaf Box   Other varieties are
microphylla   Height: to 6 ft.   taller
var. koreana   Evergreen   p. 234
                       Good for hedges,
                       topiary

**Callicarpa
americana**

French Mulberry
Height: 5–8 ft.
Violet berries in
fall

Rich soil
Full sun or light
shade
p. 234

**Calycanthus
floridus**

Carolina Allspice
Height: 4–8 ft.
Fragrant flowers in
spring
Aromatic

Rich, well-drained
soil
p. 235

**Camellia
sasanqua
'Showa no Sakae'**

*Sasanqua Camellia
Height: 6–10 ft.
Evergreen
Blooms fall to
winter*

*Moist, acid soil
May freeze in
Upper and Middle
South
p. 236*

**Caryopteris
× clandonensis**

*Bluebeard
Height: to 2 ft.
Flowers in summer
Full sun*

*For Upper and
Middle South
p. 238*

**Chaenomeles
speciosa
'Toyo Nishiki'**

Common
Flowering Quince
Height: 6–10 ft.
Blooms late winter
or early spring

Easy to grow
p. 240

**Chamaecyparis
obtusa**

Dwarf Hinoki
Falsecypress
Height: 1–8 ft.
Evergreen

Damp, acid soil
Sun
Needs humidity
p. 241

**Chamaecyparis
pisifera**

Dwarf Japanese
Falsecypress
Height: 1–8 ft.
Evergreen

Damp, acid soil
Sun
Needs humidity
p. 241

**Chimonanthus
praecox**

Fragrant
Wintersweet
Height: to 16 ft.,
but can be kept
lower

Fragrant flowers in
winter
Sometimes
damaged by cold
p. 242

Clerodendrum trichotomum

Harlequin Glorybower Height: 10–15 ft. Fragrant flowers in summer Blue berries in fall

Moist, well-drained soil p. 247

Clethra alnifolia 'Pink Spires'

Sweet Pepperbush Height: 3–8 ft. Fragrant flowers in summer

Moist, acid soil p. 248

**Daphne
× *burkwoodii*
'Carol Mackie'**

Carol Mackie
Burkwood Daphne
Height: to 3 ft.
Semi-evergreen

Fragrant flowers in
May
Temperamental
p. 253

Daphne odora

Fragrant Daphne
Height: to 4 ft.
Evergreen
Blooms in early
spring

Temperamental
p. 253

Deutzia gracilis   Slender Deutzia   Best unsheared in
                        Height: to 5 ft.   shrub border
                        Blooms in spring   p. 254

Enkianthus   Redvein   Fall color
campanulatus   Enkianthus   Best in Upper and
                        Height: 8–12 ft.   Middle South
                        Flowers in   p. 257
                        midspring

Euonymus alata

Winged
Euonymous
Height: 12–15 ft.
Brilliant fall color
Short cultivars
available

Best in Upper and
Middle South
p. 257

**Forsythia
× intermedia**

Border Forsythia
Height: to 10 ft.
Blooms in early
spring

Good for forcing
p. 261

Gardenia
jasminoides

Gardenia
Height: 4–6 ft.
Evergreen
Blooms spring to
fall

Very fragrant
Moist, acid soil
p. 262

Hamamelis
× intermedia
'Arnold Promise'

Witch Hazel
Height: to 20 ft.
Fragrant flowers
winter to spring

Fall color
p. 265

Hydrangea quercifolia

Oakleaf
Hydrangea
Height: to 6 ft.
Flower clusters to
10 in. long

Blooms in summer
Fall color
p. 271

Ilex cornuta

Chinese Holly
Height: 8–15 ft.
Evergreen
Red berries
without male plant

Specimen shrub
p. 272

Ilex crenata

*Japanese Holly
Height: 5–10 ft.
Evergreen
Tolerates shade*

*Excellent for
hedges, foundation
plantings
p. 272*

Ilex verticillata

*Common
Winterberry
Height: 5–15 ft.
Deciduous holly
Profuse red berries*

*Acid soil
Tolerates wet soil
p. 273*

Ilex vomitoria   *Yaupon*   *Tolerates salt*
  Height: 15–25 ft.   *spray, all soils*
  Evergreen   *p. 273*

Illicium   *Florida Anise Tree*   *Moist soil*
floridanum   *Height: to 10 ft.*   *p. 273*
  Evergreen

Itea virginica

Virginia Sweet
Spire
Height: 4–8 ft.
Fragrant flower
clusters in late
spring

Fall color
p. 275

Juniperus
chinensis
'Torulosa'

Hollywood Juniper
Height: 20–30 ft.
Evergreen

Easy to grow
Other cultivars for
many uses
p. 276

Kerria japonica   *Japanese Kerria*   *Tolerates shade*
                       Height: 4–6 ft.   *Useful for hedges*
                       Blooms in spring   *p. 277*

Kolkwitzia   *Beauty Bush*   *For Upper and*
amabilis   *Height: 6–12 ft.*   *Middle South*
                  Showy flowers in   *p. 278*
                  spring

**Lagerstroemia
indica
'Natchez'**

Crape Myrtle
Height: to 30 ft.
Blooms all summer
Fall color
Attractive bark in
winter

Not reliably hardy
in Upper South
p. 279

**Leucothoe
axillaris**

Dog Hobble
Height: 4–5 ft.
Evergreen
Flower clusters 1–
2 in. long in spring

Moist, acid soil
Prefers full shade
p. 281

Leucothoe fontanesiana

Fetter Bush
Height: to 6 ft.
Evergreen
Blooms in spring

Moist, acid soil
Hardiest evergreen
leucothoe
p. 282

Lonicera fragrantissima

Winter Honeysuckle
Height: 5–10 ft.
Semi-evergreen
Blooms winter to spring

Very fragrant
p. 287

**Loropetalum
chinense**

Loropetalum
Height: 6–12 ft.
Evergreen
Fragrant flowers in
spring

Prefers moist, acid
soil
p. 287

**Mahonia
aquifolium**

Oregon Grape
Holly
Height: 3–6 ft.
Evergreen
Fragrant flowers in
spring

Berries attract
birds
p. 291

Mahonia bealei   Leatherleaf
Mahonia
Height: to 12 ft.
Evergreen
Showy, fragrant
flowers in spring

Blue-black berries
attract birds
p. 291

Malus sargentii   Sargent Crabapple
Height: 6–10 ft.
Blooms in late
spring

Dark red fruit
attracts birds
p. 292

Myrica cerifera

*Wax Myrtle
Height: 10–20 ft.
Evergreen
Aromatic*

*Tolerates salt,
sandy soil
Native to eastern
U.S.
p. 295*

**Nandina
domestica**

*Heavenly Bamboo
Height: 6–8 ft.
Evergreen
Fall color
Handsome red
berries all winter*

*Hardy, easy to
grow
p. 295*

**Osmanthus
× fortunei**

*Fortune's
Osmanthus
Height: 15–20 ft.
Evergreen
Fragrant flowers in
fall*

*Acid soil
Partial shade
p. 300*

**Osmanthus
fragrans**

*Fragrant Tea Olive
Height: to 25 ft.
Fragrant flowers in
fall*

*Acid soil
Best in Lower and
Gulf South
p. 300*

Philadelphus
coronarius

Common
Mock-orange
Height: to 10 ft.
Blooms in spring
Very fragrant

Best in Upper and
Middle South
p. 307

Pieris japonica
'Wada'

Japanese Pieris
Height: 3–10 ft.
Evergreen

Sandy, acid soil
p. 310

Prunus caroliniana

Carolina Cherry Laurel
Height: 20–30 ft.
Fragrant flowers in early spring
Fruit attracts birds

Native to Southeast
Best in Middle and Lower South
p. 315

Prunus laurocerasus

Cherry Laurel
Height: to 20 ft.
Evergreen
Fragrant flowers in spring

Tolerates shade
p. 315

Pyracantha 'Navaho'

Scarlet Fire Thorn
Height: to 6 ft.,
width to 8 ft.
Evergreen

Resistant to fire
blight
Other cultivars
available
p. 317

Rhaphiolepis umbellata

Indian Hawthorn
Height: to 5 ft.
Evergreen
Fragrant flowers in
spring

Tolerates dry soil
p. 320

Rhododendron 'George Lindley Taber'

Southern Indica Hybrid Azalea Height: 8–10 ft. Evergreen

Acid soil Not reliably hardy in Middle and Upper South p. 321

Rhododendron 'Hino-Crimson'

Kurume Hybrid Azalea Height: 6–10 ft. Evergreen Blooms in early spring

Acid soil p. 321

Rhododendron austrinum

Florida Flame Azalea
Height: 6–12 ft.
Fragrant flowers in spring

Hardy, easy to grow
Native to Southeast
p. 321

Rhododendron canescens

Piedmont Azalea
Height: 6–10 ft.
Fragrant flowers in spring

Hardy southern native
p. 321

Rhododendron flammeum

Oconee Azalea
Height: 4–6 ft.
Flowers in spring

Hardy throughout
the South
p. 322

Rhododendron prunifolia

Plumleaf Azalea
Height: 6–12 ft.
Flowers July and
August

Native to Georgia,
Alabama
Hardy throughout
the South
p. 322

Rosa banksiae   *Lady Banks' Rose*   *For Gulf and*
Height: 15–30 ft.   *Lower South*
Evergreen climber   *p. 323*
Profuse flowers in
spring

Rosa   *Climbing Peace*   *Can be trained*
'Climbing Peace'   *Rose*   *against fence, wall*
Height: 8–10 ft.   *or pillar*
Long blooming   *p. 323*
season

***Rosmarinus officinalis* 'Prostratus'**

Creeping Rosemary
Height: to 2 ft., spreads to 4 ft.
Evergreen

Tolerates dry soil
p. 324

Sabal minor

Dwarf Palmetto
Height: 6–8 ft.
Good for tropical effect

Not hardy in Middle and Upper South
p. 325

| *Sarcococca* *hookerana* var. *humilis* | *Sweet Box* *Height: to 2 ft.* *Evergreen* *Small, fragrant* *flowers in spring* | *Moist, rich soil* *Tolerates shade* *p. 328* |

| *Skimmia* *japonica* | *Japanese Skimmia* *Height: 3–5 ft.* *Evergreen* *Fragrant flowers* *on male plants* | *Red berries on* *female plants* *Tolerates shade* *p. 329* |

Spirea japonica
'Little Princess'
Japanese Spirea
Height: 4–6 ft.
Blooms in spring
Very easy to grow
p. 332

Spirea
× vanhouttei
Vanhoutte Spirea
Height: 6–8 ft.
Flowers in late
spring
Tolerates city
conditions
Very easy to grow
p. 332

Stewartia
pseudocamellia

Japanese Stewartia
Height: 25–30 ft.
Flowers in early
summer

Moist, acid soil
Light shade
Not for Coastal
South
p. 333

Syringa meyeri
'Palibin'

Meyer Lilac
Height: 4–8 ft.
Blooms in spring

Best in Upper
South
p. 335

Syringa vulgaris   Common Lilac   Best in Upper and
                         Height: to 15 ft.   Middle South
                         Fragrant flowers in   p. 336
                         spring

Ternstroemia   Ternstroemia   Acid soil
gymnanthera   Height: 4–10 ft.   Not hardy in
                     Evergreen   Upper South
                     Blooms in summer   p. 337

Vaccinium
corymbosum

Highbush
Blueberry
Height: 8–12 ft.
Flowers in spring
Edible berries
Brilliant fall color

Very acid soil
p. 342

Viburnum
× carlcephalum

Carlcephalum
Viburnum
Height: 6–10 ft.
Very fragrant
flowers in late
spring

Red berries
Easy to grow
p. 344

Viburnum 'Chesapeake'

Chesapeake Viburnum Height: to 6 ft., width to 10 ft. Glossy, leathery foliage

Blooms in spring Easy to grow p. 344

Viburnum × juddii

Judd Viburnum Height: 6–8 ft. Blooms in spring Very fragrant

p. 345

Viburnum
plicatum
var. **tomentosum**

Doublefile
Viburnum
Height: 8–10 ft.
Blooms in spring
Fall color

p. 345

Viburnum tinus

Laurustinus
Height: 7–10 ft.
Evergreen
Blooms winter to
spring
Blue berries

Useful hedge in
Lower and Gulf
South
p. 345

Weigela florida   *Weigela*   *Full sun*
                      Height: 7–10 ft. *Easy to grow*
                      Blooms in spring *p. 348*

Yucca filamentosa   *Adam's Needle*   *Native to*
                        Leaves form 2–3   *Southeast*
                        ft. clump   *p. 350*
                        Flowers in summer
                        on 3–5 ft. stalk

Perennials

Achillea
× 'Coronation Gold'

Fernleaf Yarrow
Height: to 3 ft.
Blooms in summer
Sun

Best in Upper and Middle South
p. 220

Alstromeria
psittacina

Parrot Flower
Height: 2–3 ft.
Semi-evergreen

Blooms in summer
Good for cutting
p. 223

Amsonia
tabernaemontana

Blue Star
Height: to 2 ft.
Blooms in late
spring

Fall foliage yellow
Easy to grow
p. 224

Anemone
× hybrida

Japanese Anemone
Height: 1–5 ft.
Blooms in late
summer and fall
Attractive foliage

Rich, well-drained
soil
Partial shade
p. 225

Aquilegia   *Common*   *Needs good*
canadensis   *Columbine*   *drainage*
                            Height: 1–2 ft.   *p. 226*
                            Blooms in spring

Aquilegia   *Hybrid Columbine*   *Needs good*
'Dragon Fly'   *Height: 1–3 ft.*   *drainage*
                            Blooms in late   *p. 226*
                            spring

Artemisia
× 'Powis Castle'

*Powis Castle
Artemisia
Height: 30–36 in.
Does not flower*

*Best artemisia for
South
p. 226*

Aspidistra elatior

*Cast-iron Plant
Height: to 2 ft.
Evergreen*

*Tolerates shade
and dry soil
For Gulf and
Lower South
p. 227*

Aster × frikartii

Aster
Height: 2–3 ft.
Blooms late
summer to frost

Sun
p. 228

Astilbe
× arendsii
'Deutschland'

Astilbe
Height: 2–4 ft.
Blooms in spring

Needs partial
shade, moist soil
Best in Upper
South
p. 228

Boltonia
asteroides
'Snowbank'

White Boltonia
Height: 3–5 ft.
Blooms in fall

Full sun
Easy to grow
p. 232

Canna
× generalis

Common
Garden Canna
Height: 3–6 ft.
Blooms in summer

Can be left in
ground in Lower
South
p. 237

Chrysanthemum
coccineum
'Brenda'

Pyrethrum
Height: 1–3 ft.
Blooms in summer

Sun
p. 243

Chrysanthemum
leucanthemum
'May Queen'

Oxeye Daisy
Height: 2 ft.
Flowers in May
and June

Sun
p. 243

**Chrysanthemum
nipponicum**

*Nippon
Chrysanthemum
Height: 1 1/2–3 ft.
Blooms in fall*

*Sun
Good for cutting
p. 244*

**Chrysanthemum
weyrichii
'Clara Curtis'**

*Clara Curtis Daisy
Height: to 1 1/2 ft.
Blooms summer to
fall*

*Spreads rapidly in
warm regions
p. 244*

Chrysogonum
virginianum

Green-and-Gold
Height: 4–10 in.
Well-drained soil

Partial shade
Blooms in spring
p. 244

Cimicifuga
racemosa

Black Snakeroot
Height: to 6 ft.
Blooms in summer
Moist soil

Partial shade
For Upper and
Middle South
p. 245

**Coreopsis
auriculata
'Nana'**

*Eared Coreopsis
Height: 6–9 in.
Blooms in early
summer*

*Best in light shade
p. 249*

**Coreopsis
grandiflora**

*Coreopsis
Height: to 2 ft.
Blooms in summer*

*Best for meadow
gardens, not
formal borders
p. 249*

Coreopsis	*Threadleaf*	*Drought tolerant*
verticillata	*Coreopsis*	*Best in Upper*
'**Moonbeam**'	*Height: 18–24 in.*	*South*
	Blooms in summer	*p. 249*

Dianthus	*Sweet William*	*Fragrant*
barbatus	*Height: 1–2 ft.*	*Best in Upper and*
	Self-seeding	*Middle South*
	biennial	*p. 254*
	Blooms in late	
	spring	

Dianthus plumarius 'Agatha'

*Grass Pink
Height: 9–18 in.
Blooms in late
spring
Fragrant*

*Well-drained soil
Sun
p. 255*

Dicentra eximia

*Wild
Bleeding Heart
Height: 12–18 in.
Blooms spring to
fall*

*Excellent woodland
wildflower
For Upper and
Middle South
p. 255*

Echinacea   *Purple Coneflower*   *Attracts butterflies*
purpurea   *Height: 2–4 ft.*   *Drought tolerant*
Blooms summer to   *p. 256*
fall

Eupatorium   *Mist Flower*   *Invasive, best in*
coelestinum   *Height: to 2 ft.*   *wild gardens*
Blooms in late   *p. 258*
summer

Gaillardia
× grandiflora

Blanketflower
Height: 8–36 in.
Blooms in summer

Well-drained soil
Sun
p. 261

Gaura
lindheimeri

White Gaura
Height: 4–5 ft.
Blooms in summer

Well-drained soil
Drought tolerant
p. 263

**Hedychium
coronarium**

Ginger Lily
Height: 4–5 ft.
Blooms summer
through fall
Very fragrant

Not hardy in
Upper and Middle
South
p. 266

**Heliopsis
helianthoides
'Summer Sun'**

False Sunflower
Height: 2–3 ft.
Showy flowers in
late summer

Durable
Tolerates heat
p. 267

Helleborus orientalis

Lenten Rose
Height: to 18 in.
Evergreen
Blooms late winter
through early
spring

Partial shade
p. 268

Hemerocallis 'Stella d'Oro'

Daylily
Height: 12–18 in.
Other cultivars to
36 in. or higher

Long-lived and
carefree
p. 268

Hosta fortunei
'Aureo-marginata'

*Fortune's
Plantainlily
Height: 2 ft. or
taller
Lilac flowers in
summer*

*Moist soil
Partial shade
p. 269*

Hosta lancifolia

*Narrowleaf
Plantainlily
Height: 2 ft.
Blooms in late
summer*

*Moist soil
Partial shade
Fast-growing
p. 270*

**Hosta
plantaginea**

Fragrant
Plantainlily
Height: to 3 ft.
Fragrant white
flowers

Tolerates sun
p. 270

**Hosta sieboldiana
'Elegans'**

Blue Giant
Plantainlily
Height: to 2 1/2 ft.
Outstanding
specimen

Lilac flowers in
summer
Moist soil
Partial shade
p. 270

Hosta undulata
'Albo-marginata'

Wavyleaf
Plantainlily
Height: to 2 ft.
Lavender flowers

Good edging plant
or ground cover
p. 270

Iberis
sempervirens

Candytuft
Height: to 12 in.
Evergreen
Blooms in early
spring

p. 271

Bearded Iris   *Bearded Iris*   *Sun*
                         Height: to 2 ft.   *For Upper and*
                         Blooms in spring   *Middle South*
                                                  p. 274

Iris cristata   *Crested Iris*   *Moist soil*
                         Height: 4–6 in.   *Partial shade*
                         Blooms in spring   *p. 274*

Iris kaempferi
'Azure'

Japanese Iris
Height: 2–3 ft.
Blooms in summer

Moist, lime-free
soil
Sun to partial
shade
p. 275

Iris
'Louisiana'

Louisiana Iris
Height: 3–4 ft.
Blooms in spring

Prefers moist soil
Sun to partial
shade
Tolerates heat,
humidity
p. 275

Iris sibirica *Siberian Iris* *Very adaptable*
Height: 2–4 ft. *p. 275*
Blooms in early
summer

Lantana camara *Lantana* *Not hardy in*
Height: to 4 ft. *Middle and Upper*
Semi-evergreen *South*
Blooms spring to *p. 281*
fall

Liatris spicata   Blazing Star   Sun
                      Height: 3–4 ft.   Easy to grow
                      Blooms in early   p. 282
                      fall

Lilium candidum   Madonna Lily   Oldest garden
                      Height: 3–4 ft.   flower
                      Evergreen   p. 283
                      Fragrant flowers in
                      summer

**Lobelia
cardinalis**

*Cardinal Flower
Height: 3–6 ft.
Blooms in summer*

*Moist soil
Sun or partial
shade
p. 286*

**Lobelia
siphilitica**

*Blue or Great
Lobelia
Height: 2–4 ft.
Blooms in summer*

*Moist soil
Sun or partial
shade
p. 286*

Lycoris radiata   *Red Spider-lily*
                       Flower stalks 12–
                       18 in. high
                       Blooms in early
                       fall

Not reliably hardy
in Upper South
p. 288

Monarda didyma   *Bee Balm*
                      Height: 2–3 ft.
                      Blooms in summer

For Upper and
Middle South
p. 294

Narcissus
'February Gold'

Daffodil
26 species,
hundreds of
cultivars

Best bulbs for
southern gardens
'February Gold'
first to bloom
p. 296

Oenothera
fruticosa

Sundrops
Height: 1–2 ft.
Blooms all summer

Good in borders,
meadows
p. 298

Paeonia lactiflora   *Peony*   *Fragrant*
'Festiva Maxima'   *Height: 2 1/2 ft.*   *Full sun*
   Blooms spring to   *p. 303*
   early summer

Perovskia   *Russian Sage*   *Full sun*
atriplicifolia   *Height: 3–5 ft.*   *For Upper and*
   Blooms   *Middle South*
   midsummer to fall   *p. 305*

Phlox carolina
'Miss Lingard'

Carolina Phlox
Height: to 3 ft.
Blooms in early
summer

Moist, well-
drained soil
p. 307

Phlox divaricata
'Mrs.Crockett'

Wild
Sweet William
Height: to 18 in.
Blooms in spring

Moist soil
Shade
p. 307

Phlox paniculata
'Mt. Fujiyama'

*Garden Phlox
Height: 3–4 ft.
Blooms in summer
Sun or partial
shade*

*Good cultivar for
South
p. 308*

Phlox stolonifera
'Blue Ridge'

*Creeping Phlox
Height: to 12 in.
Blooms in spring*

*Partial shade
p. 308*

**Phlox subulata
'Sampson'**

*Thrift
Height: to 6 in.
Evergreen
Blooms in early
spring*

p. 308

**Physostegia
virginiana**

*False Dragonhead
Height: 4–5 ft.,
shorter in dry soil
Blooms in late
summer*

*Good cut flower
Can be invasive
p. 309*

Platycodon
grandiflorus

Balloon Flower
Height: 18–30 in.
Blooms in summer

Moist, well-
drained soil
p. 313

Polygonatum
odoratum var.
thunbergii
'Variegatum'

Variegated
Solomon's-Seal
Height: to 3 ft.
Blooms in spring

Shade
For Upper and
Middle South
p. 313

***Rudbeckia
fulgida*
'Goldsturm'**

*Orange
Coneflower
Height: 2 ft.
Blooms summer to
fall*

*Sun
Best black-eyed
Susan for South
p. 324*

***Salvia farinacea*
'Victoria'**

*Mealy-Cup Sage
Height: 1 1/2 ft.
Blooms all summer*

*Sun or partial
shade
Easy to grow
p. 326*

Salvia leucantha

Mexican
Bush Sage
Height: 3–4 ft.
Blooms summer to
fall

Drought tolerant
Not hardy in
Middle and Upper
South
p. 326

Salvia × superba
'Mainacht'

Hybrid Sage
Height: 18–48 in.
Blooms late spring
through summer

Sun
Drought tolerant
For Upper and
Middle South
p. 326

Sanguinaria canadensis

Bloodroot
Height: 4–6 in.
Blooms in early spring

Moist, acid soil
Shade
p. 327

Saponaria officinalis

Bouncing Bet
Height: 1–3 ft.
Blooms in summer
Spicy fragrance at night

Sun
Good cut flower
p. 328

**Sedum
'Autumn Joy'**

*Autumn Joy
Sedum
Height: to 2 ft.
Blooms mid- to
late summer*

*Sun to partial
shade
Good drainage
essential
p. 329*

**Smilacina
racemosa**

*False Solomon's-Seal
Height: to 3 ft.
Blooms in spring
Berries attract birds*

*Partial to full
shade
Not for Lower and
Gulf South
p. 330*

**Stachys
byzantina**

*Lamb's-ears
Height: to 18 in.
Semi-evergreen
Silvery foliage*

*Sun
Not for Lower or
Gulf South
p. 333*

Stokesia laevis

*Stokes' Aster
Height: to 2 ft.
Blooms all summer*

*Sun or partial
shade
Good cut flower
p. 334*

Tiarella
cordifolia

Foamflower
Height: to 6 in.
Evergreen
Blooms in spring

Good woodland
plant
p. 338

Tradescantia
× andersoniana
'Pauline'

Common
Spiderwort
Height: 1–2 ft.
Blooms late spring
to early summer

Sun to partial
shade
p. 340

Veronica spicata
'Sunny Border
Blue'

Spiked Speedwell
Height: 18–24 in.
Flowers summer to
fall

Recommended for
Upper and Middle
South
p. 343

Veronicastrum
virginicum

Culver's Root
Height: 2–6 ft.
Blooms in
midsummer

Rich, moist soil
Sun to partial
shade
p. 344

Ground
Covers

Ajuga reptans   *Bugleweed*   *Tolerates shade*
'Burgundy Glow' *Height: to 6 in.* *Best for Upper and*
    Flowers in spring *Middle South*
    Evergreen in mild   *p. 222*
    winters

Asarum   *Wild Ginger*   *Partial to full*
canadense   *Height: 6–8 in.* *shade*
      Moist soil
      p. 227

Convallaria majalis
Lily of the Valley
Height: 6–12 in.
Blooms in spring
Very fragrant
Partial to full shade
p. 248

Cotoneaster dammeri 'Sogsholm'
Bearberry Cotoneaster
Height: to 12 in.
Evergreen
White flowers in early summer
Red berries in fall
Full sun
p. 251

Cotoneaster
horizontalis

Rock Cotoneaster
Height: 2–3 ft.
Semi-evergreen
Pink flowers
Red fruit in fall

Full sun
Fast-growing
p. 251

Cotoneaster
salicifolius
'Scarlet Leader'

Willowleaf
Cotoneaster
Height: 2–3 ft.
Evergreen
Reddish purple in
winter
Fast-growing

Fast-growing
Full sun
p. 251

Euonymus   Winter Creeper   Tolerates shade
fortunei   Trails or climbs p. 257
'Colorata'   Evergreen
                    Purple leaves in
                    fall and winter

Hedera helix English Ivy   Tolerates shade
                    Creeps or climbs p. 266
                    Evergreen

**Juniperus
conferta
'Blue Pacific'**

*Shore Juniper
Height: to 18 in.
Evergreen*

*Good for seaside
gardens
p. 276*

**Juniperus
davurica
'Expansa'**

*Parson's Juniper
Forms 2–3 ft.
mound, 8 ft. wide
Evergreen*

*Fast-growing
p. 276*

Juniperus
horizontalis
'Bar Harbor'

Bar Harbor Juniper
Height: to 12 in.
Evergreen

Tolerates poor soil,
heat
p. 277

Lamiastrum
galeobdolon
'Herman's Pride'

Yellow Archangel
Height: to 12 in.
Yellow flowers in
spring

Good for dry
shade
p. 280

Lamium
maculatum
'White Nancy'

Spotted Dead
Nettle
Height: 6–12 in.

Shade
Easy to grow
p. 281

Liriope muscari
'Variegata'

Blue Lily-turf
Height: to 18 in.
Evergreen

Tolerates shade,
dry soil
p. 285

Liriope spicata Creeping Lily-turf Tolerates shade,
Height: to 10 in. dry soil
Evergreen Can be invasive
p. 285

Mahonia repens Creeping Mahonia Tolerates shade
Height: to 12 in. p. 291
Evergreen
Yellow flowers in
spring

***Ophiopogon
japonicus***

*Mondo Grass
Height: 8–15 in.
Evergreen*

*Drought tolerant
p. 299*

***Ophiopogon
planiscapus
'Arabicus'***

*Black Mondo
Grass
Height: 6–10 in.
Evergreen*

*Prefers partial
shade
p. 299*

Pachysandra terminalis

*Japanese Spurge
Height: to 9 in.
Evergreen*

*Tolerates dense
shade
p. 302*

Trachelospermum asiaticum

*Asiatic Jasmine
Height: to 12 in.
Tender evergreen
Slow to become
established*

*For Lower and
Gulf South
p. 339*

Verbena
canadensis

Rose Verbena
Height: 8–18 in.
Blooms spring to
late summer

Easy to grow
Native Virginia to
Florida
p. 342

Vinca major

Big Periwinkle
Height: to 18 in.
Evergreen
Blooms in spring

Prefers light shade
Best in Lower and
Gulf South
p. 346

Vinca minor   *Periwinkle*   *Blooms in spring*
                         Height: to 10 in.   *Prefers light shade*
                         Evergreen   *p. 346*

Viola odorata   *Sweet Violet*   *Light shade*
'White Czar'   *Height: to 6 in.*   *Rich, moist soil*
                         Fragrant flowers in   *p. 346*
                         spring

Vines

Akebia quinata

Fiveleaf Akebia
Tolerates partial
shade
Useful for covering
walls and arbors

Can be aggressive
p. 222

**Bignonia
capreolata**

Cross Vine
Flowers April to
August
Moist, well-
drained soil

Sun or partial
shade
Good for trellises
and fences
p. 232

**Campsis
× tagliabuana
'Mme. Galen'**

*Trumpet Creeper
Flowers in late
summer*

*Fast-growing, can
be invasive*
p. 236

**Clematis
× jackmanii**

*Hybrid Clematis
Blooms in early
summer
Dozens of other
hybrids available*

*For Upper and
Middle South*
p. 247

Clematis paniculata   *Sweet Autumn Clematis*   *Best in Upper and Middle South*
                          Flowers in late   *p. 246*
                          summer
                          Fragrant

Ficus pumila   *Creeping Fig*   *Hardy only in*
                   Evergreen   *Lower and Coastal*
                                     South
                                     p. 260

Gelsemium
sempervirens

Carolina Jessamine
Evergreen
Fragrant flowers in
spring

Not hardy in
Upper South
p. 263

Lonicera
× heckrottii

Goldflame
Honeysuckle
Semi-evergreen
Long-blooming,
spring and summer

Fragrant
Attracts
hummingbirds
p. 287

Lonicera
sempervirens

Trumpet
Honeysuckle
Semi-evergreen
Attracts
hummingbirds

Native to eastern
U.S.
p. 287

Parthenocissus
quinquefolia

Virginia Creeper
Climbs to 50 ft.
Scarlet in fall

Useful for covering
walls or fences
p. 304

| *Parthenocissus tricuspidata* | Boston Ivy
Climbs to 60 ft.
Scarlet in fall | Outstanding wall
cover
p. 304 |

| *Passiflora edulis* | Maypop
Fragrant flowers in
summer
Edible fruit | Native to South
p. 304 |

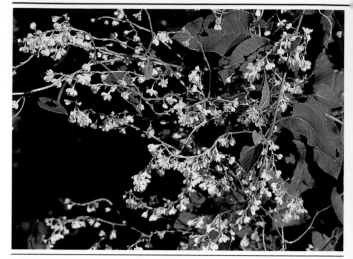

Polygonum	Silver-lace Vine	Tolerates dry soil
aubertii	Blooms late	Useful for covering
	summer to fall	eyesores
	Fragrant	p. 314

Trachelospermum	Confederate	Fragrant flowers
jasminoides	Jasmine	Best in Lower and
	Height: to 30 ft.,	Gulf South
	usually lower	p. 339
	Evergreen	

Vitis rotundifolia   Muscadine Grape   Good for shade
                        Vigorous, long-   Hardy everywhere
                        lived   but south Florida
                        Edible fruit   p. 348

Wisteria   Japanese Wisteria   Fertile, well-
floribunda   Height: to 30 ft.   drained soil
                        Showy flowers in   Full sun
                        spring   Can be invasive
                                            p. 349

Ferns and Grasses

**Adiantum
pedatum**

*Northern
Maidenhair Fern
Height: 12–24 in.*

*Moist, well-
drained soil
Light shade
p. 220*

**Athyrium filix-
femina**

*Lady Fern
Height: to 2 ft.*

*Moist, well-
drained soil
Light shade
p. 229*

Athyrium | *Japanese* | *Moist, well-*
goeringianum | *Painted Fern* | *drained soil*
'Pictum' | *Height: 10–15 in.* | *Light shade*
| | *p. 229*

Carex morrowii | *Variegated* | *Moist soil*
'Aureo-variegata' | *Japanese Sedge* | *p. 238*
| *Height: to 12 in.* |
| *Semi-evergreen* |

Chasmanthium latifolium

Upland Sea Oats
Height: to 5 ft.
Flower clusters in summer

Best in natural areas
p. 241

Cyrtomium falcatum

Holly Fern
Height: 24–30 in.
Evergreen
Good in borders

Not hardy in Middle and Upper South
p. 252

**Dryopteris
erythrosora**

*Japanese
Shield Fern
Height: 18 in.
Evergreen*

*Moist, well-
drained soil
Light shade
Not hardy in
Upper South
p. 256*

**Festuca ovina
glauca**

*Blue Fescue
Height: 8–12 in.
Evergreen*

*For Upper and
Middle South
p. 260*

Matteuccia   *Ostrich Fern*   *Wet soil*
struthiopteris   *Height: to 4 ft.*   *For Upper South*
    only
    p. 293

Miscanthus   *Maiden Grass*   *Many cultivars, all*
sinensis   *Height: to 5 ft.*   *do well in South*
'Gracillimus'   *Tolerates wet soil*   *p. 293*

Osmunda cinnamomea   *Cinnamon Fern*   *Edible fiddleheads*
Height: to 3 ft.   *p. 300*
Wet, acid soil

Osmunda regalis   *Royal Fern*   *Good accent plant*
Height: to 4 ft.   *p. 301*
Fall color
Wet, acid soil

Pennisetum alopecuroides

Fountain Grass
Height: 2–3 ft.
Silvery flower heads

Fertile soil
Sun
p. 305

Phalaris arundinacea picta

Ribbon Grass
Height: to 3 ft.
Light shade

Wet or dry soil
p. 306

Phyllostachys aurea

Golden Bamboo
Height: 20–25 ft.
Evergreen
Good for trellises,
screens

Spreads quickly
but can be
confined
p. 309

Phyllostachys nigra

Black Bamboo
Height: 15–20 ft.
Evergreen

Quick-growing
Forms lovely, open
groves
p. 309

Polystichum   *Christmas Fern*   *Rich, moist soil*
acrostichoides   *Height: 18–24 in.*   *Shade*
                           Evergreen   *p. 314*

Thelypteris   *Southern*   *Easy to grow*
kunthii   *Shield Fern*   *Not hardy in*
                      Height: 24–36 in.   *Middle and Upper*
                      Good for borders,   *South*
                      mass plantings   *p. 337*

Encyclopedia
of Plants

Abelia
A-bee'li-a
Caprifoliaceae. Honeysuckle family

Description
About 30 species of Asiatic and Mexican evergreen or deciduous shrubs. A few are popular in gardens for the clusters of small but showy flowers.

How to Grow
Plant in full sun and well-drained, humusy soil. Since flowers appear on new growth, prune in winter or early spring. Every few years, remove old stems to renew growth.

× *grandiflora* p. 102
Glossy abelia. Semi-evergreen shrub, 3–6 ft. high. Leaves oval, 1 in. long. Flowers white flushed with pink, bell-shaped, ¾ in. long. Blooms summer to fall. Good for mixed hedges, mass plantings. Abelia 'Edward Goucher' is similar but has rosy lavender flowers.

Acer
A'sir. Maple
Aceraceae. Maple family

Description
About 150 species of mostly deciduous trees and large shrubs. Many have attractive foliage that turns brilliant colors in fall. Bear clusters of small flowers in spring, followed by winged fruit.

How to Grow
Maples will grow in any good soil, preferably in full sun. During extended dry spells, irrigate deeply every two weeks or so.

ginnala p. 74
Amur maple. Shrub or small tree, to 20 ft. high, branches smooth and slender. Leaves 3-lobed, 1½–4 in. long, dark green in summer, turning scarlet in fall. Native to Asia, very hardy in U.S.

palmatum p. 74   Pictured above
Cutleaf Japanese maple. Slow-growing shrub, to 12 ft. high with weeping branches; develops into a broad mound at maturity. Leaves 5- to 9-lobed, 2–5 in. wide, the lobes deeply cut, creating a fernlike texture, turn bright red in fall. Korea and Japan. 'Bloodgood', 'Oshi Beni', 'Crimson Queen', and 'Tamukeyama' are outstanding cultivars with excellent fall color.

rubrum p. 75
Red maple. A large tree, to 70 ft. high. Leaves 3- to 5-lobed, 2–4 in. long, turning brilliant scarlet, sometimes yellow, in fall. Small but showy clusters of red flowers appear before leaves in spring. Attractive as a specimen, but because of its shallow root system, it is hard to grow other plants beneath red maple. Native Maine to Florida and Texas. 'Red Sunset' and 'October Glory' have excellent fall color.

saccharum p. 75
Sugar maple. A large tree, to 100 ft. high. Leaves 3- to 5-lobed, 4–6½ in. wide, turning red, scarlet, orange, or yellow in fall. Needs better soil conditions — moist but well-drained, not soggy — than most other maples. Use as a specimen shade tree. Native Maine to South Dakota, south to Georgia and Texas. Outstanding for fall color in the Upper and Middle South. In the Lower and Gulf South, plant *A. barbatum*, the Florida sugar maple. It is smaller, to 25 ft. high, with yellow fall color.

Achillea
A-kil-lee'a. Yarrow
Compositae. Daisy family

Description
A large genus of perennial herbs, mostly from the north temperate zone. Plants form clumps of foliage, often fernlike, and bear clusters of small flowers on upright stems. The foliage is very aromatic.

How to Grow
Plant in full sun and well-drained garden soil. Will tolerate some drought. Easily propagated by division in the spring or fall.

× 'Coronation Gold' *p. 144*
Herbaceous perennial, 3 ft. high. Leaves alternate, to 10 in. long, with a strong, spicy odor. Mustard-yellow flowers in summer, in heads 4 in. wide. Can be invasive. *Achillea* 'Moonshine', 2 ft. high, has silvery gray leaves and sulfur yellow flower in flat clusters 3–4 in. wide. New hybrid yarrows have pink, creamy, coral, and other flower colors. All yarrows do best in Upper and Middle South, may "melt" in the heat and humidity of the Lower South.

Adiantum
Ay-dee-an'tum. Maidenhair fern
Polypodiaceae. Polypody family

Description
A group of 200 or so dainty ferns, most native to temperate North America and Asia. Fronds are generally thin, delicate, and held atop wiry stalks.

How to Grow
Prefer light shade and moist, well-drained soil containing plenty of organic matter. These ferns are not drought tolerant. Divide in spring or fall.

pedatum *p. 208*
Northern maidenhair fern. A deciduous, slow-spreading fern growing 12–24 in. tall. Dark, wiry stems bears whorls of lacy fronds. Among the daintiest, most attractive ferns. Will grow

throughout the South but is better suited to cooler sections. *A. capillus-veneris,* the southern maidenhair fern, grows 10–18 in. tall and is better adapted than *A. pedatum* for gardens in the Lower and Coastal South.

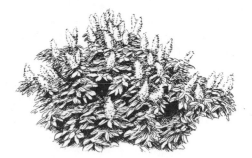

Aesculus
Es'kew-lus. Buckeyes and horse chestnuts
Hippocastanaceae. Horse-chestnut family

Description
Thirteen species of deciduous North American and Eurasian shrubs and trees. Large, long-stalked leaves have 5–9 leaflets arranged like fingers on a hand. Trees bear large clusters of very showy flowers in spring and spiny capsules containing one or two large shiny seeds called buckeyes or horse-chestnuts in fall.

How to Grow
Buckeyes or horse-chestnuts will tolerate light shade and grow in any ordinary garden soil.

parviflora p. 102   *Pictured above*
Bottlebrush buckeye. A mound-forming shrub, 8–12 ft. high and 8–15 ft. wide. Leaves have 5–7 leaflets, each 3½–8 in. long; turn yellow in fall. Outstanding in early summer when covered with 12-in.-long clusters of white flowers. An extremely handsome specimen plant for the lawn or shrub border. Native South Carolina to Florida and Alabama.

pavia p. 103
Red buckeye. A round-topped shrub or small tree, 10–20 ft. high and equally wide. Leaves have 5–7 leaflets, each 3–6 in. long; often drop early in fall. Grown for the 8-in.-long clusters of red or red and yellow flowers in late spring. A very handsome specimen tree that flowers even in moderate shade. Native Virginia to Florida and Texas.

Ajuga
Aj-oo′ga. Bugleweed
Labiatae. Mint family

Description
European annual or perennial herbs, sometimes weedy. Grown as ground covers or in borders. The leaves are opposite, oval, to 2½ in. long. Plants bear upright clusters or spikes of small 2-lipped flowers in spring or early summer.

How to Grow
Bugleweed is easy to grow in ordinary, well-drained garden soil, in full sun or partial shade. Be careful where you plant it, as it can invade lawns and other plantings.

reptans p. 184
Ajuga or bugleweed. A spreading ground cover, 3–6 in. high, with flower spikes 6–12 in. high. In the common form, leaves are green, flowers blue or purplish. There are many fine selections with variegated foliage. 'Bronze Beauty' has bronze foliage and blue flowers; 'Burgundy Glow' has green, white, and dark pink to purple foliage. All are evergreen in mild winters. Best for Upper and Middle South. Subject to southern blight and other diseases in Lower South; treat with a fungicide during hot, humid weather.

Akebia
A-kee′bi-a
Lardizabalaceae. Akebia family

Description
Four species of Asiatic woody vines. The leaves are almost evergreen and palmately compound. Plants bear loose clusters of small flowers in spring.

How to Grow
Akebia grows best in well-drained soil and sun but will tolerate partial shade.

quinata p. 198
Fiveleaf akebia. A stout, twining climber, to 30 ft. high. Leaves have 5 leaflets. The flowers are fragrant but inconspicuous. Can be aggressive; control by cutting down to the ground in late winter. Use to cover walls and arbors.

Alstroemeria
Al-stro-meer'i-a. Peruvian lily
Amaryllidaceae. Amaryllis family

Description
About 50 species of lilylike plants native to South America.
They have thick, fibrous roots, leafy stems, and showy flowers.

How to Grow
Flowers may bleach in full sun, so plant in partial shade for
a better appearance. Plant roots several inches deep in well-
drained, fertile soil. Let clumps mature in one spot for several
years; do not divide or transplant.

psittacina p. 144   *Pictured above*
Parrot flower. Semi-evergreen perennial, forms clumps of leafy
stems 2–3 ft. tall. Leaves narrow, twisted at base, 3 in. long.
Clusters of 4 or more reddish flowers top the stems in summer.
The flowers are good for cutting. Best in Lower and Gulf
South, may freeze in Middle and Upper South.

Amelanchier
Am-e-lang'ki-er. Serviceberry; shadbush; Juneberry
Rosaceae. Rose family

Description
About 25 species of deciduous shrubs or trees. Those listed
below are native to the eastern U.S. Their leaves are alternate
and toothed along the edges. Flowers are small, white or pinkish, and borne profusely in early spring. Edible fruits like tiny
purple apples ripen in early summer. These are very attractive
to birds and are sometimes used to make jellies.

How to Grow

Serviceberries grow easily in ordinary garden soil but perform poorly under drought conditions. Apply mulch and irrigate during dry spells. They will grow well in moderate shade, but flowering and fall color will be reduced. Pruning is usually unnecessary; these trees can be grown with multiple trunks.

arborea p. 76

Shadbush or serviceberry. A large shrub or small tree, 20–30 ft. tall. One of the first trees to flower in spring. (Its name comes from the fact that its bloom coincided with the run of shad, a small fish once abundant in the South.) Leaves, up to 3 in. long, turn orange in fall.

Other species of serviceberries are also excellent landscape plants. *A. canadensis* is often confused with *A. arborea,* but remains a shrub and doesn't grow into a treelike shape. *A. laevis,* Allegheny serviceberry, a tree to 35 ft. tall, has leaves that are purple-bronze in spring, bright green in summer, yellow-orange to pinkish red in fall. *A.* × *grandiflora,* apple serviceberry, is a naturally occurring hybrid of *A. arborea* and *A. laevis.* A graceful small tree, it reaches 25 ft. in height.

Amsonia

Am-sown'i-a. Bluestar
Apocynaceae. Dogbane family

Description

Twenty species of herbaceous perennials with alternate leaves and terminal clusters of small, starlike, pale blue flowers.

How to Grow

Amsonias are easy to grow in ordinary garden soil. They take full sun or partial shade. Cut back after flowering to produce fresh new foliage for summer and fall.

tabernaemontana p. 145

Blue star; willow amsonia. A bushy perennial, to 2 ft. high. Dense clusters of very pale blue flowers in late spring. Fall foliage yellow. Good in the perennial border. Native Massachusetts to Texas.

Anemone

A-nem'o-nee
Ranunculaceae. Buttercup family

Description
About 120 species of herbaceous plants native to North America, Europe, and Asia. Most have compound leaves and showy flowers. Species range from 6 in. to 4 ft. tall and bloom from spring to fall. Many are excellent for gardens.

How to Grow
Most anemones grow best in rich, well-drained soil and partial shade. Established plants need little care.

× *hybrida* p. 145   *Pictured above*
Japanese anemone. Herbaceous perennial, 1–5 ft. high, depending on the cultivar. Forms an attractive low mound of foliage in spring and summer, flowers in late summer and autumn. Flowers 2–3 in. wide, solitary, pink or white. Can be aggressive, so give it plenty of space. Best in Upper and Middle South.

Aquilegia
A-kwee-lee′je-a. Columbine
Ranunculaceae. Buttercup family

Description
About 70 species of herbaceous perennials, all from the north temperate zone. Leaves are twice- or thrice-compound. Flowers are showy, usually with long hollow spurs on the petals.

How to Grow
Columbines grow best in well-drained soil and light shade. They often die after 3–4 years, but they are easily propagated by seed and often self-sow. Leaf miners may disfigure the leaves but do not hurt the flowers.

canadensis *p. 146*

Common columbine. Herbaceous perennial, 1–2 ft. high. Flowers 1½ in. wide, with yellow petals and red sepals and spurs, in March to June. Native to dry, rocky woods from Canada to Florida and Texas. Excellent for shady or woodland gardens.

hybrids *p. 146*

Hybrid garden columbine. Herbaceous perennial, 1–3 ft. high. Flowers 2 in. wide, in shades of red, yellow, blue, white, or purple; open in late spring. Columbine foliage looks ragged after the plants bloom; combine with hostas or other plants that will hide it. 'Biedermeyer' is a good cultivar for the South.

Artemisia

Ar-te-mis′i-a

Compositae. Daisy family

Description

About 300 species of bitter or aromatic herbs and low shrubs, found in most countries and cultivated since ancient times for ornament, fragrance, and seasoning. Many have silvery leaves, often finely divided or dissected. Flowers are usually small and inconspicuous.

How to Grow

Artemisias need full sun and very well-drained soil; they will rot in wet soil or in areas with high humidity. Otherwise, they are generally easy to grow. Increase by division.

× **'Powis Castle'** *p. 147*

A cross between *A. arborescens* and *A. absinthium*, 'Powis Castle' is the best artemisia for the South. It forms a compact mound of finely divided, ferny silver foliage and does not flower. Grows 30–36 in. high. Looks wonderful in combination with pink, lavender, and blue flowers.

Asarum

Ass′a-rum. Wild ginger

Aristolochiaceae. Birthwort family

Description

Low-growing herbaceous perennials with heart- or kidney-shaped leaves. Plants spread by creeping rhizomes to form large patches. Both leaves and rhizomes have a strong, spicy, gingery aroma. The flowers hide at ground level.

How to Grow
The wild gingers need shade, humusy soil, and plenty of moisture. Given these, they spread readily and make a useful ground cover for shady woodlands or wild gardens. They are easily increased by division.

canadense p. 184
Wild ginger. 6–8 in. high. Leaves 3–6 in. wide. Flowers 1 in. wide, bell-shaped, purplish green on the outside and deep maroon inside. Native to and best in Upper and Middle South. *A. shuttleworthii,* Shuttleworth's ginger, an evergreen wild ginger with attractive white mottling on the leaves, is native to and ideal for the Middle and Lower South, but is not widely available at nurseries.

Aspidistra
As-pi-dis′-tra
Liliaceae. Lily family

Description
About 8 species of evergreen perennial herbs native to mild areas of Asia. Tough, upright leaves connect to a mat of shallow rhizomes. The flowers are inconspicuous at ground level.

How to Grow
Aspidistras do best in humus-enriched, porous soil and light shade, but tolerate conditions where little else will grow because of poor soil or low light, such as underneath live oak trees or overhanging roofs.

elatior p. 147   *Pictured above*
Cast-iron plant. Leaf blades 1–2 ft. long, 3–4 in. wide, shiny, leathery. Makes a tall ground cover for difficult spots. Hardy

only in the Gulf and Lower South; killed by hard frosts farther north or inland.

Aster
As′ter
Compositae. Daisy family

Description
An immense group of mostly perennial herbs. Most are stout plants of the woods or fields, easily grown and sometimes too weedy for borders or beds. They have alternate leaves and daisy-like flowers in clusters at tops of the stems; they bloom in late summer and fall.

How to Grow
Asters do best in full sun in soil that is fertile, moist, and well drained. During the growing season, the soil must not become dry; during the dormant season, it must not become soggy. Divide every other year.

× *frikartii* p. 148
Herbaceous perennial, 2–3 ft. high, with lavender-blue flowers 2–3 in. wide from late summer until frost. Subject to mildew and sometimes dies out in winter, but worth planting. *A. tataricus* grows up to 6 ft. tall, with lavender blooms from mid- to late fall. Other fine asters include the many cultivars of *A. novae-angliae,* New England aster, and *A. novae-belgii,* New York aster. All do best in Upper and Middle South.

Astilbe
As-til′be
Saxifragaceae. Saxifrage family

Description
A genus of herbaceous perennials mostly grown for their profuse, plumelike clusters of tiny white, pink, or red flowers.

How to Grow
Astilbes need partial shade and moist soil. Dry conditions cause leaves to turn brown and wither.

× *arendsii* p. 148
Astilbe. Perennial 2–4 ft. high with dark green or bronze leaves. Flowers in spring. Limited to Upper South, although

'Deutschland', with white flowers, seems to tolerate heat and dryness fairly well. *A. chinensis,* Chinese astilbe, does better in most of the South. It grows 1–2 ft. high, spreads readily, and has rosy purple flowers in summer. *A. tacquetii* 'Superba', 4 ft. high with lilac blooms late summer to fall, also does well in the South.

Athyrium
A-theer'ee-um
Polypodiaceae. Polypody family

Description
A group of about 25 deciduous ferns widely distributed in temperate and tropical regions around the world.

How to Grow
Prefer light shade and rich, moist, well-drained soil containing plenty of organic matter.

filix-femina p. 208
Lady fern. Lacy, light green, finely cut fronds up to 2 ft. tall. Spreads slowly. Easily divided in spring or summer. Not drought-tolerant. Native to eastern U.S.

goeringianum 'Pictum' *p. 209   Pictured above*
Japanese painted fern. Green fronds 10–15 in. tall, frosted with silver and gray. Purple stems. Striking foliage makes a colorful accent for a shady spot. Native to Japan.

Aucuba
Aw-kew'ba
Cornaceae. Dogwood family

Description
A small genus of Asiatic evergreen shrubs. The leaves are op-

posite, often variegated. Small male and female flowers are borne on different plants. Fruits are orange or scarlet, ½ in. long.

How to Grow
Aucubas do best in partial shade in moist, well-drained soil. They tolerate heavy shade, so are often grown on the north side of buildings or under trees. They are easily propagated by rooting cuttings in a jar of water.

japonica p. 103
Japanese aucuba. Evergreen shrub, usually less than 10 ft. high. Leaves glossy, dark green, more or less oval, 4–8 in. long, rather distantly toothed. Berries mostly scarlet, on female plants only. Variegated cultivars have gold dots or splotches on leaves. Damaged by severe cold, otherwise indispensable throughout the South.

Berberis
Ber'ber-iss. Barberries
Berberidaceae. Barberry family

Description
Almost 500 species of evergreen or deciduous shrubs, all more or less spiny, most native to the north temperate zone. Barberries are often planted for hedges. The leaves are simple, appearing in small clusters at the ends of short spurs, turning to scarlet, orange, or yellow in the fall. Yellow flowers bloom in spring. Many species have brightly colored berries fall and winter.

How to Grow
Barberries are easy to grow in ordinary garden soil in full sun or partial shade.

julianae p. 104
Wintergreen barberry. An upright evergreen shrub, 6–8 ft. high. Leaves 1½–3 in. long, dark green above, pale beneath.

Flower clusters 2 in. wide, berries bluish black. The hardiest of the evergreen species and one of the most popular. Native to China. Makes a mounded specimen or an impenetrable hedge.

thunbergii *p. 104 Pictured above*
Japanese barberry. Deciduous shrub, usually 4–6 ft. high. Leaves ½–1½ in. long, brilliant scarlet in fall. Flowers yellow, berries bright red. More widely cultivated than almost any other shrub, and available in many cultivars, including dwarf and purple-leaf forms. Native to Japan.

Betula
Bet'you-la. Birch
Betulaceae. Birch family

Description
A genus of medium or tall deciduous trees, rarely shrubs, native to North America and Asia. Several species are cultivated for their attractive bark; however, the white-trunked birches popular in New England don't do well in the South.

How to Grow
Birches require moist, well-drained soil for best growth. Trees drop leaves in dry weather. Leaves are also prone to insect damage; caterpillars can defoliate a 30-ft. tree in just a few days.

nigra *p. 76*
River birch; red birch. A tree, 60–80 ft. high, with reddish brown, shaggy bark. Leaves 1½–3½ in. long. Tolerates moist or even wet sites and will grow in average soil. Highly resistant to bronze birch borer. 'Heritage' is a cultivar with especially attractive bark. Native Massachusetts to Florida and westward.

Bignonia
Big-known'i-a
Bignoniaceae. Trumpet-creeper family

Description
A single species of evergreen or semi-evergreen woody vines native to the South. The leaves are compound; the flowers are funnel-shaped and slightly irregular.

How to Grow
Cross vine prefers rich, moist, well-drained soil in sun or partial shade.

capreolata p. 198   *Pictured above*
Cross vine. Woody vine climbing to 50 ft. high. Leaflets 4–6 in. long. Flowers 2 in. long, reddish orange, from April to August. Fruit a long, narrow, slightly flattened pod. A very showy vine, ideal for trellises and fences throughout the South.

Boltonia
Bole-tone'i-a
Compositae. Daisy family

Description
A small genus of erect, leafy perennials with flowers like asters. They bloom profusely in late summer.

How to Grow
Boltonias are very easy to grow in average soil. Plant in full sun, toward the rear of a bed or border. Propagate by division in spring or fall.

asteroides p. 149
White boltonia. Bushy perennial 3–5 ft. high. Covered with flower heads ¾ in. wide in fall. 'Snowbank' has white blossoms, 'Pink Beauty' is pink.

Buddleia
Bud'li-a. Butterfly bush
Loganiaceae. Buddleia family

Description

About 100 species of mostly tropical shrubs. All but one species have opposite leaves. The flowers are usually in panicles or spikes. These are among the most outstanding of late-flowering garden plants, and attract butterflies in profusion when in bloom.

How to Grow

Plant in full sun and ordinary soil. If stems are winter-killed, cut them back to the ground, as the roots usually survive. Some gardeners routinely cut stems to 12 in. above the ground in February or March.

davidii p. 105 *Pictured above*

Orange-eye butterfly bush. Shrub 6–10 ft. high, lower if cut back for the winter. Leaves lance-shaped, 6–9 in. long, finely toothed, green above, white and felty beneath. Flowers fragrant, in nodding spikes 5–12 in. long, summer to fall. Cultivars 'Pink Charm', 'White Profusion', and 'Nanho Blue' are excellent and widely available. Native to China.

Buxus

Bucks'us. Boxwood
Buxaceae. Box family

Description

Of the 30 known species of boxwood, only 2 are commonly grown. But these, and their numerous horticultural varieties, have added an atmosphere of grace, charm, and solidity to many historic gardens. The evergreen leaves are opposite and small; the flowers are small and inconspicuous but strongly scented.

How to Grow
Boxwood is very popular in the historic gardens of Virginia and other parts of the South, but it can be difficult to grow. It does best in well-drained soil in sun or light shade, and must be sheltered from cold winter winds. Because its roots are close to the surface, use a compost or bark mulch around the base to help keep them cool and reduce the need for cultivation. Boxwoods are vulnerable to winter dieback, nematodes, and various pests and diseases.

microphylla p. 105
Littleleaf box. A Japanese evergreen shrub, rarely over 6 ft. high, with leaves broadest above the middle and branchlets prominently 4-angled or winged. Var. *japonica* is a bit taller and has a more open habit. *B. sempervirens,* common box or English box, ranges from a dwarf, globular shrub to a tree 20 ft. high, the latter only in the most favorable sites. Leaves are broadest at or below the middle, ¾–1½ in. long, lustrous green on both sides. Var. *suffruticosa,* edging box, is a dwarf form used for centuries to edge beds and in formal gardens. Southern Europe, North Africa, and western Asia.

Callicarpa
Kal-li-kar′pa. Beautyberry
Verbenaceae. Verbena family

Description
A large genus of shrubs, often grown especially for their beautiful clusters of fruit in fall. The leaves are opposite; the flowers are small. The fruit is round and berrylike.

How to Grow
Plant beautyberries in full sun or light shade and rich soil. Because flowers appear on new growth, prune in spring to within 6 in. of the ground. If plants are winter-killed, they will usually come back from the base.

americana p. 106
French mulberry. Deciduous shrub, 5–8 ft. high, with leaves 4–6 in. long. Pinkish flowers ⅓ in. long in a compact bunch 1¼ in. long. Berries violet. A white-fruited variety, *C. a. lactea,* is also offered. Native Maryland to Texas and Oklahoma. *C. bodinieri,* native to China, has erect branches 6–10 ft. tall with lilac flowers and berries. *C. dichotoma,* also from Asia, has arching branches 3–4 ft. tall and violet berries.

Calycanthus
Kal-ee-kan′thus
Calycanthaceae. Sweet-shrub family

Description
Four species of deciduous shrubs native to the southeastern U.S. The leaves are opposite. All parts, including bark and wood, are aromatic. Large, fragrant flowers are brown or purple.

How to Grow
Plant in rich, well-drained soil with plenty of moisture in shade or sun. Prune after flowering. Calycanthus can spread into other plantings; control by pulling out suckers.

floridus p. 106   *Pictured above*
Carolina allspice; common sweet-shrub. A densely hairy shrub, 4–8 ft. high, with glossy leaves 3–5 in. long. Dark purple-brown flowers, 2 in. wide, have fruity fragrance, bloom in spring. Native Virginia to Florida and Mississippi.

Camellia
Ka-mee′li-a
Theaceae. Tea family

Description
Asiatic evergreen shrubs or small trees, widely grown for their waxlike, very showy, long-lasting flowers. The leaves are alternate. The flowers are nearly stalkless, 5-petaled or double, in shades of pink, red, and white.

How to Grow
Camellias need moist, well-drained, acid soil. Don't plant them too deep, and apply mulch around the roots. Camellias flower

best in partial shade. Fertilize with Epsom salts (magnesium sulfate) for good green foliage.

sasanqua p. 107
Sasanqua camellia. Evergreen shrub, 6–10 ft. high, with white to rose flowers 2–3 in. wide from fall to winter. There are dozens of cultivars with different colored flowers. Sasanqua camellias have smaller leaves and flowers, bloom earlier, and are somewhat less hardy than Japanese camellias. Likely to freeze in Upper and Middle South.

japonica
Common camellia; Japanese camellia. Evergreen shrub or small tree, 20–25 ft. high, with flowers 3–5 in. wide from late fall to spring. Several hundred cultivars are grown in the U.S., with single or double flowers ranging from white to dark red. Grown as far north as Washington, D.C., but petals are damaged by frost. New cold-hardy cultivars are being developed.

sinensis
Tea. Shrub 4–6 ft. high, with white flowers 1–1½ in. wide from early to late fall. Tolerates full sun and is more hardy to cold, heat, and drought than Sasanqua or common camellias. Native to China and cultivated for centuries as the source of tea; grown commercially near Charleston, S.C.

Campsis
Kamp′sis. Trumpet creeper
Bignoniaceae. Trumpet-creeper family

Description
Two species of handsome, deciduous, woody vines. The plants are tall-growing, climbing by aerial rootlets. The leaves are opposite and compound. The flowers are large, showy, orange or scarlet, and popular with hummingbirds.

How to Grow
Trumpet creepers are easy to grow in full sun and ordinary soil. They quickly cover rock piles, old buildings, or unsightly objects, but can become top-heavy and pull away from their support unless thinned or fastened in place. Foliage causes dermatitis in some people; they are sometimes called "cow itch" for this reason.

radicans

Trumpet creeper; trumpet vine. Stout, woody vine to 30 ft. high. Leaves have 9–11 leaflets, each 2–3 in. long. Flowers orange-scarlet, 2 in. wide, 3½ in. long, in late summer. Native to Southeast. Previously known as *Tecoma radicans* and *Bignonia radicans*.

× *tagliabuana* 'Mme. Galen' *p. 199*

A hybrid with larger, showier, salmon-red flowers. Just as vigorous and hardy as common trumpet creeper.

Canna
Kan'na
Cannaceae. Canna family

Description

A very useful and handsome genus of tropical herbs. Cannas have mostly tuberous rootstocks and stately, broad leaves that are often colored. Cultivated varieties have large clusters of very showy flowers in bright colors.

How to Grow

Over much of the country, cannas must be grown as summer bedding plants, for they are tropical and will not tolerate freezing. Plant when the soil is thoroughly warm in spring. Make raised beds of rich soil in full sun. Water during droughts. Dig the rootstocks in fall and store them in a cool, dry place. In the Lower South, cannas can be left in the ground and treated like any other perennial herb.

× *generalis* *p. 149*

Common garden canna. Herbaceous perennial 3–6 ft. high. Flowers to 4 in. across, in red, orange, pink, salmon, yellow, and white. Some cultivars have reddish or bronze leaves.

Carex
Cay'rex. Sedge
Cyperaceae. Sedge family

Description

An enormous genus of grasslike plants, some grown for their fine-textured ornamental foliage. Most form low to medium tufts of leaves and have minute green flowers atop slender, grasslike stalks.

How to Grow
Plant sedges in fertile, moist garden soil in partial shade. Increase by division. The plants are durable and easy to grow.

morrowii 'Aureo-variegata' *p. 209*
Variegated Japanese sedge. Mound-forming, to 12 in. high. Leaves flat, semi-evergreen, grasslike, with central yellow stripe. 'Variegata' has dark green leaves with white margins. Plant in groups or use as edging.

Sedges are rapidly gaining popularity and becoming more available. Look for *C. pendula,* drooping or giant sedge, 2–3 ft. tall, and *C. glauca,* blue sedge, 6 in. tall, and other species. All are excellent perennials for partial shade.

Caryopteris
Car-ry-op'ter-is
Verbenaceae. Verbena family

Description
Attractive Asiatic shrubs grown for their showy bloom. Of the 6 species, only one and its hybrids are well known, usually as bluebeard or blue spirea.

How to Grow
Bluebeards grow best in good loam in full sun. Water during dry spells. Cut the stems back in winter, since flowers grow on new wood.

× *clandonensis* *p. 107*
Bluebeard; blue spirea. A low, mounded shrub, to 2 ft. high, deciduous leaves 3 in. long. Small blue flowers in summer, in slender clusters up to 6 in. long. For Upper and Middle South.

Cedrus
See'drus. Cedar
Pinaceae. Pine family

Description
These are the true cedars, large, handsome evergreens cultivated as screen and background trees as well as specimens for lawns and parks. They are too large for most home gardens but outstanding on large properties.

How to Grow

Cedars need well-drained soil, sun, shelter from cold winds, and plenty of space. Top shoots are subject to damage by tip borers or by freezes; trees become flat-topped with age.

atlantica p. 77   *Pictured above*

Atlas cedar. These upright trees grow 40–60 ft. high and 30–45 ft. wide. The branches are stiff and angular, especially when the tree is young. Needles 1 in. long, cones 2–3 in. long. 'Glauca', blue Atlas cedar, has blue needles. *C. deodara*, deodar cedar, has drooping branch tips, softer needles. Both for Upper and Middle South.

Cercis

Sir'sis. Redbud
Leguminosae. Pea family

Description

Deciduous shrubs or small trees with showy clusters of pealike flowers in early spring, before the leaves expand. The leaves are rounded or heart-shaped and turn yellow in fall. The pods resemble flat beans.

How to Grow

Redbuds prefer well-drained, sandy loam to which lime has been added. They will tolerate partial shade. They tend to be short-lived and may die after 10–15 years, but start blooming when young.

canadensis p. 77

Eastern redbud. A small, round-headed tree, not usually over 35 ft. high, often half that height. Leaves heart-shaped, 3–5 in. long, pointed at the tip. Flowers ½ in. long, cerise-pink, in clusters 1–2 in. wide, very numerous, often borne on mature trunks and branches. Also white- and double-flowered cultivars. New York to Florida and Texas.

Chaenomeles
Kee-nom′e-lees. Flowering quince
Rosaceae. Rose family

Description
Deciduous shrubs from East Asia, grown for their colorful blossoms. Flowering quinces also bear hard, aromatic fruits, sometimes used for preserves.

How to Grow
These shrubs are easy to grow in any soil and in full sun or partial shade. They are often used for hedges. Prune after flowering.

speciosa p. 108
Common flowering quince. Shrub, 6–10 ft. high, with somewhat spiny branches. Flowers 1–2 in. wide in late winter or early spring, before the leaves open. Leaves 2 in. long, fruit yellowish green, nearly 2 in. long. There are many named cultivars. 'Cameo' has fluffy, double pink flowers; 'Spitfire' has bright red flowers and upright stems; 'Texas Scarlet' has tomato-red flowers and a spreading habit.

Chamaecyparis
Kam-ee-sip′ar-is. False cypress
Cupressaceae. Cypress family

Description
This genus has 8 species of tall, columnar evergreen trees,

native to North America and Asia. Dwarf, weeping, and variegated cultivars are very popular garden specimens. Foliage is variable. Mature needles are scalelike and minute, and press closely against the flattened, fanlike branchlets. Juvenile needles are soft and stand out from the twigs.

How to Grow
False cypresses do best in damp, acid soil. They need humidity and can't take drought or dry winds. Plant in full sun or partial shade.

obtusa p. 108
Hinoki falsecypress. Evergreen tree, 50—75 ft. high, with spreading, drooping branches. Many dwarf cultivars are very slow-growing, make compact shrubs or small trees.

pisifera p. 109   Pictured above
Japanese falsecypress. Evergreen tree, 50—75 ft. high, with a loose, open habit. Many dwarf cultivars have blue or yellow foliage and threadleaf, ferny, or furry texture.

Chasmanthium
Kas-man′-the-um
Gramineae. Grass family

Description
Five species of native perennial grasses, all strong-growing plants. Flower-spikes in flat, terminal, loose-branching clusters.

How to grow
Chasmanthiums prefer moist, well-drained, loamy soil. They do best in full sun but tolerate light shade. These grasses self-sow and can be invasive, so they are best for natural areas, not formal plantings.

latifolium p. 210
Upland sea oats, river oats. Grass to 5 ft. tall, leaves 9 in. long by 1 in. wide. Flower spikes are borne on slender, drooping stalks in graceful clusters, 8 in. long, in summer.

Chimonanthus
Ky-mo-nan'thus
Calycanthaceae. Sweet-shrub family

Description
Four species of Chinese shrubs. The one below is cultivated for its fragrant flowers, which appear before the leaves.

How to Grow
Chimonanthuses are easy to grow in any soil if drainage is good, and they will thrive in full sun or partial shade. Prune after flowering. Plant near a path or beside the house where the perfume can be enjoyed.

praecox p. 109
Fragrant wintersweet. Deciduous shrub, up to 16 ft. high, kept smaller by pruning. Opposite leaves 4–6 in. long. Yellow-purplish flowers 1 in. across, December to February, sometimes damaged by winter cold snaps but wonderfully fragrant in good years.

Chionanthus
Ki-o-nan'thus
Oleaceae. Olive family

Description
Deciduous spring-flowering shrubs or small trees, grown as handsome specimen plants.

How to Grow
Fringe trees are easy to grow in moist, fertile soil in full sun.

virginicus p. 78 *Pictured above*
Fringe tree; old-man's-beard. A shrub or tree, to 18 ft. high. Opposite leaves, 6–8 in. long. Fragrant white flowers April–May. Petals 1 in. long, in loose, hanging clusters 7 in. long

produced on previous summer's growth. Fruit fleshy, like small blue eggs, with 1 seed inside. Seed requires 2 years to germinate. Native New Jersey to Florida and Texas. *C. retusus,* Chinese fringe tree, is a multistemmed shrub 15–25 ft. high. Erect, 2–3 in. high clusters of white flowers on tips of new shoots in spring make very showy effect.

Chrysanthemum
Kris-san'thee-mum
Compositae. Daisy family

Description
An important genus of garden plants, comprising about 100 species, nearly all from the temperate or subtropical regions of the Old World. The leaves are alternate, often more or less divided, and usually strong-smelling. The flowers are borne in heads of all colors except blue and purple.

How to Grow
Plant chrysanthemums in a sunny, well-drained spot. Since they are shallow-rooted, they require moist soil and regular additions of fertilizer. Most species need pinching. When the soft growing tip is 4–6 in. long, remove it. Stop pinching plants in midsummer or when they begin flowering.

coccineum p. 150
Pyrethrum; painted daisy. Herbaceous perennial, 1–3 ft. high. Leaves fernlike. Flower heads large, often 2½ in. wide; red, pink, lilac, or white, sometimes double. Bloom in summer. Pyrethrum insecticide is extracted from the yellow disk flowers.

leucanthemum 'May Queen' p. 150 *Pictured above*
Oxeye daisy. Herbaceous perennial, 2 ft. high. Single white daisy flowers in May and June, earlier than Shasta daisies. Compact foliage. Often self-seeds.

nipponicum p. 151
Nippon chrysanthemum or daisy. Hardy border plant, 1½–3 ft. high. Glossy foliage. Pinch to keep compact. Large white flowers, 2–3 in. wide, on long stalks excellent for cutting, in September and October.

weyrichii p. 151
(Formerly called × rubellum 'Clara Curtis'.) Perennial to 1½ ft. high. Flower heads solitary, to 2½ in. across, disk yellow, rays white or pink. Blooms all summer and into the fall. Foliage finely cut with good red fall color. Spreads rapidly in warm regions and sandy soil. An old favorite.

Chrysogonum
Kris-sog'o-num. Green-and-gold
Compositae. Daisy family

Description
A single species, native to the eastern United States. Green-and-gold is an herbaceous perennial with opposite, long-stalked, bluntly toothed leaves and yellow flower heads.

How to Grow
This species does best in partial shade and poor, well-drained soil. It is subject to southern blight and "melts" if watered or fertilized too much, but it is easily propagated by division in spring or fall.

virginianum p. 152   *Pictured above*
Green-and-gold. Low-growing perennial 4–10 in. high. Flower heads solitary or a few, 1½ in. wide, yellow. Species shows regional variation. Var. *virginianum,* native in the North, grows upright. Var. *australis,* the southern form, is prostrate. Grows best in Upper and Middle South.

Cimicifuga
Sim-mi-siff'you-ga
Ranunculaceae. Buttercup family

Description
A genus of tall, rather showy, summer-blooming herbs, well suited to the wild garden or the shadiest part of the border.

How to Grow
Black snakeroot does best in moist soil that is not especially acid and in partial shade.

racemosa p. 152
Black snakeroot; black cohosh. Herbaceous perennial, up to 6 ft. high. Large, thrice-compound leaves. Flowers small, white, crowded in a dense, branched cluster, the main spike 1–3 ft. long. May need staking. Upper and Middle South.

Cladrastis
Kla-dras'tis. Yellowwood
Leguminosae. Pea family

Description
A small genus of decorative deciduous trees with alternate, compound leaves. The native yellowwood, which really does have yellow wood, is grown for its showy white flowers.

How to Grow
A well-drained soil is important, but pH is not. Prune while the tree is young to eliminate narrow crotches that might split in later years, as the wood is brittle.

kentukea p. 78 *Pictured above*
(Formerly called *K. lutea*.) American yellowwood. A smooth-barked tree, 30–35 ft. high, with fragrant pealike white flow-

ers 1 in. long, in drooping clusters 10–15 in. long. Blooms in spring. Native Georgia and North Carolina west to Illinois and Missouri. Best in Upper South.

Clematis
Klem′a-tis
Ranunculaceae. Buttercup family

Description
About 270 species of herbs or shrubby or woody vines, widely distributed in East Asia, the Himalayas, and North America. The leaves are opposite, mostly compound, the leafstalk often curling like a tendril. The flowers and fruits are often very showy.

How to Grow
Clematis grows on trellises, fences, arbors, walls, tree stumps, and other surfaces. Most species will scramble through loose shrubs and small trees into sunlight. Clematis prefers cool, rich, moist, well-drained soil. Add dolomitic lime, leaf mold, and sand when planting; never allow plants to become too dry. Provide a stable support when plants are set out, since stems are brittle and break easily in the wind. Clematis grows best with its leaves and flowers in full sun but with roots in shade. To accomplish this, mulch and underplant with a shallow-rooted ground cover, or plant on the north side of a low wall. Spring-blooming types flower on the previous year's growth; prune after flowering to preserve the plant's general shape and remove dead wood and tangled stems. Summer-flowering kinds, including large-flowered hybrids, produce flowers on the current year's wood, so prune in late winter or early spring. Young plants may be cut back to within a few inches of the ground; established plants, to 12–18 in.

armandii
Armand clematis. An evergreen vine, 15–20 ft. high. Leaves

have 3 leaflets on twisted stalks. Flowers white, 1½–2½ in. wide, in spring. Native to China. Not hardy in Upper South; excellent otherwise.

× *jackmanii*   *p. 199*   *Pictured above*
There are dozens of different hybrid clematis in this group. They are the most popular hardy vines grown in the U.S. Vines grow to 15 ft. high, with flowers 4–8 in. wide in shades of white, pink, red, blue, and purple. Bloom early summer. Upper and Middle South.

paniculata   *p. 200*
Sweet autumn clematis. Deciduous vine to 30 ft. high. Leaves have 3 leaflets, egg-shaped, 1–4 in. long, leathery. Large clusters of white flowers 1–1½ in. wide in late summer, fluffy seed heads in autumn. Different sources list this as C. *maximowicziana* or C. *dioscoreifolia*. Native to Korea, best in Upper and Middle South.

Clerodendrum
Clare-o-den'drum
Verbenaceae. Vervain family

Description
A group of over 450 species of evergreen or deciduous trees or shrubs, mostly native to the Eastern Hemisphere, many featuring showy flowers and fruits.

How to Grow
Clerodendrums prefer full sun or light shade and moist, well-drained soil. Prune in early spring.

trichotomum   *p. 110*
Harlequin glorybower. Deciduous small tree or large shrub, 10–15 feet high. Large, heart-shaped leaves. Fragrant white flowers in summer. Colorful, bright blue berries accompanied by red bracts persist into fall.

Clethra
Kleth'ra
Clethraceae. Summer-sweet family

Description
About 30 species of shrubs with very fragrant white or rosy flowers.

How to Grow
Clethras prefer moist, acid soil. They should be planted in sun or light shade.

alnifolia p. 110
Sweet pepperbush. A deciduous shrub, 3–9 ft. high. Leaves oblong, pointed, 2½–5 in. long. Erect clusters, 5 in. long, of very fragrant white flowers in summer. 'Pink Spires' and 'Rosea' have pink flowers. Native Maine to Florida and Texas.

Convallaria
Kon-va-lair'ee-a. Lily of the valley
Liliaceae. Lily family

Description
Low-growing, spreading perennials native in Eurasia and naturalized in eastern North America. Fragrant bell-shaped flowers.

How to Grow
Lily of the valley does best in partial or full shade and moist, fertile soil. Propagate by dividing local, well-established plants. Imported plants, sold in catalogs, don't grow as well as those surviving in old gardens. In favorable conditions, the plants spread to make a ground cover.

majalis p. 185   *Pictured above*
Lily of the valley. Herbaceous perennial 6–12 in. high. Upright leaves 4–8 in. long, 2–3 in. wide. Small white flowers, very fragrant, in spring.

Coreopsis
Ko-ree-op′sis
Compositae. Daisy family

Description
About 100 species of annual and perennial herbs, most with
yellow flowers.

How to Grow
Some kinds of coreopsis are almost weedlike. They are very
easy to grow in any ordinary well-drained garden soil. Divide
them in spring or fall.

auriculata p. 153 Pictured above
Eared coreopsis. Native perennial wildflower, 12–18 in. high,
with hairy leaves. Flower heads mostly solitary, 1 in. wide,
golden yellow. Cultivar 'Nana' is only 6–9 in. high. Best in
light shade, woodland margins.

grandiflora and *lanceolata p. 153*
These two native wildflowers are quite similar and often confused. Both grow up to 2 ft. tall and have golden flowers up
to 2½ in. wide. Several named cultivars bear double flowers
over a long season. Plants are short-lived but self-seed abundantly. Best for meadow gardens, not formal borders.

verticillata p. 154
Threadleaf coreopsis. Drought-tolerant native perennial 18–
24 in. high with slender threadlike leaflets. Flower heads nearly
2 in. wide in summer. 'Moonbeam' has light yellow flowers,
'Zagreb' deeper yellow flowers. Best in Upper South, but sometimes dies in winter.

Cornus
Kor'nus. Dogwood
Cornaceae. Dogwood family

Description
An important genus of deciduous garden shrubs and trees, popular for their handsome flowers, for their often brightly colored fruits, and, in some species, for the winter effect of their colored twigs. All the 45 known species are native to the north temperate zone.

How to Grow
Ordinary soil and light shade are best. Do not overfertilize, and do not plant in hot, dry, full sun. Mulch and water regularly. Our native dogwoods are beautiful trees, but unfortunately, they are subject to several insect and disease problems. In recent years, the fungus anthracnose has killed many trees in the Upper South. Ask your local extension agent for advice before planting a native dogwood.

florida p. 79
Flowering dogwood. A showy tree, up to 30 ft. high, often spreading wider. Leaves oval, 3–5 in. long, consistently coloring red or purplish for a magnificent autumn show. Flowers small, greenish, set in the midst of 4 large 3–4 in. showy, white, petal-like bracts in spring. Native to forest edges, Maine to Florida and Texas. There are many cultivars with pink or red flowers and variegated foliage.

kousa p. 79   *Pictured above*
Kousa dogwood; Japanese dogwood. An Asiatic counterpart of our native flowering dogwood. It is a smaller tree, about 20 ft. tall, and blooms about 2 weeks later. The 4 white bracts are pointed, about 2 in. wide, and unfold after the leaves have expanded. Good scarlet fall color. More trouble-free than the native dogwood, and apparently immune to anthracnose.

Named cultivars have different growth habits, larger or pink flowers. Best in Upper and Middle South.

Cotoneaster
Ko-to′nee-as-ter
Rosaceae. Rose family

Description
About 50 species of shrubs or small trees, native to Old World temperate zones. The leaves are alternate and, in some species, evergreen. White or pinkish flowers are small and appear in early summer. Small applelike fruits are borne fall and winter.

How to Grow
Plant cotoneasters in well-drained soil and full sun. Prune lightly to maintain shape. The shrubs are subject to fire blight and, in dry summers, to lace bugs and spider mites. They are useful as ground covers or trained against walls.

dammeri *p. 185   Pictured above*
Bearberry cotoneaster. Prostrate evergreen shrub to 12 in. high, with trailing branches often rooting at the joints. Leaves 1 in. long, pale beneath. Flowers white, berries bright red. Grows quickly to cover a large area.

horizontalis *p. 186*
Rock cotoneaster. Spreading shrub 2–3 ft. high, admired for its fan-shaped branching habit. Leaves nearly round, ½ in. long, reddish in fall, semi-evergreen. Flowers pinkish, fruit red. Good ground cover.

salicifolius 'Scarlet Leader' *p. 186*
Willowleaf cotoneaster. Evergreen ground cover 2–3 ft. high, spreading 6–8 ft. wide. Reddish purple winter color. Fast-growing and relatively pest-free.

× Cupressocyparis
Kew-press-o-sip′ar-is. Leyland cypress
Cupressaceae. Cypress family

Description
A hybrid species found in the garden of C. J. Leyland in Welsh-pool, England, in 1888, the offspring of *Chamaecyparis noot-katensis* and *Cupressus macrocarpa*. Leyland cypress is an upright conifer with feathery sprays of blue-green foliage.

How to Grow
This tree grows in any soil except those that are soggy, ex-tremely dry, or highly alkaline. It needs full sun, but pruning is seldom necessary. It was previously thought to be pest free, but in recent years bagworms have proven a serious problem. Heavy infestations can kill trees.

leylandii p. 80
Leyland cypress. A fast-growing, narrowly conical tree reach-ing 100 ft. at maturity. Young plants grow incredibly fast. Often grown for Christmas trees. Various named cultivars have gold or bluish foliage, upright or compact habits. Useful for quick screens, windbreaks, and hedges.

Cyrtomium
Sir-toh′mee-um
Polypodiaceae. Polypody family

Description
About 10 species of evergreen ferns, most native to the Old World.

How to Grow
These ferns prefer light shade and moist, well-drained soil containing plenty of organic matter.

falcatum p. 210
Holly fern. Glossy, deep green fronds, 24–30 in. high. Very effective in mass plantings, borders, or combined with broad-leaf evergreens. Not hardy in Middle and Upper South. 'Com-pactum' is lower-growing; 'Rochfordianum' has fringed leaf margins.

Daphne
Daf′nee
Thymeliaceae. Daphne family

Description
A genus of Eurasian shrubs, some evergreen. A few species are grown for their intensely fragrant small flowers. All parts are poisonous.

How to Grow
Daphnes are expensive, hard to find, and fussy, but their fragrance is so wonderful that they are worth a try. Sometimes they die for no apparent reason. At other times they thrive with little attention. Plant in well-drained soil that is neutral or slightly alkaline, in partial shade.

× *burkwoodii* 'Carol Mackie' *p. 111*
Carol Mackie Burkwood daphne. Semi-evergreen shrub, to 3 ft. high. Leaves 2 in. long, green with creamy edges. Terminal clusters of fragrant light pink flowers in May.

odora *p. 111*   *Pictured above*
Fragrant or winter daphne. An evergreen shrub, to 4 ft. high. Leaves 2–3 in. long. Terminal clusters of rosy purple flowers in early spring.

Deutzia
Doot′zi-a
Saxifragaceae. Saxifrage family

Description
About 40 species of deciduous shrubs, most native to Asia, with shredded bark, opposite leaves, and white flowers.

How to Grow
Deutzias are easy to grow in any ordinary garden soil.

gracilis p. 112
Slender deutzia. Deciduous shrub to 5 ft. high, usually lower and bushy. Leaves oblong, 1½–2½ in. long. Loose clusters of many white flowers, ¾ in. wide, in spring. Best in an unsheared hedge or shrub border.

Dianthus
Dy-an′thus
Caryophyllaceae. Pink family

Description
About 300 species of annual or perennial herbs, mostly Eurasian. Many have fragrant flowers that are good for cutting. Leaves are opposite, usually narrow, and sometimes evergreen.

How to Grow
Dianthus is easy to grow in well-drained soil with added lime. Plant in full sun or light shade. Plants tend to die out after 2 or 3 years but are easily propagated by seed, division, or cuttings. Cut the spent flower stalks to the base of the plant.

barbatus p. 154
Sweet William. Biennial or short-lived perennial, 1–2 ft. high, with flat, broad leaves. Fragrant flowers ½ in. across, borne in flat heads 3–5 in. across, red, rose-purple, white, or varicolored; sometimes double, in late spring. Very long-lasting as cut flowers. Best in Upper and Middle South.

gratianopolitanus
Cheddar pinks. Neat, mat-forming, evergreen perennial, 6–12 in. high. Fragrant flowers 1 in. wide, spring to fall. 'Bath Pink' is a favorite old-fashioned cultivar with soft pink flowers and

excellent foliage. 'Tiny Rubies' is a compact plant with rich pink flowers on short stalks.

plumarius p. 155 *Pictured above*
Grass pink. Mat-forming herb 9–18 in. high, with smooth, bluish gray foliage. Flowers 1½ in. across, fragrant, rose-pink to purplish, white or variegated colors, petals fringed, sometimes double.

Dicentra
Dy-sen'tra
Fumariaceae. Bleeding heart family

Description
A small genus of slender herbs from Asia and North America. They have fleshy rootstocks and feathery leaves. The unusual flowers are heart-shaped or long-spurred.

How to Grow
Grow bleeding hearts in fertile, moist soil with plenty of organic matter, in light shade. They will self-sow and form pleasant natural drifts.

eximia p. 155
Wild bleeding heart. Herbaceous perennial 12–18 in. tall, with finely divided fernlike leaves and narrow, heart-shaped, magenta-pink flowers. Blooms spring to fall. Native New Jersey to Tennessee and North Carolina. An excellent woodland wildflower for the Upper and Middle South.

Dryopteris
Dry-op'ter-is
Polypodiaceae. Polypody family

Description
A group of about 150 species of ferns native to temperate and tropical areas of the world.

How to Grow
These ferns prefer light shade and moist, well-drained soil containing plenty of organic matter.

erythrosora p. 211
Japanese shield fern, autumn fern. Evergreen fern, 18 in. tall, native to China and Japan. Beautiful arching fronds emerge with a striking coppery red color in spring. Clump-forming. Not hardy in Upper South.

marginalis Pictured above
Marginal shield fern, leatherwood fern. Handsome, upright, evergreen fern, 2 ft. tall. Clump-forming. Not as fussy as most ferns. Tolerates drought if grown in shade. Native Canada south to Georgia and Alabama. Easy to grow throughout the South.

Echinacea
Ek-in-ay′see-a. Purple coneflower
Compositae. Daisy family

Description
Echinaceas are easy-to-grow native perennial wildflowers. Their roots are thick and black; the leaves are alternate. Daisylike flower heads are borne on long stalks.

How to Grow
Purple coneflower prefers well-drained, sandy, loamy soil. It tolerates full sun and drought.

purpurea p. 156
Purple coneflower. Perennial 2–4 ft. high. Leaves coarsely toothed. Flowers 3 in. wide, ray flowers pink, rosy, or white; disk flowers coppery or orange-brown. Blooms summer to fall, attractive to butterflies. Good cut flower.

Enkianthus
En-ki-an′thus
Ericaceae. Heath family

Description
Asiatic shrubs, some cultivated for their yellow-orange flowers and fine red color in the fall.

How to Grow
Plant enkianthus in full sun to partial shade, in a well-drained, moderately acid soil like that needed for rhododendrons. Do not move established plants.

campanulatus p. 112
Redvein enkianthus. Deciduous shrub, 8–12 ft.; can grow to 30 ft. high. Alternate leaves, 1–3 in. long. Drooping clusters of ½-in. long bell-shaped flowers, yellow with red veins, cover the bush in midspring. Best in Upper and Middle South.

Euonymus
You-on'i-mus
Celastraceae. Spindle-tree family

Description
About 170 species of shrubs, vines, and trees with smooth opposite leaves that are sometimes evergreen. All have small, inconspicuous flowers in spring and bear inedible fruits from midsummer to frost.

How to Grow
Grow euonymus in any soil or exposure. Scale insects are often a problem, but they can be controlled with horticultural oil sprays.

alata p. 113   *Pictured above*
Winged euonymus. A deciduous shrub, 12–15 ft. high, with stiff cork-winged twigs. Leaves 2 in. long, brilliant rosy red

in fall. Fruit red, ½ in. long. 'Compacta' is a smaller, globe-shaped cultivar. Used as a colorful specimen or in hedges. Native to East Asia. Best in Upper and Middle South.

americanus
Strawberry bush or hearts-a-burstin'. A deciduous shrub, 4–6 ft. high, native to woodlands in eastern North America. Bland-looking most of the year, but noteworthy in fall when scarlet fruits pop open.

fortunei p. 187
Winter creeper. A trailing or climbing evergreen vine with oval leaves ¾–2 in. long. Mostly used as a ground cover but will climb trees or walls. There are many cultivars. 'Colorata' has deep purple leaves in autumn and winter. 'Kewensis' is a fine-textured trailing form to 2 in. high, with small whitish-veined leaves ¼ in. wide.

Eupatorium
You-pa-toe′ri-um
Compositae. Daisy family

Description
A large genus of chiefly tropical American herbs, a few reaching temperate regions and grown in flower gardens. The flowers are showy, in numerous small heads crowded in clusters.

How to Grow
These plants are easy to grow in ordinary soil and light shade.

coelestinum p. 156
Mist flower; hardy ageratum. Herbaceous perennial, to 2 ft. high. Leaves thin, coarsely toothed. Flower heads numerous, small, light blue or violet-blue. Best in wild gardens; can be invasive.

Fagus
Fay′gus. Beech
Fagaceae. Beech family

Description
A genus of 10 species of deciduous trees native to the Northern Hemisphere. The leaves are alternate and toothed. Inconspi-

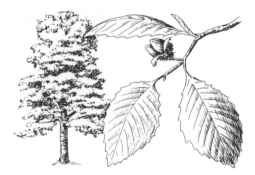

cuous flowers bloom in spring; small, woody, prickly nuts appear in fall.

How to Grow
Beeches prefer moist but well-drained acid soil. Growth and foliage are best in full sun. Allow plenty of space for specimen trees to develop their characteristic beauty. Do not underplant, because beech roots are shallow.

grandifolia p. 80   *Pictured above*
American beech. A tree to 100 ft. high, with smooth light gray bark. Leaves 4–7 in. long, green in summer, yellow-bronze in fall, often persisting through the winter. Native to and best in Upper and Middle South.

sylvatica p. 81
European beech. A tree to 100 ft. high. Leaves 3½–5 in. long. There are many cultivars. 'Pendula' has weeping branches; 'Cuprea' has coppery leaves, 'Purpurea' has purple leaves, and 'Tricolor' has variegated pink, purple, and white leaves. Upper and Middle South.

Festuca
Fess-too′ka. Fescue
Gramineae. Grass family

Description
Nearly 100 species of annual or perennial grasses, usually tufted. Some are grown for turf or ornament.

How to Grow
Fescues need light, well-drained soil and full sun. They some-

times "melt" in high heat and humidity. Renew them by division every few years. Use as specimens, for edging, or as a ground cover.

ovina glauca p. 211
Blue fescue. Evergreen grass with slender stems 8–12 in. high and silvery blue, threadlike leaves to 6 in. long. Upper and Middle South.

Ficus
Fy′kus. Fig
Moraceae. Mulberry family

Description
A large genus of chiefly tropical trees, shrubs, and vines, including the common fig and many ornamentals. Nearly all have milky sap. The leaves are alternate, deciduous or evergreen.

How to Grow
Grow figs in fertile soil in sun or shade. They are outstanding on the walls of courtyard gardens in Savannah, Charleston, Mobile, and New Orleans. Do not plant them by hot south- or west-facing walls.

pumila p. 200
Creeping fig; climbing fig. Evergreen vine to 40 ft. high. Leaves dense, very numerous. Young stems grow neat and flat against walls, have small leaves. Prune to remove older, fruiting stems, which stick out, have coarse leaves, and bear inedible figs. Hardy only in Lower and Coastal South.

Forsythia
For-sith′i-a
Oleaceae. Olive family

Description
Very handsome, spring-blooming, Asiatic shrubs, widely planted for their profuse, usually yellow flowers, which bloom before or while the leaves unfold.

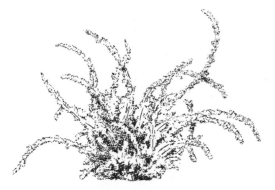

How to Grow
Easy to grow in any garden soil, forsythias are extremely effective when planted in large masses, especially against an evergreen background. Prune after flowering.

× *intermedia* p. 113   *Pictured above*
Border forsythia. Deciduous shrub, to 10 ft. high, with arching or spreading branches. Opposite leaves, 3–5 in. long, sometimes turning purple in fall. Stems are covered with clusters of yellow flowers, 1½ in. long, in early spring. There are several cultivars, including 'Arnold Dwarf', low-growing and useful as a ground cover, and 'Lynwood', with bright gold flowers.

Gaillardia
Gay-lar'di-a
Compositae. Daisy family

Description
North American wildflowers, some popular as garden plants. They are leafy, erect, branching herbs with handsome flower heads.

How to Grow
Gaillardias do best in loose, well-drained soil and full sun. Winterkills are frequent in heavy, wet soils. Renew by division every few years.

× *grandiflora* p. 157
Blanketflower. Herbaceous perennial 8–36 in. high, with slightly hairy leaves. Flowers red and yellow, 3–4 in. wide. 'Goblin' is a low-growing cultivar with large flowers.

Gardenia
Gar-dee′ni-a
Rubiaceae. Madder family

Description
A genus of 200 species of tropical Old World shrubs and trees with fragrant white flowers and glossy evergreen leaves.

How to Grow
Plant in moist, acid soil with plenty of organic matter. Gardenias grow best in sun or light shade, are hurt by frost and drought. They are fussy but worth the trouble. The leaves turn chlorotic (yellow) in alkaline soil. Plants are attacked by aphids, scale, mealybugs, and spider mites. Fragrant flowers over a long season justify the effort.

jasminoides p. 114   Pictured above
Gardenia. Evergreen shrub, 4–6 ft. high. Leaves 3–4 in. long, thick and glossy. Very fragrant white flowers 2–3½ in. wide. Popular cultivars include 'Mystery', an upright shrub with large double flowers; 'Radicans', a low creeping shrub with small flowers; and 'Veitchii', 3–4 ft. high, a very good bloomer from spring to fall. China. Lower and Gulf South.

Gaura
Gau′ra
Onagraceae. Evening primrose family

Description
About 20 species of perennial North and South American wildflowers. They are stout herbs with alternate leaves and terminal flower spikes.

How to Grow
Gauras are very easy to grow in full sun and ordinary garden soil. They need good drainage and tolerate droughts. Divide in spring or fall.

lindheimeri p. 157
White gaura. Herbaceous perennial to 5 ft. high; bushy. Flowers white fading to light pink, ½–1 in. long, in erect, wandlike stalks, over long season. Good for back of border. Native to Louisiana and Texas.

Gelsemium
Gel-see′mi-um
Loganiaceae. Buddleia family

Description
A few species of evergreen woody vines native in East Asia and eastern North America. The leaves are opposite; the flowers are funnel-shaped and attractive.

How to Grow
Plant in fertile, well-drained soil in sun or light shade. Gelsemiums are attractive on a trellis, fence, or lamppost, or as a ground cover.

sempervirens p. 201 *Pictured above*
Carolina, or yellow, jessamine or jasmine. Evergreen vine climbing 10–20 ft. high. Shiny leaves 2–4 in. long. Covered with clusters of fragrant bright yellow flowers in spring. All parts of the plant are poisonous. Not hardy in Upper South.

Gordonia
Gor-doh′-nee-a
Theaceae. Tea family

Description

About 30 species of evergreen trees and shrubs native to the warmer parts of the southern United States and Asia.

How to Grow

Gordonias prefer sun or light shade and moist, acid soil. They grow wild in swamps and bogs and can be temperamental in home landscapes.

lasianthus p. 81

Upright evergreen tree growing 25–40 ft. high. Features showy, white, camellia-like blooms in spring and summer. Can make a striking specimen or grouping. Not hardy in Middle and Upper South.

Halesia
Ha-lee'zi-a
Styracaceae. Storax family

Description

Handsome, medium-sized trees with white, bell-shaped flowers hanging gracefully along twigs of previous year's growth, especially interesting when viewed from below.

How to Grow

Halesias prefer partial shade but tolerate full sun. They grow best along stream banks, in acid, moist but well-drained soil. Hardy and pest-free.

carolina p. 82   *Pictured above*

Silver-bell tree; snowdrop tree. Deciduous tree, usually reaching 30–40 ft. high. Leaves 2–4 in. long, yellow-green in fall. Numerous drooping clusters of white flowers in spring, followed by dry 4-winged fruits 1½ in. long. A fine, pest-resistant small tree, spectacular against taller evergreens. The related mountain silver-bell, *H. monticola,* is a larger tree with larger flowers. Both native to the South.

Hamamelis
Ha-ma-mell′is. Witch hazel
Hamamelidaceae. Witch hazel family

Description
A small genus of shrubs and small trees native to North America and East Asia. Grown for its fragrant flowers in winter and early spring and brilliant fall foliage. The leaves are alternate, more or less wavy-toothed. Flowers are yellow or reddish, crumpled in the bud, the 4 petals strap-shaped. Seedpod pops open dramatically, shooting its 2 shiny black seeds a considerable distance.

How to Grow
Witch hazel is very easy to grow in ordinary or moist garden soil, in full sun or light shade. Pest-free.

× *intermedia* *p. 114*
Hybrid witch hazel. Deciduous shrub or small tree, to 20 ft. high. Leaves 3–4 in. long, turning yellow to red in fall. Flowers on bare twigs, winter to spring. There are many cultivars. 'Arnold Promise' has fragrant yellow flowers; 'Jelena' has copper-colored flowers and orange-red fall color; 'Ruby Glow' has coppery-red flowers and orange-red foliage in fall. All are wonderful shrubs.

Hedera
Hed′er-ra. Ivy
Araliaceae. Aralia family

Description
Evergreen woody vines from northern Eurasia and North Af-

rica. Leaves are alternate, usually lobed. There are two growth forms. Juvenile stems are vining; mature stems, erect and spreading, bear flowers and berries.

How to Grow

Ivy thrives in rich, moist soil. It grows well in shade; full sun will scorch some varieties. Aerial rootlets cling to masonry, brick, and tree bark. Ivy will hide a chain link fence, but it does not twine and must be woven into the links. It makes a good ground cover under trees where grass cannot be maintained. Its deep roots help control soil erosion on banks. Common ivy grows fast and can be invasive. Prune heavily or shear for desired habit and compact growth.

Fancy-leaved cultivars are increasing in popularity. They are hardy but less aggressive than common English ivy. Ideal in containers or as specimens or accent plants.

helix   p. 187   *Pictured above*

English ivy. Evergreen vine, creeping or climbing to 50 ft. high. Juvenile leaves 3- to 5-lobed, 2–5 in. long; leaves on flowering branches of mature plants are larger, squarish, not lobed. A vigorous and versatile vine. Fancy-leaved cultivars include 'Needlepoint', 'Deltoidea', 'Fan', 'Dragon's Claw', and many others. All are suitable throughout the South.

Hedychium
Hed-ee'kee-um
Zingiberaceae. Ginger family

Description

About 50 species of herbaceous perennials, many grown for their fragrant, showy flowers.

How to Grow

Ginger lily prefers partial sun or light shade and moist, fertile, well-drained soil. Divide plants in late fall or early spring.

coronarium   p. 158

Ginger lily or butterfly ginger. Herbaceous perennial, 4–5 ft. high, with large, coarse foliage on upright stalks. White, very fragrant flowers from summer through fall. Kahili ginger (*H. gardneranum*) bears fragrant yellow flowers with red stamens. Red ginger lily (*H. coccineum*) has red or salmon-red flowers. Not hardy in Upper and Middle South.

Heliopsis
He-li-op′sis
Compositae. Daisy family

Description
Sunflowerlike North American herbs, useful for informal borders or wild gardens. They have opposite, rather coarsely toothed, 3-veined leaves, often very rough. The flower heads are long-stalked and showy, the long rays generally yellow, the disk flowers darker.

How to Grow
Heliopsis is easy to grow in average soil, preferably in full sun. It wilts unless watered in hot, dry weather. Propagate by seed or by division.

helianthoides p. 158   *Pictured above*
False sunflower. Herbaceous perennial, 2–3 ft. high. Flower heads 4 in. wide, bright yellow. A durable and showy plant that is a mainstay of the late-summer perennial garden. 'Summer Sun' is the best cultivar for the South; it tolerates heat well and blooms for weeks.

Helleborus
Hell-e-bore′us
Ranunculaceae. Buttercup family

Description
A small genus of Eurasian herbs with thick, fibrous roots and divided evergreen leaves. Flowers are showy, nodding, very long lasting in the garden.

How to Grow

Helleborus prefers moist soil and partial shade, but will grow in most garden soils. It forms clumps and also spreads by self-sowing. A pest-free and long-lived perennial, excellent for the South.

orientalis p. 159

Lenten rose. Evergreen perennial, to 18 in. high. New leaves come up in spring. Bears clusters of 2–6 flowers, 2 in. wide, in cream, purplish pink, or greenish white fading to brown, on leafless stems; blooms from late winter through early spring. Related Christmas rose, *H. niger,* does not do well in the South.

Hemerocallis
Hem-mer-o-kal′lis. Daylily
Liliaceae. Lily family

Description

About 15 species of perennial flowers, native from Central Europe to Japan. Basal clumps of long narrow leaves, with clusters of lilylike flowers atop upright stalks. There are thousands of hybrid cultivars. Daylilies are easy to grow and very popular in the South.

How to Grow

Plant daylilies in ordinary, well-drained soil, in sun or partial shade. They have few problems with pests or diseases. Plants are long-lived and form vigorous clumps. Divide clumps every few years.

hybrids *p. 159 Pictured above*

Daylily. Herbaceous perennials generally 2½–3½ ft. high. Some have evergreen foliage, others die back to the ground each winter. Flowers range from 2–7 in. wide and come in shades of cream, yellow, orange, salmon, rose, pink, lavender, and bicolors. Some have ruffled petals; some are fragrant; most have one or more bursts of flowering between early June to late September. Compact varieties have flower stalks 12–18 in. high, tall cultivars reach 36 in. or higher.

Daylilies are excellent in perennial beds and borders, in massed plantings, or naturalized in open areas or on slopes. A mixture of daylilies and daffodils makes a carefree planting with a long season of bloom. The new small daylily cultivars, such as the very popular 'Stella d'Oro', do well in containers.

Hosta
Hos'ta. Plantain-lily
Liliaceae. Lily family

Description
About 25 species of herbaceous perennials, all from China, Korea, and Japan. Numerous cultivars are grown for their handsome basal leaves; they have white, lilac, or blue flowers in midsummer.

How to Grow
Hostas are very easy to grow and make fine specimens that improve with age. A clump can grow in the same place for 20 years or more. Propagate by dividing clumps in summer. Hostas do best in partial shade and moist soil. Use metaldehyde bait to control slugs and snails that feed on leaves; traps or cats to control pine voles, which eat hosta roots; and Terrachlor fungicide to treat southern blight, a fungus disease that weakens the leaf bases.

fortunei 'Aureo-marginata' *p. 160*
Fortune's plantainlily. Perennial, 2 ft. or more high. Leaf blades to 5 in. long, egg-shaped, green with yellow or gold border. Flowers lilac to violet, to 1½ in. long.

lancifolia p. 160

Narrowleaf plantainlily. Perennial, 2 ft. high. Leaf blades 4–6 in. long, lance-shaped or narrower, often with a long point. Flowers violet, to 2 in. long. A fast-growing hosta that forms a cascading mound of leaves.

plantaginea p. 161   *Pictured above*

Fragrant plantainlily. Perennial, to 3 ft. high. Leaf blades to 8 in. long, heart-shaped, medium green or sometimes yellowish. Flowers pure white, very fragrant, to 4 in. long. 'Royal Standard' has greener foliage, even more fragrant flowers. Both tolerate more sun than most hostas do.

sieboldiana 'Elegans' p. 161

Blue giant plantainlily. Perennial, to 30 in. high. Leaf blades 10–15 in. long, heart-shaped, with rich blue-green color and seersuckerlike texture. Flowers lilac, to 1½ in. long, on stalks shorter than the leaves. Mature clumps are outstanding specimens.

undulata 'Albo-marginata' p. 162

Wavyleaf plantainlily. Perennial, to 2 ft. Leaf blades to 6 in. long, egg-shaped, green with cream or white borders. Flowers lavender, to 2 in. long. Often used as an edging or ground cover.

Hydrangea
Hy-dran'jee-a
Saxifragaceae. Saxifrage family

Description

Deciduous garden shrubs and woody vines, often cultivated for their showy flower clusters in summer.

How to Grow
Hydrangeas need rich, well-drained, moist soil and full sun or partial shade. Water well during dry periods.

quercifolia   p. 115   *Pictured above*
Oakleaf hydrangea. A coarse-textured shrub, to 6 ft. high, with hairy, reddish twigs and flaky bark. Large oak-shaped leaves with 3–7 toothed lobes, often turning a rich reddish purple in fall. Showy upright clusters of flowers, white in June, turning pink or tan later in the summer. Named cultivars, including 'Snowflake' and 'Snow Queen', have larger, heavier, flower clusters. Native Georgia to Florida and Louisiana.

Iberis
Eye-beer′is
Cruciferae. Mustard family

Description
About 30 species of annual and perennial herbs, mostly from the Mediterranean region, some grown in flower gardens.

How to Grow
Iberis needs well-drained soil and full or partial sun. They are easily propagated by division.

sempervirens   p. 162
Candytuft. Evergreen perennial, to 12 in. high, with narrow leathery leaves. Clusters of small white flowers cover the plant for several weeks in early spring. Useful as edging, in rock gardens, or on slopes. Prune after flowering.

Ilex
Eye′lecks
Aquifoliaceae. Holly family

Description
A large genus of evergreen and deciduous trees and shrubs, many grown as ornamentals. The leaves are alternate, sometimes spiny-toothed. Male and female flowers, borne on separate plants, are inconspicuous, white or greenish. Fruits, on female plants only, are often bright red and showy. Male and female plants must be planted together to produce berries.

How to Grow

Most hollies do best in moist, well-drained, slightly acid soil; plant them in sun or partial shade.

× *attenuata* 'Fosteri' *p. 82*

Foster's hybrid hollies. Evergreen shrubs or small trees, 10–25 ft. high. Most have small, light green, few-toothed narrow leaves and scarlet berries. This hybrid group includes 'East Palatka', 'Foster's', and 'Savannah' hollies. All are popular as foundation plants, hedges, and specimens.

cornuta *p. 115*

Chinese holly. Dense-branched, spiny-textured, evergreen shrub or tree, usually 8–15 ft. high. The angular, lustrous leaves have 3 spines at the tip and 1 or 2 along the sides. Red berries, ½ in. wide, are produced without fertilization, so it is not necessary to have a male tree nearby. The female cultivar 'Burfordii' can reach 20–25 ft.; it has bright green wedge-shaped leaves with only a few spines at the tip. Although often used as a foundation planting, this cultivar grows much too large and will soon hide the house. It is better to use it as a large specimen shrub or prune it into a tree shape.

crenata *p. 116*

Japanese holly. An extremely handsome evergreen shrub 5–10 ft. high, with small, fine-toothed leaves. Fruit is black but inconspicuous. This holly requires slightly acid soil; don't plant near concrete, which is alkaline. Tolerates shade. There are several cultivars with compact, spreading, or upright growth form. Much used in foundation plantings and hedges.

× 'Nellie R. Stevens' *p. 83*

Nellie R. Stevens holly. Large shrub or small tree, 15–25 ft. high, evergreen. Lustrous dark green leaves with 2 or 3 spines on each side. Heavy crops of red berries. A vigorous, fast-growing holly. One of the best for the South.

opaca p. 83
American holly. Evergreen shrub or tree to 50 ft. but usually 15–30 ft. high. The leaves are 1½–4 in. long, pea-sized red berries usually single. Grows best in acid soil. Native Massachusetts to Florida, west to Texas. There are hundreds of named cultivars.

verticillata p. 116   *Pictured above*
Common winterberry. A deciduous, usually spreading shrub 5–15 ft. high, grown mostly for its bright red fruits, which are more profuse than in any other holly and persist over most of the early winter. The leaves are 1½–3 in. long, toothed but not spiny. It prefers acid soil, tolerates poor drainage. Native Canada to Florida, west to Missouri. There are many named cultivars.

vomitoria p. 117
Yaupon. An evergreen shrub or small tree, 15–25 ft. high. The leaves are 1½ in. long, the margins wavy-toothed. Scarlet fruit is borne on old wood. There are many cultivars, including several dwarf forms. This is a versatile holly, tolerant of wet or dry, acid or alkaline soil. Highly recommended for hedges and foundation plantings in the South. Tolerates coastal salt spray. Native Long Island to Florida, west to Texas.

Illicium
Il-liss'i-um
Illiciaceae. Anise family

Description
A genus of 40 species of shrubs and trees with aromatic, evergreen leaves. Two are native to the South, others are Asian. The woody, star-shaped, fragrant fruits of Chinese or star anise (*I. verum*) are used as a spice.

How to Grow
Anises need moist or even wet soil with plenty of organic matter. Plant in shade or sun.

floridanum p. 117
Florida anise tree. Evergreen shrub to 10 ft. high. The leaves

are elliptical, 6 in. long, resin-scented. Odd maroon flowers in spring. The related Ocala anise, *I. parviflorum,* has yellow flowers, more upright habit. Both are native to Georgia, Florida, and Louisiana but hardy up into the Middle South. Pest-free.

Iris
Eye'ris
Iridaceae. Iris family

Description
Over 150 species of herbaceous perennials, mostly from the north temperate zone. There are thousands of horticultural varieties. Irises have stout rhizomes or bulbous rootstocks; narrow, often sword-shaped, leaves; and showy flowers. Flowering occurs from winter to summer, depending on species.

How to Grow
Care varies, but most irises do best in sun and well-drained soil. Some tolerate dampness and shade. Plant rhizome-producing irises with the rhizome showing and the fan of leaves pointing in the direction you want the plant to grow. Propagate species by seed and hybrids by division.

Bearded iris *p. 163   Pictured above*
A huge group of hybrid cultivars, all with creeping rhizomes, erect flat leaves, and showy flowers in a wide range of colors. Depending on cultivar, flower stalks are 8–36 in. high. Easy to grow in well-drained soil. Upper and Middle South.

cristata *p. 163*
Crested iris. Leaves and flower stalks 4–6 in. high. Flowers are lavender-blue with yellow crest, outer segments 1½ in. long, faintly fragrant. Plant in partial shade and moist humusy soil. Spreads to form wide clumps. Native Maryland to Georgia and Arkansas.

kaempferi p. 164
(Also called *I. ensata*.) Japanese iris. Leaves and flower stalks 2–3 ft. high. The popular cultivars have very large, flat flowers, up to 8 in. wide, in rich shades of blue, purple, red-violet, and white. Plant in lime-free soil and keep constantly moist.

Louisiana hybrids p. 164
A group of hybrids based on several species native to southern wetlands. Most grow 3–4 ft. high. Flowers up to 7 in. wide, in shades of blue, purple, pink, copper, and yellow. Good for areas with hot, humid summers. They prefer but do not require moist soil.

sibirica p. 165
Siberian iris. Leaves and flower stalks 2–4 ft. high. There are hundreds of cultivars, with blue, violet, or white flowers, smaller and more graceful than bearded iris. Native to Eurasia. Plants can grow for years without being divided. They are tough, reliable, and pest-free.

Itea
It'ee-a
Saxifragaceae. Saxifrage family

Description
A small genus of shrubs or trees cultivated for their showy flowers.

How to Grow
Virginia sweet spire is easy to grow in well-drained, moist soil. Plant it in sun or partial shade.

virginica p. 118
Virginia sweet spire. Deciduous shrub, 4–8 ft. high with grace-ful arching branches. The leaves are oval, 2–4 in. long, bright red in fall. Clusters 4–6 in. long of small, white, fragrant flowers bloom from late spring to early summer. Native New Jersey to Florida and Texas.

Juniperus
Jew-nip'er-us. Juniper
Cupressaceae. Cypress family

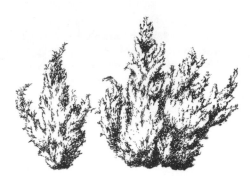

Description
About 70 species of evergreen conifers, ranging from low, prostrate shrubs to tall, slender trees. On young plants and vigorous branches, the leaves are usually needle-shaped; on adult plants, leaves are generally small, scalelike, pressed close to twigs. Flowers are inconspicuous, fruit is berrylike. Wood, foliage, and berries are all fragrant.

How to Grow
Plant junipers in ordinary soil and full sun. Spider mites and bagworms are occasional pests. Use upright forms as specimens and hedges. Low, spreading types are excellent for covering slopes.

chinensis cultivars *p. 118   Pictured above*
Very popular junipers selected from a Chinese species. Dozens of named cultivars are grown as ground covers, specimens, foundation plantings, and hedges. 'Torulosa', with rich green needles, artistic twisted form, and dense erect branches, grows 20–30 ft. high. 'Pfitzeriana' has gray-green needles; its branches spread at a 45-degree angle, easily reaches 5 ft. high and 10 ft. wide. All are vigorous, easy to grow, hardy to cold and heat.

conferta *p. 188*
Shore juniper. Handsome prostrate shrub to 18 in. high. Leaves sharply pointed. New growth is light green, later becoming blue-green. Native to Japan, it does very well in sandy soil, seaside gardens. Most used as a ground cover, but can also be planted in containers or trained over walls. 'Blue Pacific' and 'Emerald Sea' are especially dense and low-growing.

davurica 'Expansa' *p. 188*
Parson's juniper. Low-growing shrub with branches that

spread just above the ground, eventually forming a mound 2–3 ft. high and 8 ft. across. Native to east Asia. Vigorous and adaptable, it does very well in the South. White- and yellow-variegated forms are also available. Good specimen plant or ground cover.

horizontalis cultivars   *p. 189*

Creeping junipers. Prostrate shrubs with long, spreading branches, widely planted as ground covers. They tolerate poor soil and hot, dry, sunny locations. Native to eastern North America. There are dozens of cultivars. 'Bar Harbor' forms a dense mat to 12 in. high and has steel-blue foliage turning silvery purple in winter. 'Plumosa' has ascending branches to 18 in. high with feathery light green foliage, tinged purplish in winter. 'Wiltonii' has prostrate branches forming a silver-blue carpet 6 in. high; it trails nicely over a wall or large rock.

Kerria

Ker′ri-a
Rosaceae. Rose family

Description

One species of deciduous shrubs, grown for its yellow flowers. Native to China.

How to Grow

Kerria is easy to grow in ordinary garden soil. Plant in partial or full shade. Prune the shrub after flowering; remove old stems every few years.

japonica   *p. 119*   *Pictured above*

Japanese kerria. Deciduous shrub with slender green branches, growing 4–6 ft. high. Leaves are 1½–4 in. long. Bright yellow flowers, 1½ in. wide, in spring. 'Shannon' has larger flowers, 'Pleniflora' has double flowers. Useful for mass plantings, hedges.

Koelreuteria
Kel-roo-teer'i-a. Golden-rain tree
Sapindaceae. Soapberry family

Description
A small genus of deciduous Asiatic trees often planted for their yellow, summer-blooming flower clusters and fall seedpods.

The trees have deep roots and are not invasive, so annuals and perennials can be planted beneath them.

How to Grow
Golden-rain tree is not fussy about soil, but does best in full sun. It withstands drought and heat and is fairly pest-free.

paniculata p. 84
Golden-rain tree. A fine specimen tree, usually 30–40 ft. high. Compound leaves are 9–18 in. long, the leaflets coarsely toothed. Very showy clusters, 12–15 in. long, of bright yellow flowers in summer are followed by yellow-tan papery pods, 2 in. long, lasting through fall. Hardy in Upper and Middle South. *K. bipinnata,* Chinese flame tree, reaches 60 ft. high, has yellow flowers in late summer and rosy pink pods. Branch tips may freeze in Upper and Middle South, but trees recover and bloom on new wood.

Kolkwitzia
Kolk-wit'zi-a. Beauty bush
Caprifoliaceae. Honeysuckle family

Description
One species of Chinese shrub, cultivated for its showy flowers.

How to Grow
Beauty bush is easy to grow. Plant it in full sun in any type of soil. Remove old stems after flowering.

amabilis p. 119
Beauty bush. Deciduous shrub, 6–12 ft. high, with upright, arching stems. Pink, bell-shaped flowers, ½ in. long, in spring. A hardy, tough, old-fashioned favorite for the Upper and Middle South.

Lagerstroemia
Lay-ger-stree′mi-a
Lythraceae. Loosestrife family

Description
About 55 species of decorative shrubs and trees from warm regions of the Old World. One species, crape myrtle, is a spectacular, summer-flowering shrub or tree.

How to Grow
Crape myrtles need full sun or nearly so, and warm summers. Plant in acid to neutral soil with plenty of organic matter. Since blossoms form on new growth, prune before buds show in late winter or early spring. Crape myrtles respond well to pruning; they may be cut almost to the ground each spring for perpetual shrubbiness or trained to a single trunk or multiple-trunked small trees. Japanese beetles are a major pest in some areas, eating all the flowers and buds.

indica p. 120 *Pictured above*
Crape myrtle. Deciduous large shrub or small tree, up to 30 ft. tall. The leaves are opposite, 1–2 in. long, bright yellow, orange, or red in fall. Mottled, flaking, bark is especially attractive in winter. Flowers with crinkly petals, white, pink, red, lavender, or purple, 1¼ in. wide, in clusters 6–8 in. long. Blooms all summer. Many named cultivars have different color flowers. Not reliably hardy in Upper South.

National Arboretum hybrids
These outstanding new crape myrtles, hybrids of *L. indica* and *L. fauriei,* have improved winter hardiness, mildew resistance, large foliage with excellent fall color, larger flowers summer to fall, and handsome bark. Developed at the National Arboretum in Washington, D.C.

Lamiastrum
Lay-mee-as'trum
Labiatae. Mint family

Description
One species of low-growing perennial herbs, native to Europe and planted as a ground cover. Opposite leaves have a pungent odor.

How to Grow
Lamiastrum is easy to grow in average soil in shade. It is an excellent ground cover for dry shade; also useful for covering old foliage of daffodils. Though prey to slugs, it is otherwise pest-free. Increase by cuttings or division.

galeobdolon p. 189
Yellow archangel. Herbaceous ground cover to 12 in. high. Leaves are heart-shaped, 1½ in. long. Dense clusters of yellow flowers in spring. 'Variegatum' has silvery leaves with green-spotted margin, 'Herman's Pride' has silvery leaves veined with green.

Lamium
Lay'mium. Dead nettle
Labiatae. Mint family

Description
About 40 species of Old World herbs with opposite leaves, square stems, and clusters of small 2-lipped flowers. Can be weedy.

How to Grow
Lamium is easy to grow in ordinary moist garden soil in shade. Propagate by division or cuttings.

maculatum p. 190 *Pictured above*
Spotted dead nettle. A spreading herbaceous ground cover, 6–12 in. high. Variegated leaves are 1½ in. long. Many cultivars are available; 'Chequers', with violet flowers, is best for the South. Others may "melt" in heat and humidity.

Lantana
Lan-ta′na
Verbenaceae. Verbena family

Description
About 155 species of very ornamental tropical or subtropical shrubs, grown for their bright, cheerful flowers.

How to Grow
Plant lantanas in ordinary soil and full sun. They are tough and drought tolerant when established. Prune hard in spring to prevent woodiness.

camara p. 165
Lantana. Semi-evergreen shrub to 4 ft. high and wide. Leaves are oval, 2–6 in. long. Flowers are yellow, orange, or red, in clusters 1–2 in. wide, spring to fall. Use in planters, on slopes, or as low hedge. Native Central America north to Texas and Florida. Not hardy in Middle and Upper South.

Leucothoe
Lew-koth′o-ee
Ericaceae. Heath family

Description
Ornamental shrubs grown for their handsome dark foliage, graceful habit, and attractive fragrant flowers.

How to Grow
Leucothoes need moist, acid, peaty soil or sandy loam with plenty of humus added. They prefer full shade but will grow in full sun if kept constantly moist. Leaf spot diseases can disfigure the foliage.

axillaris p. 120
Dog hobble. Evergreen shrub with arching branches, 4–5 ft. high. Leathery, pointed leaves, 2–4 in. long. White flowers in

axillary clusters, 1–2 in. long, in spring. Native Virginia to Florida and Mississippi.

fontanesiana p. 121
Fetter bush. Evergreen shrub, to 6 ft. high, with slender, arching branches. White flowers in drooping 3-in.-long clusters along the branches in spring. Native Virginia to Georgia and Tennessee; hardiest of the evergreen leucothoes. Cultivar 'Rainbow' has bright white, pink, and coppery new growth.

  Agarista populifolia, also called fetter bush, is closely related to and used to be grouped with the leucothoes. It is an evergreen shrub, 10–12 ft. high, with arching branches. Small, bright green leaves turn red or bronze in winter. Honey-scented white flowers in spring. It is good for a quick screen or hedge and makes a large foundation plant if pruned. Native to the Coastal Plain, but hardy throughout the Lower and Middle South.

Liatris
Ly'a-tris
Compositae. Daisy family

Description
About 40 species of showy North American wildflowers with stiff, narrow, alternate leaves and handsome spikes or racemes of rose-purple flowers in summer or early fall.

How to Grow
Grow liatris in ordinary, moist soil and full sun. Do not over-fertilize. Divide plants in spring.

spicata p. 166
Blazing star, gayfeather. Herbaceous perennial, 3–4 ft. high, with narrow grasslike leaves that extend up the flower stalks. Dense spikes, 6–12 in. long, of purple flowers in early fall. Easy to grow. Looks attractive with yellow-flowered heliopsis, rudbeckia, or goldenrods. Other species of liatris are also attractive.

Lilium
Lil'i-um. Lily
Liliaceae. Lily family

Description
Erect, leafy-stemmed, perennial herbs with scaly bulbs and very showy flowers. There are about 100 species and a great many hybrids and cultivars.

How to Grow
Lilies prefer light, loamy soil with a deep organic mulch and require perfect drainage. Some do better in partial shade, others in sun. Lilies have a mixed reputation as garden plants for the South. Only a few types survive as perennials and bloom reliably year after year. Others succumb to heat or disease. Sometimes the bulbs are eaten by squirrels or other animals. The lilies that do succeed form large showy clumps. Divide the clumps every few years and replant excess bulbs immediately, before they dry out.

candidum p. 166   *Pictured above*
Madonna lily. Bulbous perennial native to Asia Minor; the oldest garden flower in cultivation. Plant bulb 1 in. deep in late summer or early fall. Forms a rosette of hostalike leaves that stay green all winter. Flowering stalk reaches 3–4 ft. tall in early summer and bears 12–20 pure white, very fragrant flowers 4–5 in. wide. Best on well-drained, limey soils.

longiflorum
Easter lily. Plant bulbs 5–6 in. deep. Leafy stems to 3 ft. high topped with fragrant pure white flowers nearly 7 in. long. This lily is forced in greenhouses for Easter bloom; it flowers in midsummer in the garden. Hardy only in Lower and Gulf South. Needs good drainage.

tigrinum
Tiger lily. Bulbous perennial long cultivated in China as a food plant; the bulbs are edible. Leafy stalks reach 4–5 ft. tall, bear

8–20 dark-spotted orange flowers in summer. Increase by planting the small black bulbils which form at the leaf bases. Tiger lilies tolerate heavy, acid, soil better than other lilies. There are several cultivars with white, yellow, pink, red, or gold flowers.

Liriodendron
Lir-i-oh-den′dron. Tulip tree
Magnoliaceae. Magnolia family

Description
Two species of deciduous trees, one from the eastern U.S. and the other from China. The leaves have a distinctive truncated maple leaf shape, and the flowers look like yellow-orange tulips.

How to Grow
Deep, moist, slightly acid soil is best. Apply mulch, and water deeply during drought. Aphids can be a problem.

tulipifera p. 84   *Pictured above*
Tulip tree, tulip poplar. A columnar or broadly upright tree, to 100 ft. high. Leaves 3–5 in. long, turn yellow in fall. A fast-growing shade or specimen tree.

Liriope
Li-ri′o-pe. Lily-turf
Liliaceae. Lily family

Description
Asiatic herbs with grasslike evergreen leaves. They spread to form thick mats and are often grown as ground covers. Spikes of small white, blue, or violet flowers in summer; round black fruits in fall.

How to Grow

Easy to grow in ordinary soil and partial shade. Mow in late winter to shear off old leaves and promote new growth. Increase by division. Very useful ground covers.

muscari p. 190   *Pictured above*

Blue lily-turf. To 18 in. high. Flowers lilac-purple to white, ⅛ in. wide. The plant forms clumps, but the arching, straplike leaves make it useful as a ground cover. Some cultivars have yellow- or white-striped leaves.

spicata p. 191

Creeping lily-turf. To 10 in. high. Leaves are narrow, grasslike. Flowers are pale lilac to nearly white, to ¼ in. long. Spreads by rhizomes and can be invasive.

Lobelia
Lo-bee′li-a
Lobeliaceae. Lobelia family

Description

A large genus of showy-flowered perennials or annuals. Popular for borders, wild gardens, and edgings.

How to Grow
Lobelias need moist soil and sun or partial shade. Increase by
dividing clumps in spring or fall. Plants may self-seed.

cardinalis *p. 167   Pictured above*
Cardinal flower. Herbaceous perennial, 3–6 ft. high. Stems
are topped with clusters of scarlet flowers, 1½ in. long, in
summer. May rot in wet winters; to improve survival, keep
leaf litter and mulch off the rosettes. Plant against a dark
background of ferns to display the brilliant flowers. Native to
damp sites throughout eastern North America.

siphilitica *p. 167*
Blue or great lobelia. Herbaceous perennial, 2–4 ft. high.
Stems topped with clusters of blue flowers 1 in. long. Blooms
longer and is easier to grow than cardinal flower. Native to
damp sites throughout eastern North America.

Lonicera
Lon-iss'er-ra. Honeysuckle
Caprifoliaceae. Honeysuckle family

Description
About 180 species of shrubs and woody climbers found
throughout the northern hemisphere, many popular as garden
plants. The leaves are opposite, sometimes evergreen. Flowers
are abundant, often showy and sweetly scented. The white,
yellow, orange, red, blue, or black berries are quite ornamental
and a favorite food for birds.

How to Grow
Honeysuckles are easy to grow in ordinary soil, in sun or
partial shade. Prune after flowering. Plant vining forms against
a trellis or fence for support.

fragrantissima p. 121
Winter honeysuckle. Semi-evergreen shrub, 5–10 ft. high, with spreading branches that form a rounded mass. Leaves oval, thick, 1–2 in. long. Numerous small white flowers, very fragrant, in late winter and early spring. An old garden favorite that is coming back into fashion. Native to China.

× *heckrottii* p. 201   *Pictured above*
Goldflame honeysuckle. Semi-evergreen vine to 12 ft. high, with spreading, sometimes twining branches. Leaves oval, 1–2½ in. long; upper pairs unite to form a round disk. The flower buds are reddish; open flowers are pink outside, yellow within, 1½ in. long. Flowers are fragrant, especially at night, and popular with hummingbirds. Blooms spring and summer, sporadically into fall.

sempervirens p. 202
Trumpet honeysuckle; coral honeysuckle. Semi-evergreen vine to 8 ft. high. Leaves are oval, 1–3 in. long; upper pairs unite to form a round disk. Flowers in terminal clusters, bright orange or red outside, yellow within, 2 in. long; late spring through summer. Flowers are not fragrant but attract hummingbirds. A yellow-flowered form is also popular. Native to eastern United States.

Loropetalum
Lor-o-pet′a-lum
Hamamelidaceae. Witch hazel family

Description
One species of Chinese shrub with evergreen leaves and fragrant white flowers.

How to Grow
This shrub prefers moist, well-drained acid soil but can tolerate some dryness. Plant in sun or shade.

chinense p. 122
Evergreen shrub 6–12 ft. high. Grows naturally in a casual rounded shape but is often rigidly pruned. Clusters of small flowers line the stems in spring for a magnificent effect. Useful as specimen, hedge, or foundation plant.

Lycoris
Ly-ko'ris
Amaryllidaceae. Amaryllis family

Description
About a dozen species of bulbous perennials with showy clusters of fragrant flowers. Straplike leaves emerge in fall and die back in spring. Flowers are borne on naked stalks in summer. These long-lived plants often mark old home sites in the South. Native to Asia.

How to Grow
Plant bulbs about 6 in. deep in ordinary soil in full sun or partial shade. Divide every few years, after flowering.

radiata p. 168 *Pictured above*
Red spider-lily. Leaves are ½ in. wide, 4–6 in. long, in winter. Flowers, deep red, 1½ in. long, have stamens that extend far beyond the petals. Flower stalks 12–18 in. high; blooms in early fall. Not reliably hardy in Upper South.

squamigera
Magic lily, hardy amaryllis. Very showy, hardier than other species. To 2 ft. high. Leaves are about 1 in. wide and 12 in. long. Beautiful flowers, nearly 3 in. long, rosy pink, in late summer. Foliage is very shabby as it dies down in late spring. Bulbs multiply fast.

Magnolia
Mag-no'li-a
Magnoliaceae. Magnolia family

Description
About 125 species of evergreen and deciduous trees and shrubs native to North America, Central America, and Asia. Many are grown as beautiful spring-flowering ornamental trees. The leaves are alternate, usually large. Flowers are large and showy, with 6–20 petals. Fruits are conelike structures that split open to reveal scarlet seeds.

How to Grow
Plant magnolias in full sun or partial shade, in deep, moist, acid or neutral soil. Cover the root zone with mulch and avoid disturbing the fleshy roots — even by planting bulbs. If possible, magnolias should not be transplanted. Irrigate during drought. Prune after flowering, only for form or maintenance. Magnolias seldom have serious pest problems.

grandiflora p. 85
Southern magnolia; bull bay. Large evergreen tree of noble proportions, becoming 80 ft. high. Oblong leaves 5–8 in. long, leathery, shiny green above and rusty-woolly beneath. Giant silky buds open into creamy white, richly fragrant flowers, 6–8 in. wide, from late spring to midsummer, occasionally until fall. Brown fruit, 4 in. long, has red seeds. A fine specimen tree for southern landscapes. 'Little Gem' is a small, even shrublike cultivar. 'Main Street' has upright growth. 'Symmes Select' has spreading branches all the way to the ground. Native North Carolina to Florida and Texas.

macrophylla p. 85
Bigleaf magnolia. A deciduous tree, to 30–40 ft. high, with the largest leaves of any native tree, up to 32 in. long and 10 in. wide. Grown as a showpiece, also for a tropical effect. The showy white flowers are very fragrant. Plant in a sheltered spot, since wind can shred the huge leaves. Native to rich forests throughout the Southeast.

× *soulangiana* p. 86

Saucer magnolia. Deciduous large shrub or small tree, reaching 20–30 ft. tall and equally wide, often grown with several trunks. Flowers appear in early spring before the leaves; they are cup-shaped, 6 in. across, purplish to white, scentless or fragrant. Hard frost in spring can damage the buds or flowers, turning petals limp and brown. An excellent small specimen tree. There are numerous cultivars; consult local authorities about the best for your area.

stellata p. 86 Pictured above

Star magnolia. A much-branched, spreading shrub or small tree, to 15 ft. high. Oval leaves 1½–5 in. long, dark green in summer, yellow in fall, deciduous. Fragrant white flowers, 3 in. wide, appear before leaves; petals turn brown if frosted. There are many cultivars. Native to Japan.

virginiana p. 87

Sweet bay magnolia. Semi-evergreen tree, eventually reaching 60 ft. high in the South. Leaves oblong, green above and silvery beneath, 3–5 in. long. Flowers, 2–3 in. wide, white, very fragrant, open intermittently over a 6-week period in spring and early summer. Fruit 2 in. long, red in summer and fall. Grows well in wet places and endures shade. Native to the Coastal Plain and Piedmont regions of the Southeast.

Mahonia
Ma-ho′ni-a
Berberidaceae. Barberry family

Description

About 70 species of evergreen shrubs native to North America and Asia. Compound leaves have spine-tipped, leathery leaflets; blue-green in summer, often turning purple in cold weather. Terminal clusters of small, fragrant, yellow flowers in spring. Fruit, blue-black, like a small grape, is edible but mostly eaten by birds.

How to Grow

Plant mahonias in ordinary moist soil and partial shade, in sites sheltered from winter wind and sun. They are useful specimen plants for shrub borders, shady corners, and foundation plantings.

aquifolium p. 122

Oregon grape holly. Evergreen shrub, 3–6 ft. high. Compound leaves 6–12 in. long. Named cultivars vary in height and leaf color. Attractive in all seasons. Native British Columbia to Oregon.

bealei p. 123 *Pictured above*

Leatherleaf mahonia. Evergreen shrub with stout, upright stems, to 12 ft. high. Compound leaves are coarse and prickly. Very showy clusters of lemon-yellow, fragrant flowers in spring; blue-black berries last until the birds eat them. The upright stems and stiff leaves give this shrub a striking silhouette. Remove a few of the older stems each year to promote bushy new growth. Native to China.

repens p. 191

Creeping mahonia. Evergreen spreading shrub, rarely more than 12 in. high. Leaves leathery and spiny, purple in winter. Yellow flowers in spring. Makes a handsome ground cover. Native British Columbia to Mexico.

Malus

May′lus. Apple, crabapple
Rosaceae. Rose family

Description

About 25 species of mostly deciduous trees and shrubs, native to the north temperate zone. All bear white to pink or carmine flowers in spring. Regular fruiting apple trees are in this genus but are not described in this book. Crabapples have fruit 2 in. or less in diameter; colors include purple, red, orange, and yellow. The edible fruit is enjoyed by birds.

How to Grow
Crabapples do best in moist, acid, well-drained soil and full sun. Prune after flowering to shape the tree and remove suckers. They are subject to a wide range of pest and disease problems. Ask your extension agent for advice about the problems most common in your area.

'Callaway' *p. 87*
Callaway crabapple. Deciduous small tree, 15–25 ft. high, with round crown. White flowers, 1 in. wide, March to April; maroon fruits summer to fall. One of the best crabapples for the South; it flowers reliably, resists disease, tolerates heat and humidity.

floribunda *p. 88*   *Pictured above*
Japanese crabapple. Deciduous tree to 25 ft. high with round crown. Buds red, flowers pale pink, almost white, 1½ in. wide. Fruit red and yellow, ⅜ in. wide. A dependable tree.

sargentii *p. 123*
Sargent crabapple. Deciduous shrub, reaching 6–10 ft. high and spreading twice as broad as high. Branching is dense, often criss-crossing. Pink buds open to white flowers, 1 in. wide; bloom is sometimes prolific and sparse in alternate years. Blooms later than many other crabapples. The small, shiny dark red fruit is popular with birds. Good for mass plantings, low screens, hillsides.

Matteuccia
Ma-too'chee-a
Polypodiaceae. Polypody family

Description
Three species of large ferns found in temperate North America, Europe, and Asia.

How to Grow
Ostrich ferns prefer full sun or light shade and wet soil. They are not suited to the Middle and Lower South. Easily transplanted in fall or spring.

struthiopteris *p. 212*
(Also called *M. pensylvanica.*) Ostrich fern. Large, deciduous, clump-forming fern growing to 4 feet tall. A very showy fern for the Upper South; it cannot take much heat and humidity. Native Canada to Virginia, west to Missouri.

Miscanthus
Mis-kan′thus
Gramineae. Grass family

Description
About 20 species of tall perennial Old World grasses; some cultivated as ornamentals. Erect, mostly clump-forming. Leaf blade has a distinct white midrib and rough margins. Flower plumes have a feathery appearance.

How to Grow
Miscanthus grows in ordinary soil that is moist but well drained, in full sun or light shade. Withhold fertilizer; soil that is too rich causes stems to fall over. Cut foliage to the ground in late winter. Divide old large clumps in spring, using a saw if necessary to cut woody roots. To prevent self-seeding, which can be a problem, cut off flower stalks before seeds mature.

sinensis *p. 212   Pictured above*
Maiden grass. Graceful, fine-textured grass to 5 ft. high; leaves are narrow and curving; flower plumes beautiful. 'Silver Feather' has showy silver plumes in summer, good for arrangements. 'Variegatus' has leaves with creamy stripes, buff-colored in winter. 'Zebrinus' has upright, narrow form; leaves have horizontal yellow bands, turn buff-colored in winter. The many other fine cultivars all do well in the South.

Monarda
Mo-nar′da
Labiatae. Mint family

Description
A North American genus of 12 aromatic herbs, some grown for their showy flowers. The leaves are opposite on square stems; flowers are rather large, white, red, purplish, yellow, or mottled, often with showy, colored bracts.

How to Grow
Bee balm is a coarse plant but often very brilliant in color. It is easily grown in any good soil in full sun or partial shade. Spreads quickly and can be invasive. Susceptible to rust and powdery mildew. Divide every few years, in spring.

didyma p. 168   *Pictured above*
Bee balm; Oswego tea. Herbaceous perennial, 2–3 ft. high, with hairy, aromatic stems and leaves. Scarlet flowers, nearly 2 in. long, in terminal clusters, surrounded by red-tinged bracts. Cultivars 'Cambridge Scarlet' and 'Croftway Pink' are most commonly sold. Native Quebec to Georgia and Tennessee; for Upper and Middle South only.

Myrica
Mir-i′ka
Myricaceae. Bayberry family

Description
About 50 species of shrubs and trees, many pleasantly aromatic. Several are attractive, useful shrubs for dry, sandy soils.

Flowers are inconspicuous, with male and female on separate plants. Fruits are waxy blue-gray berries.

How to Grow
Wax myrtle grows well in ordinary soil and tolerates poor soil. Plant in full sun or partial shade. Renew old, leggy plants by cutting stems to the ground.

cerifera p. 124
Wax myrtle; southern wax myrtle. A shrub or small tree, to 10–20 ft. high. Leaves, slender 1–3 in. long, are evergreen or very persistent. Leaves and berries are aromatic, often brought indoors for Christmas decorations. Tolerates salt and sandy soil. Winter cold in Upper South may kill the leaves; 'Evergreen' is a cultivar with improved cold hardiness. *M. pensylvanica,* northern bayberry, is similar to wax myrtle but has a shorter, spreading habit. Both are native to eastern U.S.

Nandina
Nan-dy′na
Berberidaceae. Barberry family

Description
A single species of evergreen shrub, native to China and Japan, grown often in the South for its columnar form, bright red berries, and brilliant fall foliage. Alternate leaves are pinnately compound.

How to Grow
Nandina prefers moist soil but tolerates ordinary soil. Plant in sun or partial shade. It is actually a tough plant, often surviving years of neglect. Remove a few of the older canes each year to promote bushy growth. New compact cultivars require no pruning. All are pest-free.

domestica p. 124
Heavenly bamboo, nandina. Evergreen shrub, 6–8 ft. high, with erect stems. Large compound leaves with small, narrow leaflets. Clusters of small white flowers in spring; showy red berries last all winter. The large shrub is considered old-fashioned; dwarf cultivars such as 'Fire Power' and 'Harbour Dwarf' are more popular now. These form low dense mounds of foliage, brilliant red or red-purple in winter. Excellent for edging, masses, or containers.

Narcissus
Nar-sis'sus. Daffodil; jonquil; narcissus
Amaryllidaceae. Amaryllis family

Description
About 26 species of bulbous plants, widely grown for orna-ment or fragrance. Basal leaves are rushlike or flat, flowers white or yellow, often nodding. There are thousands of hor-ticultural forms. The genus *Narcissus* includes all the plants commonly called narcissus, daffodils, or jonquils.

How to Grow
Easy to grow in ordinary well-drained soil, in full sun or partly shaded by deciduous trees. Plant bulbs in fall after soil has cooled below 70 degrees F. Fertilize annually in the fall or just when new leaves poke through the ground. Resist the urge to trim off leaves after the flowers fade. Let the leaves mature and die back naturally; they feed the bulb and provide for next year's flowers. Use hostas, daylilies, or other perennials or annuals to hide the dying leaves. Naturalized plantings around old home sites thrive for decades with no care. In the garden, large clumps of daffodils should be divided every few years. Dig clumps when the leaves start to yellow, shake the soil off the roots, separate the many individual bulbs, and replant them promptly.

'February Gold' and other narcissus *p. 169*
Narcissus are the best bulbs for southern gardens, offering a sequence of bloom for three months or more in spring. Daf-fodil enthusiasts describe several divisions based on flower shape and size. The center part of the flower is called the corona or cup; the spreading petals and sepals are collectively called the perianth. The following types are especially popular in the South.

Trumpet narcissus have a large trumpet-shaped corona, as long as the perianth segments. Leaves and flower stalks 16–20 in. tall, flowers 3–4 in. wide. 'Unsurpassable' is yellow, 'Mount Hood' white. Early to midspring.

Large-cupped narcissus have coronas more than a third but less than the total length of perianth segments. Flat leaves 14–20 in. tall, flowers up to 4½ in. wide. 'Carlton' is yellow, 'Ice Follies' white. Early to midspring.

Double narcissus have more than one layer of petals. Flat leaves, 14–18 in. tall, flowers 2–3 in. wide. 'Cheerfulness' is white, 'Tahiti' is yellow marked with red. Mid- to late spring.

Triandrus narcissus have a cuplike corona about half as long as perianth segments. Leaves are rushlike or round, to 12 in. tall, flowers 1–1½ in. wide. 'Thalia' has white flowers, 'Hawera' is yellow. Early spring.

Cyclamineus narcissus have flowers with long coronas and distinctly turned-back perianth segments. Leaves are flat, 6–10 in. tall, flowers ½–2 in. wide. 'February Gold' is the first narcissus to bloom in spring. 'February Silver' and 'Tte Tte' are also very popular.

Jonquilla narcissus have very fragrant flowers in clusters of 3–6. Reedlike leaves, 12 in. tall, flowers ½–1 in. wide. 'Suzy' has yellow perianth, orange cup; 'Trevithian' is yellow. Mid- to late spring.

Tazetta narcissus have very fragrant, almost flat flowers in clusters of 4–8. Leaves are flat, 18 in. tall, flowers ½–1¼ in. wide. 'Paperwhite', hardy only in Lower and Gulf South, is very early, sometimes blooming at Christmas. 'Geranium', white with orange cup, is hardy throughout the South, blooms in late spring.

Nyssa
Nis'sa. Tupelo
Nyssaceae. Tupelo family

Description
A few species of North American and Asiatic deciduous shade trees, noted for their fine fall foliage. The leaves are alternate and simple. Flowers and fruit are inconspicuous.

How to Grow
Tupelos are native to swampy sites, but they tolerate most soils and withstand drought. Light shade will lessen fall color but not growth. Hardy and pest-free.

sylvatica p. 88

Black gum; tupelo. Deciduous tree, to 85 ft. high. One of the finest native trees for fall color; its leaves turn early to a brilliant scarlet. An excellent specimen or shade tree for the South. Native Maine to Michigan, south to Florida and Texas.

Oenothera

Ee-noth'er-ra. Evening primrose, sundrops
Onagraceae. Evening primrose family

Description

About 80 species of North American annual and perennial wildflowers. Flowers are very showy, day- or night-blooming, usually yellow but sometimes white or rose. Bloom all summer.

How to Grow

These flowers are easy to grow in sunny, sandy, or loamy sites. Propagate by division.

fruticosa p. 169

(Also called *O. tetragona.*) Sundrops. Herbaceous perennial with flowering stems 1–2 ft. high. Shiny yellow flowers, 2 in. wide, with 4 petals, open during the day. Basal leaves form an attractive reddish purple mat in winter. Flea beetles may attack the leaves in early spring; dust with rotenone. Native Canada to Mississippi and South Carolina. Plant in borders, meadows, along woodland edges.

O. *missouriensis,* Missouri primrose or Ozark sundrops, is a low, spreading, perennial with yellow flowers up to 5 in. wide. O. *speciosa,* showy evening primrose, grows up to 18 in. tall and has white to pink flowers 1–2 in. wide. It spreads rapidly in good soil; better for natural landscapes than formal borders.

Ophiopogon

O-fi-o-po'gon. Lily-turf
Liliaceae. Lily family

Description

Evergreen perennials with grasslike leaves that form turflike masses. The few species are all natives of East Asia. Small,

nodding flowers are usually borne in small clusters that do not extend above the foliage. Similar to *Liriope,* but with blue instead of black fruit.

How to Grow
Mondo grass grows well in ordinary garden soil in light shade. Propagate by division. If foliage becomes shabby in winter, cut back hard in early spring. A good substitute for grass in shady areas. Tolerates drought.

japonicus p. 192   *Pictured above*
Mondo grass. A good sod-forming ground cover, 8–15 in. high. Dark green leaves, to 15 in. long, arise from underground stolons; the roots bear small tubers. Pale lilac flowers are almost hidden by foliage. Fruit is pea-size, blue. 'Nana' and 'Nippon' are dwarf cultivars.

planiscapus 'Arabicus' p. 192
Black mondo grass. Spreading perennial ground cover, 6–10 in. high, with distinctive purple-black leaves. Lilac-pink flowers, dark berries. This variety is hard to find and slow to spread, but it provides excellent contrast with bright green plants. Cultivars 'Nigra' and 'Ebony Knight' are similar in size and color.

Osmanthus
Oz-man'thus
Oleaceae. Olive family

Description
About 20 species of evergreen shrubs or small trees, nearly all Asiatic or Polynesian. The leaves are opposite. Flowers, not showy, are often very fragrant.

How to Grow

These shrubs are easy to grow in acid soil in partial shade. Use for hedges, espaliers, or in containers.

× *fortunei* p. 125

Large, dense, rounded evergreen shrub reaching 15–20 ft. tall. Leaves are leathery, 2–4 in. long. Small white flowers, extremely fragrant, in fall. Use as a specimen or hedge; too large for foundation plantings.

fragrans p. 125　*Pictured above*

Fragrant tea olive. Evergreen shrub or small tree, to 25 ft. high. Leaves leathery, 2–5 in. long. Small white flowers, extremely fragrant, in fall. Grows larger than O. × *fortunei* and is more tender to frost. Best in Lower and Gulf South.

Osmunda
Oz-mun′da
Osmundaceae. Flowering fern family

Description

About 10 species of large ferns native to temperate and tropical regions of Asia and the Americas.

How to Grow

These ferns prefer light shade and acid, wet soil containing plenty of organic matter. They need constant moisture and are not drought tolerant.

cinnamomea p. 213   *Pictured above*

Cinnamon fern. Deciduous, clump-forming fern to 3 feet tall. Handsome light green fronds surround striking, cinnamon-brown, spore-bearing fronds. Fiddleheads are edible. Will grow throughout the South.

regalis p. 213

Royal fern. Deciduous, clump-forming fern up to 4 feet high. Its pronounced upright habit and widely spaced leaflets give this fern a distinctive look. Rich green fronds turn bright yellow in fall. Showy golden-brown spore cases. Makes a good accent. Will grow throughout the South.

Oxydendrum

Ok-si-den'drum. Sourwood
Ericaceae. Heath family

Description

A single species of deciduous tree, native to the eastern U.S. and grown for the flowers, fruit, and fall foliage. Ornamental in all seasons. Also an important "honey tree," much used by bees.

How to Grow

Like rhododendrons, to which it is related, sourwood needs an acid soil (pH 4.0–5.5 preferable), moist and well drained. Full sun is best for flowers and fall color, but it will grow well in shade. Avoid disturbing soil over the shallow roots. Mulch the tree and water well during drought in first few seasons.

Established plants endure dryness fairly well. Sourwood has no serious pests.

arboreum p. 89 *Pictured above*
Sourwood, sorrel tree. Deciduous tree, usually 20–30 ft. high in gardens, up to 50 ft. in the wild. Alternate leaves, 3–8 in. long, are bright green in summer, turning scarlet, gold, or purple in fall. Very handsome drooping clusters, 8–10 in. long, of small, fragrant white flowers in summer. Fruits are gray hairy capsules, for a time in fall almost as attractive as the flowers. An excellent specimen tree for home gardens.

Pachysandra
Pack-i-san'dra
Buxaceae. Box family

Description
Five species of low-growing perennial herbs or subshrubs native to North America and East Asia. Useful as shade-tolerant ground covers.

How to Grow
Pachysandra is easy to grow in moist, ordinary soil. It is widely used as a ground cover for partly shady places; foliage yellows in full sun. Propagate by taking cuttings in summer and planting in an equal mixture of sand and soil. Water well and keep shaded until rooted. For a quick ground cover, plant them 8 in. apart.

terminalis p. 193
Japanese spurge. Evergreen herbaceous ground cover, to 9 in. high. Dark glossy green leaves are thick, spoon-shaped. Upright spikes of small white flowers in spring, followed by small white berries. Makes a thick ground cover and tolerates dense shade where little else will succeed. Subject to leaf blight and other diseases; apply recommended fungicides. Cultivars 'Silver Edge' and 'Variegata' have white-marked leaves, are attractive but less vigorous than the green form. Native to Japan.

procumbens
Allegheny spurge. Semi-evergreen herbaceous perennial, native from West Virginia to Florida and Louisiana. Leaves wider than in Japanese spurge, and mottled with brownish purple.

Handsome spikes of pinkish white flowers in spring. A very attractive native ground cover, adapts well to cultivation. Vulnerable to southern blight; treat with Terrachlor.

Paeonia
Pee-o'nee-a. Peony
Paeoniaceae. Peony family

Description
About 33 species of outstanding perennials and shrubs with very beautiful flowers in spring to early summer. Most are native to Eurasia.

How to Grow
Peonies are easy to grow in well-drained, moisture-retentive, average soil in full sun to partial shade. Plant with buds right at the soil surface. Early, single-flowering cultivars are best for the Lower South. Standard cultivars and the shrublike "tree" peonies do well from Atlanta north.

lactiflora 'Festiva Maxima' *p. 170*
Herbaceous perennial, 2½ ft. high. This cultivar is an old (mid-19th-century) favorite. Erect stems carry large, solitary, fragrant, fully double white flowers flecked with dark red.

Parthenocissus
Par-then-o-sis'sus
Vitaceae. Grape family

Description
Woody climbers from East Asia and North America, grown

chiefly for their foliage, some brilliantly colored in autumn. Small, inconspicuous flowers and small dark berries.

How to Grow

These vines are not particular about soil, but they grow more vigorously in fairly moist loam in sun or light shade.

quinquefolia p. 202   *Pictured above*

Virginia creeper; woodbine. Vigorous deciduous vine, to 50 ft. high. Compound leaves have 5 pointed leaflets, 2–5 in. long. Leaves turn scarlet in autumn. Not dense but useful for covering fences or walls, or as a ground cover. Self-seeds and can be a pest. May be ravaged by Japanese beetles.

tricuspidata p. 203

(Formerly called *Ampelopsis tricuspidata*.) Boston ivy. Climbs to 60 ft. high and clings firmly. Leaves to 10 in. long, simple or compound, usually shiny on both sides. Foliage brilliant scarlet in autumn. Outstanding wall cover, the leaves overlapping like shingles. 'Veitchii' has smaller leaves that are purple when young.

Passiflora

Pass-i-flo'ra. Passion-flower
Passifloraceae. Passion-flower family

Description

Tendril-climbing vines, most of the 400 species are native to the New World, and several are cultivated for ornament. The leaves are alternate, lobed or undivided. The flowers are showy.

How to Grow

Passion-flowers grow best in light, evenly moist soil and full sun. They may die to the ground in winter but will resprout if the roots live. Useful for a fence or trellis, or for rambling over shrubs.

edulis p. 203

(Formerly *P. incarnata*.) Maypop; wild passion-flower. Deciduous vine, to 20 ft. high. Native to the South and more cold-hardy than the exotic tropical passion-flowers. Leaves have 3 lobes. Fragrant, white or purplish pink flowers, 2 in. wide, in summer. Egg-sized yellow fruits have edible pulp.

Pennisetum
Pen-i-see′tum
Gramineae. Grass family

Description
About 80 species of chiefly tropical annual or perennial grasses, a handful grown for ornament. Flat, narrow, sometimes colored leaf blades on erect stems. Spikelike clusters of flowers. Grow in masses or as single clumps.

How to Grow
Pennisetum grows best in fertile soil in full sun. Increase by dividing clumps in spring.

alopecuroides p. 214   *Pictured above*
Fountain grass. Slender-stemmed perennial, 2–3 ft. high, with hairy stems, bright green leaves. Silvery, cylindrical flower heads. 'Hameln' is a dwarf cultivar, growing only 1–2 ft. high.

Perovskia
Per-ov′ski-a. Russian sage
Labiatae. Mint family

Description
Small Central Asian genus of herbs or subshrubs with fragrant, gray, dissected leaves and small flowers.

How to Grow
Russian sage is easy to grow in full sun and well-drained soil. Plants in shade will sprawl. Deadhead to promote flowering into the fall. Cut to the ground each spring to promote vigorous new growth.

atriplicifolia p. 170
Russian sage. Shrubby, 3–5 ft. high. Bruised foliage smells like

sage. In summer, tiny blue flowers in clusters along and at tips of stems. Gray foliage complements other plants in a mixed perennial border. Upper and Middle South.

Phalaris
Fal'ar-is
Gramineae. Grass family

Description
About 15 species of grasses from the north temperate zone.

How to Grow
Ribbon grass is easy to grow in most soils. It does best in light shade, grows more sparsely in deep shade. Useful as a ground cover in difficult conditions.

arundinacea picta p. 214
Ribbon grass, gardener's garters. Perennial, to 3 ft. Narrow leaves striped green and white, 12 in. long. An old-fashioned favorite, it can spread out of place in a garden.

Philadelphus
Fill-a-del'fus. Mock-orange
Saxifragaceae. Saxifrage family

Description
About 60 species of North American and Eurasian deciduous shrubs, widely grown for their fragrant flowers in late spring.

How to Grow
Mock-orange is easy to grow in any soil, in sun or partial shade. Plants tend to become leggy, so prune yearly immedi-

ately after blossoming, as flowers appear on the previous year's growth.

coronarius *p. 126   Pictured above*
Common mock-orange; sweet mock-orange. Deciduous shrub, to 10 ft. tall and equally wide. Can be kept smaller by pruning. Pointed oval leaves, 1½–4 in. long. Grown for the clusters of creamy white, very fragrant, 1½-in.-wide flowers in spring. Best in Upper and Middle South.

Phlox
Floks
Polemoniaceae. Phlox family

Description
About 60 species of perennial and annual herbs, usually hardy, native mostly to North America. Some are strong and erect, others trailing. Lance-shaped leaves, clusters of showy flowers, usually with a conspicuous eyelike marking in the center. Garden favorites with a long season of bloom.

How to Grow
Most phlox are easy to grow. All but *P. subulata* benefit from humus-enriched, moist soil. Most prefer sun or partial shade. Propagate from seeds, cuttings, or division. Powdery mildew may blemish the foliage but will not seriously harm the plants.

carolina *p. 171   Pictured above*
(Also called *P. suffruticosa*.) Carolina phlox. Herbaceous perennial, stems to 3 ft. tall, topped with loose clusters of smallish flowers in early summer. Clumps are not fast-spreading. 'Miss Lingard' has white flowers; 'Rosalinde' is pink.

divaricata *p. 171*
Wild sweet William; blue woodland phlox. Perennial, to 18

in. high. Spreads rapidly by creeping stems. Upright stems bear loose clusters of pale mauve flowers in spring. 'Fuller's White' has white flowers. A similar and related phlox, *P.* × *chatta-hoochee,* has flowers with an arresting purple eye.

paniculata p. 172
Garden phlox; perennial phlox. Strong stems to 3–4 ft., topped with large, spreading clusters of pink, white, red, or pale blue flowers in summer. Foliage is prey to powdery mildew and spider mites, often looks ratty. Remove faded flowers to prevent self-seeding, which crowds out choicer cultivars. 'Mt. Fujiyama', with large white flower heads, does well in the South.

stolonifera p. 172
Creeping phlox. Perennial to 12 in., spreads by creeping, flowerless stems that root. Best in partial shade. Dense clusters of small purple or violet flowers in spring. 'Blue Ridge' has larger, pale blue flowers.

subulata p. 173
Thrift; ground pink; moss pink. Evergreen creeper forms a dense mat 6 in. high. Stems are crowded with small needlelike leaves. Plants are covered with bright purple, pink, or white flowers in early spring. Prefers poor, well-drained soil and full sun. Shear or mow stems to 3 in. high after flowering to promote denser growth.

Phyllostachys
Fill'oh-stack'is
Gramineae. Grass family

Description
About 30 species of mostly tall, evergreen, rhizomatous, bamboos native to temperate East Asia and the Himalayas.

How to Grow

These bamboos prefer full sun or light shade and fertile, moist, well-drained soil. They can be invasive in moist, rich soil. Use metal or concrete barriers to contain the roots and restrict spreading. The following species are quite cold-hardy; tops may freeze, but new growth will sprout from underground.

aurea p. 215

Golden bamboo or fishpole bamboo. Can grow to 20–25 ft. The bright yellow stems are of good quality for fishing poles, trellises, and other uses. Spreads quickly but can be confined. Good for color accent or tall screen.

nigra p. 215 Pictured above

Black bamboo. To 15–20 ft., with bright green leaves and shiny black stems. Forms lovely open groves, attractive year-round.

Physostegia
Fy-so-stee′ji-a
Labiatae. Mint family

Description

Some 12 species of native perennial wildflowers. The leaves are opposite, toothed; showy flowers are borne at top of stem.

How to Grow

Physostegia is easy to grow in moist soil in full sun; in shadier sites, plant in drier soil. Propagate by seed or by division of clumps.

virginiana p. 173

False dragonhead; obedient plant. Herbaceous peremnial with stalks up to 4–5 ft. high, shorter in dry soil. Bears hot-dog-size spikes of purple-red, rose-pink, or lilac flowers in late summer. A good cut flower, but plants can be invasive. Plant in back of border or in informal garden.

Pieris
Py-ear′is
Ericaceae. Heath family

Description

About 8 species of valuable broad-leaved evergreen shrubs or small trees, widely planted for their flowers and shiny foliage. Slow-growing plants, useful for gateway plantings, as accent plants, and for the rock garden.

How to Grow

Plant pieris in peaty, somewhat sandy, moderately acid soil mulched with leaves.

japonica p. 126

(Often sold as *Andromeda japonica.*) Japanese pieris. A splendid evergreen shrub, usually 3–10 ft. high. Leaves are oblong, 1½–3½ in. long, dark green when mature, reddish when young. Hanging clusters, 3–5 in. long, of small, slightly fragrant flowers in spring. 'Forest Flame' and 'Mountain Fire' have especially vivid new growth.

Pinus
Py'nus. Pine
Pinaceae. Pine family

Description

Magnificent evergreen trees of outstanding value for ornamental uses and timber. Most pines have upright trunks with tiers or whorls of branches bearing clusters of needles and woody cones. Many pines are native to the South and dominate parts of the landscape.

How to Grow

Most pines grow well in ordinary well-drained soil and full sun. Plant pines singly or in groups as specimens in a lawn, or use for hedges, screens, and windbreaks. Pines can be shaped by pruning. For more compact growth, snap off the ends of the new shoots (called "candles") when they first elongate in spring.

Southern hard pines *p. 89*

This group includes several native pines that are widespread in the Coastal Plain and Piedmont regions of the South. They sprout quickly in abandoned fields and cut-over forests. Existing trees are usually preserved when new homes are built in these areas. These pines are also planted for timber and landscape use. Most have yellow-colored wood and are often called yellow pines.

P. echinata, shortleaf pine, has needles 3–5 in. long in groups of 2, prickly cones that hang on the branches for years, and dark reddish brown bark. Very fast-growing, to 50–60 ft. tall. Young trees have conical shape, older trees have a narrow, open crown.

P. palustris, longleaf pine, has needles 8–18 in. long in groups of 3, large tapered cones, light-colored scaly bark. Slow-growing, eventually reaches 100 ft. with large upright trunk and irregular open crown.

P. taeda, loblolly pine, has needles 6–9 in. long in groups of 3, medium-sized spiny cones, bright reddish brown furrowed bark. Very fast growing, usually reaches 50 ft. high with an open, rounded crown.

P. virginiana, Virginia pine (*pictured above*), bears stiff twisted needles 1½–3 in. long in groups of two, and groups of 2–4 egg-sized prickly cones. Fast-growing and very tolerant of poor soil conditions, including heavy clay and dry sand. Widely used in Christmas tree plantations in the South, and useful as a quick tree cover for barren sites. Conical shape when young; older trees look straggly.

strobus p. 90

Eastern white pine. A beautiful tree with soft, bluish green needles 3–5 in. long in groups of 5, cylindrical cones 4–8 in. long, and gray bark. Young trees are conical, older trees have branching crowns, reach 50–80 ft. tall. Fast-growing. There are also dwarf, weeping, and columnar forms. Native from New England south through the Appalachian Mountains; suitable for the Upper and Middle South.

thunbergiana p. 90

(Often called *P. thunbergii.*) Japanese black pine. Picturesque tree with stiff, twisted needles 2–4 in. long in groups of 2, small oval cones, and dark bark. Variable growth habit, often irregular in outline. Can reach 20–80 ft. tall. Tolerates salt spray and is useful for exposed, windswept places along the seacoast. Vigorous and attractive tree. Native to Japan.

Pistacia
Pis-tash'i-a. Pistachio
Anacardiaceae. Sumac family

Description
Some 10 species of aromatic shrubs or trees. The species below is a shade tree with handsome foliage and fruit. (*P. vera* is the source of pistachio nuts.)

How to Grow
Chinese pistache needs full sun. It grows best in good, well-drained soil, but does well in poor, dry soil. Withstands wind and drought and has no serious pests. May need early pruning to develop a symmetrical rounded shape.

chinensis p. 91
Chinese pistache. Rounded deciduous tree, to 60 ft., sometimes much lower and shrublike. The compound leaves have 10–12 leaflets 2–4 in. long, turning orange-red in fall. Clusters of small fruits in fall. Excellent for lawn planting. Native to China.

Platycodon
Plat-i-ko'don
Campanulaceae. Bellflower family

Description
Single species of showy perennial herb from East Asia. A handsome border plant that blooms in summer.

How to Grow
Platycodon is easy to grow in moist, well-drained soil. Increase by spring division. Because it is slow to emerge in the spring, mark its location to prevent accidentally digging it up during spring cleanup.

grandiflorus p. 174 *Pictured above*
Balloon flower. Herbaceous perennial, forming a clump of
stems 18–30 in. high. The leaves are opposite, oval. Puffed-
out buds open into bell-shaped flowers, 2–3 in. wide, dark
blue, white, or pink. Upper and Middle South.

Polygonatum
Pol-lig-o-nay'tum. Solomon's-seal
Liliaceae. Lily family

Description
About 30 species of generally hardy herbaceous perennials
distributed throughout the northern hemisphere. Stems arise
each spring from thick rootstocks; leaves are borne on upper
parts of stems. Small tubular flowers, single or in clusters,
hang from the axils of the leaves.

How to Grow
Solomon's-seal is easy to grow in partial or full shade in moist
soil. The species below will tolerate dry soil in full shade.
Propagate by division of rootstocks in fall.

odoratum var. *thunbergii* 'Variegatum' p. 174 *Pictured
above*
Variegated Solomon's-seal. Herbaceous perennial with stems
3 ft. tall. Leaves have white tips and edges. Smallish white
flowers, 2 to a cluster, in spring. Spreads slowly to form an
attractive patch of stems that all bend in the same direction,
as if combed. Native to Japan. Upper and Middle South.

Polygonum
Pol-lig'o-num. Smartweed; knotweed
Polygonaceae. Knotweed family

Description
About 150 species erect, trailing, or climbing annual or perennial herbs found throughout the world. Some species are weedy, others very ornamental. Generous clusters of small flowers, usually pink or white.

How to Grow
The species below is easy to grow in average soil in full sun.

aubertii p. 204
Silver-lace vine; fleece-vine. Hardy, twining, perennial vine with slender stems, to 25 ft. high. Leaves to 2½ in. long. Loose clusters of fragrant white flowers cover the vine in late summer. Very vigorous and useful for covering fences, sheds, eyesores. Prune hard in late winter.

Polystichum
Polly-stick'um
Polypodiaceae. Polypody family

Description
About 120 species of terrestrial woodland ferns native to temperate areas around the world.

How to Grow
Christmas fern prefers shade and rich, moist soil containing plenty of organic matter.

acrostichoides p. 216
Christmas fern. Evergreen, clump-forming fern very common in moist woods. It tolerates wet or well-drained soil, transplants easily. Fronds reach 18–24 in. tall.

Prunus
Proo'nus
Rosaceae. Rose family

Description
More than 400 species of deciduous and evergreen shrubs and trees, nearly all from the north temperate zone. The genus includes all the plums, cherries, apricots, peaches, and almonds. The varieties below are grown for ornament, not fruit.

The leaves are alternate, nearly always sharply toothed. Flowers are white or pink, sometimes with 5 petals, sometimes double.

How to Grow

Most cherries need full sun and reasonably moist, well-drained soil. Because stress of any sort increases the trees' susceptibility to various insects and diseases, cherries as a group are short-lived — about 30 years unless coddled. Spread organic mulch beneath the branch spread and water deeply and regularly during drought.

caroliniana p. 127

Carolina cherry laurel. Large shrub or small tree, 20–30 ft. high, almost as wide. Oblong evergreen leaves, 2–3 in. long. Small clusters of tiny, white, fragrant flowers in early spring. The small fruits are popular with birds; seedlings sprout everywhere from bird droppings. Space plants close together and prune for a hedge or screen. Southeastern native; best in Middle and Lower South.

cerasifera p. 91

Cherry plum; myrobalan plum. Small deciduous tree, 15–30 ft. high and wide, with flowers in early spring. The species is seldom grown for landscape purposes. Several cultivars have rich reddish purple leaves. Look for 'Newport' (very early pale pink to white flowers), 'Thundercloud' (pink flowers), and 'Krauter Vesuvius' (light pink flowers).

laurocerasus p. 127

Cherry laurel; English laurel. Evergreen shrub or small tree, to 20 ft. Leaves 2–7 in. long. Small, fragrant, white flowers in short clusters in spring. Small dark purple fruit. Tolerates shade. There are many cultivars, differing in leaf and plant shape and in hardiness. 'Otto Luyken' has a compact habit, 4 ft. high with a spread of 6–8 ft., and tolerates deep shade. 'Schipkaensis', an unusually hardy cultivar, has narrow, dark green leaves and usually grows 4–5 ft. high with a wider spread. 'Zabeliana' has an especially low, broad habit, reaching 2–3 ft. high and 12 ft. wide at maturity. Good for foundation planting.

mume p. 92

Flowering apricot. Small deciduous tree, to 20 ft. Notable for its January to March bloom of pale rose flowers on long, naked stems. The fruit is inedible. Prefers full sun. Cultivars are available with white, red, rose, single or double flowers; one has a weeping form.

serrulata p. 92 *Pictured above*

Oriental cherry. Vase-shaped deciduous tree, to 30 ft. Sometimes grown with several trunks rising from close to the ground, but usually grafted at a height of 4–6 ft. on a single trunk. Leaves are 3–5 in. long, bronzy when unfolding, orange-bronze in fall. Large deep pink double flowers appear before leaves in spring. 'Kwanzan' is one of the many popular cultivars.

subhirtella 'Autumnalis' p. 93

Higan cherry. Deciduous tree 20–40 ft. high, 15–20 ft. wide. Small pink or white flowers on bare twigs may open over a long season from late fall to early spring. Slender branches, often weeping; narrow leaves, 1–3 in. long. Grow as a specimen for winter bloom.

yedoensis

Yoshino cherry. Very showy deciduous tree, to 40 ft. tall. Leaves 2–5 in. long. Clusters of 1¼-in.-wide flowers, white or pink, faintly fragrant, in spring. Many of the famous cherry trees of Washington, D.C., are this species. Widely cultivated in many named Japanese forms. 'Akebono', also called 'Daybreak', has blush-pink flowers.

Pyracantha

Py-ra-kan'tha. Fire thorn
Rosaceae. Rose family

Description

A small genus of thorny evergreen shrubs native to Asia. Most are grown for their fine foliage and bright red or orange fruits that persist in winter. Small white flowers in spring. There are both upright and spreading growth forms.

How to Grow

Plant in full sun in well-drained soil for best fruiting. Long thorns make these shrubs useful for hedges but painful to prune, so place them where they will have room to spread. If pruning is necessary, you can do it at any time. Problems include lacebug (serious) and fire blight (sometimes). Pyracanthas suffer winterkill in severe winters.

coccinea and related hybrids *p. 128*

Scarlet fire thorn. Vigorous shrubs 6–18 ft. tall. Semi-evergreen to evergreen with stiff thorny branches. Used for hedges, barriers, espalier. Outstanding crops of bright-colored berries in fall. 'Navaho' has rounded shape, 6 ft. high, 7–8 ft. wide, orange-red berries; resistant to fire blight. 'Lalandei' is vigorous, to 10–15 ft., widely grown and quite hardy. 'Mohave' is an upright shrub, growing to 10 ft. 'Teton', with yellow-orange fruit, grows to 15 ft. and is nearly twice as tall as wide. Native to the Mediterranean region.

koidzumii and related hybrids

Formosa fire thorn. Similar to but less hardy than the *P. coccinea* group. Tolerates heat and drought. 'Victory' is vigorous, with upright arching growth and dark red berries that last for months, 'San Jose' and 'Santa Cruz' are spreading forms used as woody ground covers; all have good scab resistance. Native to Formosa.

Quercus
Kwer′kus. Oak
Fagaceae. Beech family

Description
About 450 species, including fine hardwood timber trees and many beautiful species for planting on lawns, parks, and streets. Nearly all are from the north temperate zone, a few from mountainous regions in the tropics. Some are deciduous, others evergreen. All produce acorns.

How to Grow
Oaks grow best in full sun, though most will tolerate light partial shade. They like a rich, deep soil without hardpan. Mulch but do not disturb the root zone, which may reach 3 times the branch spread. Trenching, grade changes, or soil compaction in the root zone can seriously harm or kill the tree.

acutissima p. 93
Sawtooth oak. Deciduous tree, 35–45 ft. tall. Tapering leaves, 3½–7½ in. long, lustrous dark green. Golden catkins (flowers) in spring; large acorns. A fast-growing tree for lawn and shade. Native to Japan, Korea, China.

alba p. 94
White oak. Magnificent, round-headed deciduous tree. Slow-growing, in cultivation it will reach 80 ft. in 100 years. Bluntly lobed leaves, brownish to purple in fall. Probably the largest of all the native oaks, the trunks of old specimens being more than 20 ft. in circumference. Prefers a heavy, damp clay soil. Transplant young trees only. Native Maine to Florida, west to Texas.

coccinea p. 94

Scarlet oak. An upright, roughly cylindrical tree, growing 50–80 ft. high in cultivation. Deeply lobed deciduous leaves, shiny green in summer, brilliant scarlet in fall. Similar to *Q. palustris* (see below) but more tolerant of alkaline soils. Prefers a light sandy loam. Transplant when small for best results. Native Maine to Florida.

laurifolia p. 95

(Often grouped with *Q. hemisphaerica*.) Laurel oak. Tough, handsome, medium-size trees, usually reaching 40–60 ft. tall with spread of 30–40 ft. Lustrous semi-evergreen leaves are slender, toothless, 1–4 in. long. Fast-growing and trouble-free. Often planted as a street tree. Native to the Coastal Plain.

palustris p. 95

Pin oak. A broad, conical tree with lower branches that droop and often sweep the ground. Reaches 100 ft. tall in the wild, shorter in gardens. Deciduous leaves, 4–5 in. long, sharply and deeply lobed, turn bright bronze or red in fall. Tolerant of city conditions and wet soils; prefers a heavy, damp clay soil. Leaves turn yellow in alkaline soil. Can be transplanted at a larger size than many other oaks and grows quickly. Native New England to Arkansas.

virginiana p. 96   *Pictured above*

Live oak. Large evergreen tree, usually round-headed and not more than 70 ft. high. Old trees may be twice as wide as high, often draped with Spanish moss in the southern part of the range. Oblong leaves, 3–5 in. long, green above, white and felty beneath. Temperatures below 0 degrees F will kill leaves. Native Virginia to Florida and Mexico. Lower South (especially useful along South Atlantic and Gulf coasts).

Rhaphiolepis
Ra-fi-ol′e-pis
Rosaceae. Rose family

Description

Handsome Asiatic shrubs widely planted in warm areas for their leathery green foliage, showy flower clusters.

How to Grow

These shrubs are easy to grow in a variety of soils in full sun

or partial shade. They tolerate some drought. Useful in borders, hedges, and mass plantings.

umbellata p. 128

Indian hawthorn, Yeddo rhaphiolepis. Evergreen shrub, to 5 ft. tall and equally wide. Leathery, pointed leaves, 2–3 in. long. Many named cultivars have flowers that range from pure white to deep pink; some are dwarf or compact shrubs. This species is very similar to *R. indica,* and it is uncertain which species the cultivars belong to. Not hardy in Upper South, marginal in Middle South.

Rhododendron
Ro-do-den'dron
Ericaceae. Heath family

Description

A very large genus of evergreen or deciduous shrubs, chiefly from the north temperate zone, that includes the plants commonly called azaleas. Azaleas are mostly deciduous and have funnel-shaped flowers, while rhododendrons are usually evergreen with larger, bell-shaped flowers borne in terminal clusters. These distinctions are not always reliable, so it is best to know the scientific and cultivar name of the plant you want to grow.

How to Grow
Plant rhododendrons in well-drained soil containing ample amounts of organic matter. If your soil does not drain well, plant on mounded soil or use raised beds. Almost all species require acid soil. Use mulch to conserve moisture and reduce the need for cultivation around the plants, which can damage the shallow roots. (Do not mulch close to stem.) Partial sun or light shade is best for most types. Deciduous species need more sun to bloom well than evergreen species. All species benefit from afternoon shade in South. Protect evergreen species from drying winds and direct sun in winter. Prune, if necessary, just after flowering.

Kurume hybrid azaleas *p. 129*
Generally dense, slow-growing, upright shrubs, 6–10 ft. at maturity. Small, glossy, evergreen leaves. Flowers mostly single, open early in spring, in shades of white, pink, rose, salmon, red, lavender, or purple. Will grow throughout the South. Among the most popular selections are 'Coral Bells' (bicolor pink), 'Hino Crimson' (bright red), 'Snow' (white), and 'Hinodegiri' (rose-red).

Southern Indica hybrid azaleas *p. 129*
A group of plants developed in South Carolina in the late 19th century. Generally tall, vigorous shrubs, 8–10 ft. tall and wide, with evergreen leaves and large flowers in midseason. Blooms are usually single, colors ranging from white to pink, red, or purple. Not reliably hardy in the Middle and Upper South. Among the most popular selections are 'Formosa' (purple), 'George Lindley Taber' (pink with deeper blotch), 'Mrs. G. G. Gerbing' (white), and 'Pride of Mobile' (pink with deeper blotch).

austrinum *p. 130*
Florida flame azalea. Vigorous deciduous shrub, 6–12 ft. high, with fragrant yellow or golden flowers in spring. Native to the Southeast. Hardy and easy to grow.

canescens *p. 130*
Piedmont azalea. Common deciduous woodland shrub, 6–10 ft. tall with slightly fragrant pink or white flowers in spring. Another native azalea with extremely fragrant white flowers is *R. alabamense*. Both spread by suckers; old colonies can

cover several acres! Both are native to and hardy throughout the South.

flammeum p. 131
Oconee azalea. Stoloniferous deciduous shrub growing 4–6 ft. high with orange, red, salmon, yellow, or pink flowers in spring. Not fragrant. Native to Alabama, Georgia, South Carolina. Hardy throughout the South.

prunifolia p. 131
Plumleaf azalea. Deciduous shrub, 6–12 ft. tall with bright orange or red flowers in July and August. Not fragrant. Native to Georgia and Alabama. Hardy throughout the South.

Rosa
Ro'za. Rose
Rosaceae. Rose family

Description
About 200 species of prickly shrubs or vines grown throughout the region (and everywhere else) for their beautiful, often fragrant flowers, ranging from small, 5-petaled wild types to extravagant, many-petaled hybrids.

How to Grow
Roses grow well in fertile, well-drained soil free of tree roots; they need at least 6 hours of sunlight daily. Most species roses require no special care and seem to have fewer insect problems than many modern roses, though they can be bothered by aphids, mites, and Japanese beetles. Black spot, powdery mildew, and canker are common diseases. Species roses are good for borders or for naturalizing. Climbing roses can be trained on fences and trellises.

banksiae *p. 132*   *Pictured above*

Lady Banks' rose; banksia rose. More like a vine than a shrub, this rose is long-lived and easy to grow. Long, vigorous canes make it outstanding for fences and arbors or for cascading from trees. It can climb 15–30 ft. high. Leaves are evergreen; stems have few or no thorns. Profuse clusters of small flowers in spring. Single white and yellow forms exist, but commonest are 'Alba Plena', double white with the fragrance of violets, and 'Lutea', double yellow. Disease resistant. Native to China. Hardy only in Gulf and Lower South.

'Climbing Peace' and other garden roses   *p. 132*

There isn't space in this book to describe all the wonderful roses that southern gardeners enjoy growing. Hybrid tea roses, like the famous 'Peace' and its cousin 'Climbing Peace', are very popular and bloom over a long season in the South, but they require considerable maintenance. 'Climbing Peace' has large blooms of creamy yellow edged with pink. Can be trained against a fence, wall, or pillar 8–10 ft. high.

Old-fashioned shrub roses and modern "landscape" roses make attractive hedges and mass plantings and add color and fragrance to perennial beds and borders. In general, these roses are easier to care for than hybrid teas. For more information on roses, contact your local rose society and read *Taylor's Guide to Roses*.

Rosmarinus

Ros-ma-ry′nus. Rosemary
Labiatae. Mint family

Description

A few species of evergreen shrubs, native to the Mediterranean region, one widely cultivated as a culinary and sweet herb; also an attractive ornamental plant.

How to Grow
Rosemary tolerates hot sun and poor soil, but good drainage is essential; grows best in soil that is not too rich. Prune after flowering to improve tidiness and prevent excessive woodiness.

officinalis p. 133
Rosemary. Upright or spreading evergreen shrub with fragrant evergreen leaves ½–1 in. long, small light blue flowers fall to spring. Often trained into a standard or pruned to form a low hedge. 'Arp' is a particularly hardy cultivar, surviving outdoors throughout the South. 'Prostratus', or creeping rosemary, has trailing branches spreading to 4 ft. wide and mounding to 2 ft. high. It makes a good ground cover in the Lower and Gulf South.

Rudbeckia
Rood-beck′i-a. Coneflower
Compositae. Daisy family

Description
About 25 species of hardy North American annual, biennial, or perennial herbs. Large daisylike flowers, generally yellow with brown or black centers — often called black-eyed (or brown-eyed) Susan. Useful border plants.

How to Grow
Rudbeckias are easy to grow in moist or average well-drained soil in full sun. Propagate by seeds or by division in early spring.

fulgida '**Goldsturm**' p. 175   *Pictured above*
Orange coneflower. Stems 2 ft. high. Flowers, 3–4 in. across,

deep yellow rays surrounding a nearly black disk, rise above clump of deep green foliage. The best black-eyed Susan for the South. Unlike many cultivars, 'Goldsturm' does come true from seed.

Sabal
Say'bul ·
Palmaceae. Palm family

Description
About 14 palms native to coastal and inland areas around the Caribbean Sea. Most are dwarf, stout palms with fanlike fronds.

How to Grow
These palms will grow in either wet or dry soil, but growth in dry soil is quite slow. They prefer sun or partial shade.

minor p. 133   *Pictured above*
Dwarf palmetto. Small shrublike palm, 6–8 ft. tall. Large palmate leaves 5–8 ft. across give plant a coarse texture. Makes a good understory for natural areas, or use for tropical effect. Difficult to transplant but easy to grow from seed. Not hardy in Middle and Upper South.

Salvia
Sal'vi-a. Sage
Labiatae. Mint family

Description
About 900 species of annual, biennial, or perennial herbs, subshrubs, or shrubs distributed throughout the tropical and

temperate zones. Many have fragrant foliage; some are used for seasoning. Whorls or spikes of often showy, tubular flowers.

How to Grow
The sages below are easy to grow in full sun or partial shade, in average to dry, well-drained soil. They are easy to propagate from seeds or by division in fall or early spring.

farinacea p. 175   Pictured above
Mealy-cup sage. Perennial grown as annual in colder regions. Gray-green leaves, 4 in. long. Forms a leafy mound 1½ ft. high, topped with many-whorled spikes of small violet-blue or white flowers. Blooms all summer. Native to Texas.

leucantha p. 176
Mexican bush sage. Graceful arching shrub to 3–4 ft., with gray-green leaves and long, slender, velvety spikes of purplish pink bracts and small white flowers in summer and fall. Drought tolerant. Cut plants back after flowering. Not hardy in the Middle and Upper South.

× *superba* p. 176
Hybrid sage. Herbaceous perennial with upright stems, 18–48 in. high, 3 ft. wide. From late spring through summer, the stems are topped with dense spikes of vivid flowers. 'Mainacht' ('May Night') has deep indigo flowers, 'Blue Queen' rich violet, and 'East Friesland' deep purple. All are drought tolerant. Great plants for the Upper and Middle South.

Sanguinaria
San-gwin-air′ee-uh. Bloodroot
Papaveraceae. Poppy family

Description
One species of perennial wildflower native to woodlands in eastern North America. When broken, the creeping rhizome bleeds a bright red sap.

How to Grow
Bloodroot prefers shade and acid to neutral, moist, well-drained soil containing plenty of organic matter. It will self-sow on bare soil.

canadensis *p. 177*   *Pictured above*
Bloodroot. Herbaceous perennial with showy white flowers, 1–3 in. wide, in early spring. Handsome, deeply lobed foliage, 4–6 in. high, dies back in late summer. 'Multiplex' has double flowers with many petals.

Saponaria
Sap-o-nair′i-a. Soapwort
Caryophyllaceae. Pink family

Description
About 30 species of hardy annual or perennial herbs with showy flowers in loosely branched clusters. Native to the Mediterranean region.

How to Grow
Bouncing Bet is easy to grow in average, well-drained soil in full sun. Propagate by division in spring or fall. Hardy, long-lived, and pest-free.

officinalis p. *177*
Bouncing Bet; soapwort. Herbaceous perennial, stems 1–3 ft. high, topped with dense clusters of small pink or white flowers. Spicy fragrance, especially at night. Native to Eurasia, it has naturalized in this country. Common at old home sites. Var. *flore-pleno,* with double flowers, is good for cutting.

Sarcococca
Sar-ko-kok′a. Sweet box
Buxaceae. Box family

Description
A small genus of Asiatic and Malayan evergreen shrubs; 4 of the 14 known species are planted for ornament. The species below has handsome foliage and fragrant flowers.

How to Grow
Sweet box grows best in moist, humus-enriched soil. The foliage looks good even in deep shade, but flowers and fruits do better in light shade. Protect from winter sun. Slow to establish, the plants spread by suckers. Increase by dividing established clumps. Plant along a path or as a ground cover under high-pruned trees.

hookerana var. *humilis* p. *134*
Sweet box. Low-growing, mounded shrub to 2 ft. high. Narrow, shiny, dark green leaves, 1–3 in. long. White flowers in spring are inconspicuous except for their sweet fragrance. Small black berries. Native to western China. *S. ruscifolia* is bigger (to 3 ft. high and wide) with red fruit, not as hardy as above.

Sedum
See′dum. Stonecrop
Crassulaceae. Stonecrop family

Description
About 600 species of low-growing, chiefly perennial herbs, found throughout the northern hemisphere. Succulent foliage and small flowers in white, yellow, pink, red, or rarely blue.

How to Grow

Sedums are particularly adapted to the rock garden, but a few species can be used in flower borders or as a ground cover. They are easy to grow in average soil in sun or partial shade. Good drainage is essential, particularly in winter. Easily propagated by cuttings taken from spring through fall.

'Autumn Joy' *p. 178   Pictured above*

Autumn Joy sedum. Perennial to 2 ft. high. Plump leaves crowded along succulent stems. Small pink to rusty red flowers in clusters that resemble broccoli heads. Tolerant of moist soil. Cut back halfway in June to keep plants from getting leggy. Rot can be problem in humid summers. Also sold as 'Indian Chief'.

Skimmia

Skim′i-a

Rutaceae. Citrus family

Description

Somewhat tender Asiatic evergreen shrubs, several species grown for their showy flowers and attractive foliage and fruit.

How to Grow

Plant in moist, acid soil with plenty of organic matter. Tolerate partial to full shade.

japonica *p. 134*

Japanese skimmia. Low, densely branching shrub, 3–5 ft. high, often lower. Yellowish green leaves, 3–5 in. long, more or less crowded at the ends of twigs. Small yellowish white male and female flowers, usually on different plants, in spring. Male flowers are larger and very fragrant. Female plants have small bright red berries. You must have both male and female plants to ensure having berries. Native to Japan.

Smilacina
Smy-la-see'na. False Solomon's-seal
Liliaceae. Lily family

Description
About 25 species of herbaceous perennials, native to North America and temperate Asia. Forms dense stands of medium-high leafy stems.

How to Grow
Grow false Solomon's-seal in lime-free, humus-rich soil. It needs partial or full shade, does not tolerate heat. Do not disturb roots after planting. Propagate older plants by division. Long-lived and trouble-free. A showy plant for shady borders.

racemosa p. 178   Pictured above
False Solomon's-seal. Arching stems, to 3 ft. high, are clothed with long slender leaves, topped with showy clusters of bright white flowers. Small red berries are attractive and popular with birds. Native Canada to Virginia and Tennessee; cannot take the heat of the Lower and Gulf South.

Sophora
So-for'ra
Leguminosae. Pea family

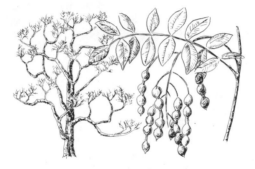

Description

About 50 species of handsome, profusely flowering shrubs or trees native to Asia and North America. The species below is a popular summer-flowering deciduous ornamental tree.

How to Grow

Sophoras grow best in acid or neutral sandy loam soil, in full sun. Established trees are quite hardy and tolerate heat, drought, and air pollution.

japonica p. 96   *Pictured above*

Japanese pagoda tree; Chinese scholar tree. Spreading, round-headed tree, 40–70 ft. high, sometimes more. Compound deciduous leaves, 6–10 in. long. Long drooping clusters of fragrant, cream-colored, pealike flowers are very showy in late summer. Beanlike pods, 3–8 in. long, last all winter. The cultivar 'Regent' grows faster, has better foliage, and blooms at an earlier age. Native to China and Korea. Upper and Middle South.

Spirea

Spy-ree'a. Spirea
Rosaceae. Rose family

Description

Nearly 100 species of handsome flowering deciduous shrubs, mostly from the north temperate zone. Showy clusters of white or pinkish flowers in spring or summer.

How to Grow

Spireas are very easy to grow. They thrive in a variety of soils and all sorts of exposures, with less attention than many other flowering shrubs. Do best in a reasonably moist site in open sunshine. Most species require little pruning. Easy to transplant. They are popular for mixed borders, hedges, and mass plantings.

japonica p. 135
Japanese spirea. Upright shrub, 4–6 ft. high, with delicate twigs. Oval or oblong leaves, 1–4 in. long. Small pale pink flowers in clusters 2–6 in. wide in spring. There are many named cultivars, some with darker rose flowers, some with golden foliage. *S. × bumalda* 'Anthony Waterer' is similar, with bright crimson flowers in mid to late summer and yellow-variegated leaves that turn maroon in fall. Often massed in public landscapes in the Upper and Middle South.

thunbergii
Thunberg spirea. Loose, arching shrub with slender branches, 3–5 ft. tall and wide. Tiny leaves are yellow-green in summer, turn orange-bronze in fall. White flowers in early spring, before the leaves. Prune after flowering to keep shrub neat. Japan and China.

× *vanhouttei* p. 135
Vanhoutte spirea. Slender shrub, 6–8 ft. high, with beautifully arching branches. Oval leaves to 1½ in. long. Small clusters of tiny, pure white flowers in late spring. One of the most commonly cultivated spireas in America, it tolerates city conditions better than most. A tough plant and an old favorite.

Stachys
Stack'iss
Labiatae. Mint family

Description
About 300 species of annual or perennial herbs, most native

to the temperate zones. Some are grown for ornament or herbal use.

How to Grow
Lamb's-ears is easy to grow in very well-drained soil in full sun. It is useful as a border edging or ground cover. Can take dry soil but "melts" in hot, humid weather.

byzantina p. 179 *Pictured above*
Lamb's-ears. Herbaceous semi-evergreen perennial. Forms a low mat of leaves and stems covered with soft, white, woolly hairs. Small purple flowers in dense whorls on stalks up to 18 in. high. Cultivar 'Silver Carpet' does not produce flowers. Native to Caucasus and Iran. Does not do well in the Lower or Gulf South.

Stewartia
Stew-ar'tee-uh
Theaceae. Tea family

Description
About 6 species of deciduous shrubs or small trees with showy white flowers, native to the temperate zones of eastern North America and eastern Asia.

How to Grow
Stewartias prefer light shade and moist, acid, well-drained soil containing plenty of organic matter. Pruning is seldom necessary.

pseudocamellia p. 136
Japanese Stewartia. Small, slow-growing shrub or tree to 25–30 ft. White flowers, 2 in. across, with orange anthers, appear in early summer. Very handsome peeling bark. Leaves turn purple in fall. Needs afternoon shade and well-mulched soil to prevent leaf scorch during summer. Not recommended for Coastal South.

There are several other species of stewartias. *S. monadelpha,* which does well in the South, is a tall shrub or 25-ft. tree with peeling brown bark and 1–1½ in. white flowers. *S. malacodendron,* the silky camellia, is a shrub or small tree, 10–12 ft. high, with white flowers 4 in. wide. It is native to the Coastal Plain and Piedmont of the Southeast.

Stokesia
Sto-kee′zi-a; stokes′i-a
Compositae. Daisy family

Description
A single species of hardy perennial wildflower, native to the Coastal Plain from South Carolina to Louisiana.

How to Grow
Easy to grow in full sun in average well-drained soil; sandy loam is best.

laevis p. 179   *Pictured above*
(Also sold as *S. cyanea*.) Stokes' aster. Herbaceous perennial, stems to 2 ft. high. Handsome flower heads, up to 5 in. wide, are good for cutting. Blooms all summer. Recommended cultivars include 'Alba', with white flowers, and 'Blue Danube', with lavender-blue flowers.

Styrax
Sty′rax
Styracaceae. Storax family

Description
About 100 species of shrubs or small trees with showy white flowers. Native to the warm temperate or tropical regions of the Northern Hemisphere.

How to Grow
Japanese snowbell prefers full sun or light shade and moist, acid, well-drained soil containing plenty of organic matter. Prune after flowering.

japonicus *p. 97*
Japanese snowbell. Small, fine-textured deciduous tree, 20–30 ft. tall. Layered branches have a distinct zigzag pattern. Great profusion of small bell-shaped flowers in late spring or early summer. Handsome orange-brown bark. *S. obassia* is similar, with larger leaves and fragrant flowers. Both are native to Asia. Not recommended for Coastal South.

Syringa
Suh-ring′uh. Lilac
Oleaceae. Olive family

Description
About 30 species of deciduous shrubs or small trees with showy flowers, native to eastern Asia, southeastern Europe, and the Himalayas.

How to Grow
Lilacs prefer full sun and slightly acid to neutral, moist, well-drained soil that contains plenty of organic matter. Prune immediately after flowering.

laciniata
Cutleaf lilac. Large shrub, 8–12 ft. high, with small, finely dissected foliage. Branched clusters of mildly fragrant lavender flowers in midspring. Not susceptible to powdery mildew. Native to China. This is the best lilac for the Lower and Coastal South. Satisfactory blooming reported in Florida. Will grow throughout the South.

meyeri 'Palibin' *p. 136*
Meyer lilac. A handsome lilac with a dense, broad, mounded habit, 4–8 ft. high. Short, branched clusters of violet-purple flowers. One of the best lilacs for total flower effect. Native to China. Best in Upper South.

vulgaris p. 137 *Pictured above*
Common lilac. Handsome, widely cultivated shrub (sometimes
a small tree) to 15 ft. high. Heart-shaped to oval leaves, 2–6
in. long. Clusters, 6–8 in. long, of very fragrant flowers, usually lilac-colored. There are many forms, with white, pink,
blue, and purple flowers. Native to southeastern Europe.
Upper and Middle South.

Taxodium
Tacks-o′di-um
Taxodiaceae. Bald cypress family

Description
Magnificent coniferous trees, one evergreen from Mexico, two
native to the southeastern U.S.

How to Grow
Bald cypress is native to swampy sites. It will grow in dry soil,
but it must be acid; otherwise the foliage may yellow. Best in
full sun. Easy to transplant. Pest-free.

distichum p. 97 *Pictured above*
Bald cypress; southern cypress. Deciduous tree, to 100 ft., but
usually shorter farther north. When growing in moist soil, the
tapering trunk is often buttressed at the base, and the roots
form "cypress knees," thick, woody projections 4–6 ft. high.
Graceful, feathery, light green needles turn russet brown before
dropping in the fall. A handsome specimen tree. Southeastern
native, hardy throughout the region.

Ternstroemia
Tern-stro′mi-a
Theaceae. Tea family

Description
About 85 species of tropical trees and shrubs, one of which is grown for its ornamental foliage.

How to Grow
This shrub does best in sun or partial shade but tolerates heavier shade. In full sun, provide plenty of moisture. Requires acid soil. Pinch out the growing tips to produce compact growth.

gymnanthera p. 137
(Commonly sold as *Cleyera japonica*.) Low-growing evergreen shrub 4–10 ft. high. Glossy, oval leaves, to 3 in. long, are deep green in the shade but almost purple in full sun. Small, fragrant, yellowish flowers in summer. Small yellowish or reddish fruit. Native India to Japan. Not hardy in the Upper South.

Thelypteris
Thuh-lip′ter-is
Polypodiaceae. Polypody family

Description
About 500 species of ferns native to the tropical and warm temperate regions of the world.

How to Grow
These ferns prefer shade and moist, well-drained soil containing plenty of organic matter. They like hot weather and are quite drought tolerant if grown in shade. Tolerate sun if given moist soil. Divide in spring or fall.

kunthii p. 216
Southern shield fern. Deciduous fern, 24–36 in. tall, with light green, fine-textured fronds. Spreads steadily by rhizomes but is not invasive. Good for borders or mass plantings. Easy to grow but not widely available. Native to the Southeast, but not hardy in the Middle and Upper South.

Tiarella
Ty-a-rell'a
Saxifragaceae. Saxifrage family

Description
A small genus of low-growing, spring-flowering, perennial woodland wildflowers.

How to Grow
Foamflower grows best in woodland conditions with moist but well-drained, humus-rich soil in light shade. It will not make a dense cover in deep shade. Propagate by seed or division in the fall. Susceptible to disease in wet springs.

cordifolia p. 180   *Pictured above*
Foamflower; false mitrewort. Mostly evergreen perennial, to 6 in. high, spreading by stolons. Heart-shaped leaves, 3–4 in. wide. Small white flowers in a dense finger-shaped cluster on a slender stem, 8 in. high, in spring. The var. *collina* (sometimes called *T. wherryi*) is taller and clump forming, with showier flowers. Both make attractive ground covers for shady spots. Native Canada to Georgia and Alabama, in the Appalachian Mountains.

Trachelospermum
Tra-kell-o-sper'mum
Apocynaceae. Dogbane family

Description
Some 20 species of Indo-Malayan or Chinese woody vines, most with fragrant, showy flowers.

How to Grow

These plants tolerate a variety of soils with average watering, but are slow to become established. Plant in full sun or partial shade. Prune older plants occasionally to prevent excessive woodiness.

asiaticum p. 193

Asiatic jasmine. Tender evergreen ground cover, generally less than 12 in. high. Leathery dark green leaves, 1–2 in. long. Flowers are infrequent. Useful as a ground cover in the Lower and Gulf South.

jasminoides p. 204 *Pictured above*

Confederate jasmine, star jasmine. Twining evergreen vine can reach 30 ft. high, but is usually much lower. Provide support by training it on a post, wall, or trellis. Can also be grown as a ground cover, but spreads slowly. Oval, evergreen leaves 2–4 in. long. Small white flowers resembling pinwheels are wonderfully fragrant, especially at night. Best in Lower and Gulf South. 'Madison' is more cold-hardy, may survive in Middle South.

Tradescantia

Tray-des-kan'ti-a. Spiderwort
Commelinaceae. Spiderwort family

Description

About 65 species of herbaceous perennials, native to North and Central America. Most have weak, sprawling stems; slender, grasslike leaves; and flowers with 3 showy petals. Popular for flowerbeds and containers.

How to Grow

Spiderworts need well-drained soil and sun or partial shade. They are easy to divide in spring; detached joints of stems will usually root in moist, sandy soil.

× *andersoniana* p. 180

(Often listed as *T. virginiana*.) Common spiderwort. Dense grasslike foliage, 12–24 in. high. Smallish 3-petaled flowers, blue to purple; each lasts only a day, but many are produced. Cut foliage back after flowering to produce a neater clump. Self-sows but is easily controlled by hand weeding. Cultivars include 'Pauline', with pink flowers, 'Zwaanenberg Blue', with blue flowers, and 'Snowcap', with white flowers.

Tsuga
Soo'ga. Hemlock
Pinaceae. Pine family

Description

About 10 species of beautiful evergreen conifers, chiefly from North America and East Asia. The one below is an excellent hedge, screen, or specimen tree.

How to Grow

Hemlocks need cool, well-drained, acid soil and adequate moisture. They do best in full sun but will tolerate full shade. Fare poorly in windy spots with dry summer air, and in dry or alkaline soils. Hemlock casts a dense shade; few plants will grow underneath it.

canadensis p. 98

Canada hemlock; eastern hemlock. Magnificent evergreen tree to 90 ft., usually shorter. Branches droop gracefully in age. Small needlelike leaves, lustrous dark green above, bluish beneath. Small cones. 'Pendula' (also called 'Sargentii') is compact, bushy, usually broader than high, with pendulous branches, one of the most graceful of all plants. Native Canada to Alabama, does best in Upper and Middle South. Used as a specimen tree or for hedging.

Ulmus
Ul'mus. Elm
Ulmaceae. Elm family

Description

Some 18 species of trees, mostly deciduous, all from the north
temperate zone of North America, Europe, and Asia. Excellent
shade trees, broadly upright and high-branching, creating a
canopy of dappled shade.

How to Grow

Elms are easily transplanted and grow in all but very wet or
very dry soils. Best in full sun. Prune young trees to eliminate
narrow crotches, which are likely to split in later years.

parvifolia p. 98   *Pictured above*

Chinese elm; lacebark elm. Small, quick-growing tree, usually
not more than 60 ft. high and inclined to forking. Bark is
attractively mottled and peeling in multicolored patterns, on
some trees better than others. Serrated leaves, 1–2½ in. long,
may turn yellowish or reddish purple in fall. Flowers and fruit
are inconspicuous. Relatively immune to Dutch elm disease.
Many named cultivars are available. Native to East Asia.

Vaccinium
Vak-sin′i-um
Ericaceae. Heath family

Description

Over 150 species of erect or prostrate shrubs, including blueberries and huckleberries. Most have small bell-shaped flowers, leathery leaves, and finely branched twigs. Native from
the Arctic Circle to the summits of tropical mountains.

How to Grow

Plant highbush blueberries in moist, acid soil in sun or partial shade. Use ammonium sulfate fertilizers, not those containing ammonium nitrate. Add sulfur to reduce pH. Use mulch to control weeds; cultivation can damage roots that are close to the surface. Prune plants after fruiting.

corymbosum p. 138
(This species includes plants previously sold as *V. ashei*.) High-bush blueberry. Spreading, bushy shrub, 8–12 ft. high. Oval leaves, 2–3 in. long, turn yellow or red in fall. Small white or pinkish flowers in spring. Bushes are very ornamental, make fine hedges. You can eat the berries if the birds don't get them first. Native to swamps in eastern North America.

Verbena
Ver-bee′na. Vervain
Verbenaceae. Verbena family

Description
About 200 species of tender or hardy annual or perennial herbs, most native to the Americas.

How to Grow
Verbenas are easy to grow, almost weedy, in ordinary soil and full sun. Useful for borders and informal massed plantings.

canadensis p. 194   *Pictured above*
Rose verbena. Herbaceous perennial that forms broad dense mats. Spreading stems reach 8–18 in. high, root where they touch ground. Deeply lobed, sticky-feeling leaves 1–3 in. long. Showy clusters of small, tubular, red to pink flowers from spring to late summer. Native Virginia to Florida.

Veronica
Ver-on'i-ka. Speedwell
Scrophulariaceae. Snapdragon family

Description
More than 250 species of herbaceous perennials, many popular for borders or rock gardens. Some species are upright, others are prostrate and good for ground cover or edging.

How to Grow
Most veronicas are easy to grow in average, well-drained soil, in sun or partial shade. Increase by division after flowering.

spicata p. 181
Spiked speedwell. Perennial, 10–36 in. high, 24 in. wide. Lance-shaped, glossy leaves, 2 in. long. Tiny deep blue to white flowers on small dense spikes for a month or more in summer. There are many cultivars and related hybrids. 'Sunny Border Blue' is highly recommended for the Upper and Middle South. Grows 18–24 in. tall with violet-blue flowers midsummer to fall.

Veronicastrum
Ve-ro-ni-kas'trum
Scrophulariaceae. Snapdragon family

Description
One species of perennial wildflower native to eastern North America. Formerly included in the genus *Veronica*.

How to Grow
Culver's root prefers rich, moist soil and full sun or partial shade.

virginicum p. 181 *Pictured above*
Culver's root; blackroot. Herbaceous perennial, 2–6 ft. high.
A striking plant for the perennial border. Slender leaves in
whorls around the stems. Tiny white flowers in spikes 6–8 in.
long in midsummer. 'Rosea' has pink flowers. Upper and Middle South.

Viburnum
Vy-bur'num
Caprifoliaceae. Honeysuckle family

Description
About 150 species of chiefly deciduous shrubs and small trees
of the north temperate zone. Many are cultivated for their
attractive clusters of spring flowers and their often showy
fruits, which are favorites of birds.

How to Grow
Viburnums are generally easy to grow. They prefer moist, well-
drained, slightly acid soil. Prune after flowering if necessary.

× *carlcephalum* p. 138
Carlcephalum viburnum. Rounded deciduous shrub 6–10 ft.
high and wide. Oval, hairy, dark green leaves, to 4 in. long,
turn reddish purple in fall. Very fragrant white flowers in 5-
in.-wide clusters in late spring. Berries are red, changing to
black. One of the latest viburnums to flower.

'Chesapeake' p. 139
Chesapeake viburnum. A compact shrub, to 6 ft. tall and 10
ft. wide, with glossy, leathery foliage. Pink buds open to showy
white flowers in spring. Red to black berries in fall. A new
cultivar developed by the USDA.

'Eskimo'

Eskimo viburnum. A compact semi-evergreen shrub, to 4–5 ft. tall and wide. Glossy foliage is resistant to leaf spot. Fragrant flowers in 3-in.-wide "snowballs." Another new USDA introduction.

× *juddii* p. 139

Judd viburnum. Rounded deciduous shrub 6–8 ft. high. Very fragrant clusters, about 3 in. wide, of tiny white flowers (pink in bud).

plicatum var. *tomentosum* p. 140   *Pictured above*

Doublefile viburnum. Rounded deciduous shrub, 8–10 ft. high, with horizontal branches. Flat clusters of creamy white flowers lie atop the spreading branches in spring. Berries are red, turning black. Leaves are a striking reddish purple in fall. Makes a very handsome specimen.

tinus p. 140

Laurustinus. Evergreen shrub, 7–10 ft. high and somewhat less wide. Dark green leaves, 2–3 in. long. White or pinkish flower clusters, 3 in. wide, unpleasantly scented, bloom winter to spring. Fruit is blue, turning black. Useful hedge in Lower and Gulf South.

Vinca

Ving′ka

Apocynaceae. Dogbane family

Description

About 12 species of erect or trailing perennial evergreen vines or vinelike shrubs, native to the Old World. Excellent ground covers.

How to Grow

Vinca makes a thick carpet in moderately fertile garden soil.

It tolerates full sun but grows best in light shade. May be sheared annually to encourage dense growth. Easy to propagate by cuttings or division.

major p. 194
Big periwinkle. Trailing evergreen vine, the stems thin and wiry, mounding to 18 in. high, usually lower. Shiny, dark green, heart-shaped leaves and blue flowers, 1–2 in. wide. 'Variegata' has yellowish white leaf margins. Much used in containers and as a ground cover. It is less cold-hardy and more open in growth habit than *V. minor*. Best in Lower and Gulf South.

minor p. 195
Periwinkle; creeping myrtle. Hardy evergreen vine with trailing stems to 10 in. high. Dark green oval leaves to 2 in. long. Small light blue flowers. Good ground cover for shady places. 'Bowles' Variety' has large bright blue flowers; 'Alba' has white flowers.

Viola
Vy-o′la. Violet
Violaceae. Violet family

Description
About 500 species of hardy perennial and annual plants, native to temperate regions. This genus includes violets and pansies.

How to Grow
Violets grow best in rich, moist soil, where they may spread by runners or by self-seeding. Light shade is best. Suitable for shady ground cover, border edging, or naturalizing.

odorata p. 195   *Pictured above*
Sweet violet. Clump-forming perennial to 6 in. high, with long runners. Heart-shaped basal leaves, to 3 in. wide. Sweet-

scented flowers, deep violet or white, open from fall to spring. Spreads to form a ground cover. Named cultivars have deep purple, blue, or white flowers.

Many species of violets are native to the region. One of the most widespread is the Confederate violet (*V. sororia*), a clump-forming violet with woolly leaves and blue-gray flowers. Other native species bloom in shades of white, yellow, blue, and purple.

Vitex
Vy'tex
Verbenaceae. Verbena family

Description
About 270 species of ornamental trees or shrubs found chiefly in the tropical and warmer regions of the world. The species below makes a handsome small tree in the South.

How to Grow
Plant in any good, moist, well-drained soil, in full sun. Prune the tree after flowering, as the flowers appear on new wood.

agnus-castus p. 99
Lilac chaste tree. Deciduous shrub or small tree, 7–20 ft. high. The leaves are compound, with leaflets up to 4 in. long, pleasantly scented when bruised. Fragrant lilac-blue flowers in dense, showy terminal spikes 1 ft. long in summer. 'Alba', with white flowers and larger leaves, is one of the best of the cultivated forms. 'Latifolia' has shorter, broader leaves. Native to Europe.

Vitis
Vy'tis. Grape
Vitaceae. Grape family

Description
A group of woody deciduous vines native to the Northern Hemisphere. They climb by means of tendrils and produce pulpy, edible berries.

How to Grow
Grapes prefer full sun and moist, well-drained soil that con-

tains some organic matter. Provide good air circulation around plants. Propagate by seeds or cuttings.

rotundifolia p. 205   Pictured above
Muscadine grape. Very vigorous, long-lived, disease-resistant grape bearing bronze, reddish, or purple-black fruit. The fruit is used for wine, jelly, jams, pies, fresh eating. To prevent overproduction and poor fruit quality, prune canes back to 8 to 12 buds each in late winter. Will grow throughout the South, except South Florida. Recommended selections include 'Carlos' (reddish) and 'Noble' (purple); both are self-pollinating. Grape vines are very popular for shading patios and arbors or covering trellises and fences.

Weigela
Wy-gee'la
Caprifoliaceae. Honeysuckle family

Description
About 12 species of very handsome Asiatic shrubs, most flowering in late spring.

How to Grow
Weigela is easy to grow in any ordinary garden soil in full sun. Prune after flowering.

florida p. 141
Deciduous shrub 7–10 ft. high, often wider. Elliptical leaves are 4 in. long. Small clusters of funnel-shaped flowers, 1½ in. long, are typically rose-pink, but there are white, pink, and darker forms. Native to Korea and northern China.

Wisteria
Wis-tair′i-a. Wisteria
Leguminosae. Pea family

Description
Beautiful woody vines, 2 species native to the U.S., the other 5 Asiatic, widely grown for their profuse bloom.

How to Grow
Wisteria grows best in fertile, well-drained soil. It tolerates some shade, but flowers best in full sun. Slow to become established, so provide extra fertilizer and water when young. Can be very invasive. May be trained as a single-stemmed or multistemmed vine over a porch, trellis, or dead tree. May also be grown as a small weeping tree or as ground cover. Wisterias require several years to reach blooming size. Discourage excessive vegetative growth by pruning roots and fertilizing with phosphate to promote flowering.

floribunda *p. 205*
Japanese wisteria. Deciduous woody vine, to 30 ft. high. Compound leaves with many oblong leaflets, 2–3 in. long. Violet-blue or violet flowers in clusters nearly 18 in. long, in spring. Selections have been made for white or pink flowers or for length of flower clusters. Chinese wisteria (*W. sinensis*) is similar, with bluish violet flowers in clusters 12 in. long. The native *W. frutescens* has shorter clusters of fragrant pale lilac-purple flowers in June–August. May be hard to obtain.

Yucca
Yuck′a
Agavaceae. Agave family

Description
About 40 species of evergreen succulents, a few cultivated for

their rosettes of tough, leathery, sword-shaped leaves and showy clusters of white or creamy flowers that are often fragrant at night.

How to Grow
Yuccas do best in full sun but will tolerate light shade. Soil should be fast draining. Roots are strong and deep, making yuccas difficult to transplant. Not all plants will bloom every year, so planting in small groups is recommended.

filamentosa p. 141   *Pictured above*
Adam's needle. Long-lived perennial forms clump of evergreen leaves 2–3 ft. long. Flower stalk appears in early summer, reaching 3–5 ft. or higher. Creamy white flowers are 2 in. long. Native to the Southeast.

Zelkova
Zel-ko′va
Ulmaceae. Elm family

Description
Five species of elmlike Asiatic deciduous shrubs and trees. The species below, a neat, hardy shade tree, is free of the pest that plagues many elms.

How to Grow
Zelkova can grow in acid to alkaline soils. It quickly becomes wind and drought tolerant and endures city air reasonably well. Does best in deep, moist soil with mulch and irrigation.

serrata p. 99
Japanese zelkova. Vase-shaped when young, rounded with age, often umbrellalike. Grows to about 70 ft. in a century. Leaves are sharply toothed, 2–3 in. long, turning purplish in fall. Named cultivars such as 'Green Vase' have the best growth forms.

Appendices

Pests and Diseases

It's said that in this life, there's no free lunch. And that certainly applies to gardening. For every prized flower, fruit, or vegetable you harvest, you can bet a bug, blight, or bacterium has its eyes on the next one.

Controlling such pests is especially difficult in the South. The long growing season encourages insects to reproduce faster and more often. Insects that produce a single generation per year in Maine may go through four generations in Florida. Moreover, fungal diseases have a field day in the South, thanks to the high number of warm, humid days. And as if all this weren't bad enough, a number of imported, foreign insects — fire ants, Asian tiger mosquitoes, and "killer bees" — have either invaded the South already or will do so shortly.

Despite this grim scenario, you can win the fight against garden pests. The key is to determine what you're up against, then apply the proper control.

We can generally separate garden pests into four categories: insects and mites, nematodes, diseases, and environmental stresses.

Insects and Mites

More bugs plague the Southern garden than the average person cares to hear about. But the most common ones, those most likely to show up in your yard, can be controlled. The best way to begin is to divide them into groups according to how they feed.

Chewers. Grasshoppers, caterpillars, and beetles, for instance, are chewing insects. They chomp away on leaves and stems, like a Doberman presented with a juicy steak. If their numbers are small, you can pick them off by hand. Otherwise, you can spray their intended meal with a stomach insecticide, which kills when ingested. Carbaryl, malathion, and diazinon are stomach insecticides. They also kill on contact. For caterpillars, you may also want to try *Bacillus thuringiensis,* a biological insecticide that's completely nontoxic to humans, animals, and bees.

Tunnelers, borers, and suckers. Leafminers make tunnels inside leaves. To inhibit them, spray the plant with a systemic insecticide, such as Orthene or Cygon, that's absorbed into plant tissue. Borers chew their way through the insides of branches and stems. Stomach and systemic insecticides applied to plant surfaces may keep young borers from entering, but once they are inside the plant, most chemicals don't work. Aphids, scales, and mealybugs suck the juice from plants, as do spider mites. Most stomach and systemic insecticides work against sucking pests. But the safest control is insecticidal soap.

Nematodes

Nematodes are microscopic roundworms; some species attack roots, while others attack leaves. Either usually results in poor plant growth. Nematodes are an especially serious problem in the coastal South and Florida, infesting vegetables, fruit trees, roses, and even lawns. While nematicides or soil sterilants may be called for in extreme cases, the best ways to foil nematodes are to plant nematode-resistant selections and to rotate susceptible crops every year. You may also want to try Clandosan, a recently introduced natural control. Don't move plants from infested areas to clean soil. You'll only spread the pests.

Diseases

Diseases make themselves known in a variety of ways. They can show up as leaf spots, blights, mildews, or wilts. Leaf spots look just like their name and may be black, brown, purple, or orange. Often, they result in defoliation. Blights cause entire stems, shoots, and branches to wither suddenly. Just to confuse things, they can also appear as leaf spots. Mildews usually form grayish, powdery layers on plant surfaces. They distort and destroy leaves and flowers. Wilts induce entire plants suddenly to shrivel and die. They usually enter plants from the soil.

Gardeners rely on a wide variety of fungicides to treat plant diseases. One of the oldest, safest, and most reliable is garden sulfur. However, it's easily washed off by rain and has no residual action. Before using any other fungicide, first identify the disease pest, then carefully read the fungicide's label to see whether this product will control it.

Environmental Stresses

Occasionally, plant damage that at first appears caused by an insect or disease turns out to be the fault of the environment. Winter cold, summer heat and drought, salt spray, air pollution, nutrient deficiencies, poor drainage, high winds, and lawn mower injury can all make plants suffer. The best way to avoid such problems is to learn as much as you can about the growing conditions each plant prefers and match them as closely as possible.

Sanitation: A Clean Garden Is a Healthy Garden

Good sanitation will go a long way toward reducing problems with insects, mites, nematodes, and diseases. First, remove and destroy infested leaves, stems, and fruits (don't compost them). This will remove eggs and spores that could result in future infestations. Second, eradicate weeds near your garden — they often harbor insects and diseases. Third, thin your plants so that air and light can easily pass through the canopy of leaves. Fourth, remove and destroy withered leaves, stems, and fruits from plants at the end of the growing season. Finally, when using hand pruners or loppers to remove diseased stems and branches, disinfect the tool after each cut. Dip it in a solution of a cup of bleach to a gallon of water.

Pesticides Do's And Don'ts

Pesticides, when used correctly, can greatly benefit the home gardener. Unfortunately, most people have no idea of what chemical they're spraying or what its effects can be. As a result, they produce more problems than they solve. To be sure you use pesticides properly, safely, and effectively, follow these guidelines.

Always read the label. The label tells you what pests a particular product controls, how much to use, when to spray, and what precautions to take.

Know what pest you're spraying. Fungicides won't kill insects and insecticides won't kill fungi. Don't expect a single product to control everything.

Apply pesticides only when there is a problem. Coating plants with pesticides won't eliminate problems. Unfortunately, the overuse of pesticides leads to resistant, "super" insects and fungi that are nearly impossible to control. So spray only when you see a pest, not before.

Use natural controls if possible. Natural controls have fewer environmental repercussions. They include biological controls, such as *Bacillus thuringiensis;* natural pesticides, such as insecticidal soap, rotenone, Clandosan, pyrethrin, and garden sulfur; row covers; and beneficial insects, such as ladybugs, lacewings, and parasitic wasps.

Don't spray flowers. Doing so may kill honeybees, which pollinate countless trees, shrubs, vegetables, and flowers. Spray in early morning or late afternoon, when bees aren't active.

Wear protective clothing. This includes rubber gloves and boots, long pants and a shirt, and a mask over your nose and mouth.

Learn to accept a few bugs or leaf spots. A totally insect- and fungus-free environment isn't natural. As long as we don't upset the balance, the environment will keep most pests from becoming a plague.

A Final Word of Advice

The best way to limit the number of insects, mites, nematodes, and diseases in your garden is to avoid growing plants susceptible to these pests. There are many hundreds of annuals, perennials, shrubs, vines, vegetables, fruits, and trees available today. Pick the ones that have the least problems — ask your nurseryman or county agricultural extension agent if you're not sure. You'll be glad you did.

Sources of Seeds and Plants

Gardeners in the South are fortunate in having a great many regional nurseries from which to buy plants. There are so many, in fact, that we can mention only a fraction. We encourage you to seek out local nurseries, where the staff will be familiar with the plants and problems of your area. Some of the nurseries listed below sell only through the mail; others sell on site. Some have display gardens open to the public. Some sell a wide range of plants, others are more specialized. We have indicated this information in each entry (see the key), but you should call the nursery to confirm it before ordering plants or making a trip there.

Key:
[S]: seeds
[P]: plants
MO: mail order
Nu: on-site sale
Gdn: display garden
appt: some restriction on visits, call for appointment

Alabama

Heritage Lawn and Garden Center [P,S]
3420 Old Columbiana Rd.
Birmingham, AL 35226
205 822-3172
Nu

Magnolia Nursery & Display Garden [P]
12615 Roberts Rd.
Chunchula, AL 36521
205 675-4696
Southeastern native plants
Catalog: $2
MO, Nu (appt), Gdn (appt)

Plant Odyssey [P,S]
3000 Clairmont Ave.
Birmingham, AL 35205
205 324-0566
Nu

Village Arbors [P]
1804 Saugahatchee Rd.
Auburn, AL 36830
205 826-3490
Herbs and perennials for the South
Nu, Gdn

Wayside Nursery and Garden Center [P,S]
2247 Montgomery Highway
Pelham, AL 35124
205 988-9171
Nu

Delaware

Winterthur Museum and Gardens [P]
Kennet Pike, Rte. 52
Winterthur, DE 19735
302 888-4600
Catalog: $1
Heirloom, rare, and unusual perennials, shrubs, and trees
MO, Nu

Florida

Native Nurseries [P,S]
1661 Centerville Rd.
Tallahassee, FL 32308
904 386-8882
Nu, Gdn

Tallahassee Nurseries [P,S]
2911 Thomasville Rd.
Tallahassee, FL 32312
904 385-2162
Nu, Gdn

Georgia

Eco-Gardens [P]
P.O. Box 1227

Decatur, GA 30031
404 294-6468
Native and exotic plants hardy in Piedmont region
Catalog: $1
MO, Nu (appt), Gdn (appt)

Goodness Grows, Inc. [P]
P.O. Box 311
Highway 77 North
Lexington, GA 30648
404 743-5055
Wide variety of perennials and herbs
Nu, Gdn

Hastings Nature and Garden Center [P,S]
2350 Cheshire Bridge Rd., N.E.
Atlanta, GA 30324
404 321-6981 or 800 334-1771 (mail order)
Full-service garden center
Catalog: free
MO, Nu

Piccadilly Farm [P]
1971 Whippoorwill Rd.
Bishop, GA 30621
404 769-6516
Hostas, hellebores, perennials
Catalog: $1
MO, Nu (appt), Gdn (appt)

Thomasville Nurseries, Inc. [P]
P.O. Box 7
1840-42 Smith Ave.
Thomasville, GA 31799
912 226-5568
Roses, daylilies, azaleas, and liriopes
MO, Nu, Gdn

Transplant Nursery [P]
Rte. 2, Parkertown Rd.
Lavonia, GA 30553
404 356-1658
Catalog: $1
MO, Nu, Gdn

TyTy Plantation [P]
P.O. Box 159
Highway 82

TyTy, GA 31795
912 386-1919
Cold-hardy plants for the South
Catalog: free
MO, Nu, Gdn

Kentucky

Dabney Herbs [P,S]
P.O. Box 22061
Louisville, KY 40252
502 893-5198
Variety of plants including natives
Catalog: $2
MO

Louisiana

Louisiana Nursery [P]
Rte. 7, Box 43
Opelousas, LA 70570
318 948-3696
Many plants; specialize in magnolias, daylilies, Louisiana irises
Catalog: $5 (also 2 other, more specialized catalogs)
MO, Nu, Gdn

Maryland

Behnke Nurseries [P,S]
11300 Baltimore Ave.
Beltsville, MD 20705
301 937-4037
Full-service garden center
Nu

Carroll Gardens [P]
P.O. Box 310
444 E. Main St.
Westminster, MD 21157
301 848-5422 or 800 638-6334
All types of plants, including unusual and hard-to-find
Catalog: $2
MO, Nu, Gdn

Cavano's Perennials, Inc. [P]
6945 Sunshine Ave.
Kingsville, MD 21087

301 592-2377
Perennials, herbs, ferns, wildflowers, daylilies, grasses
Nu

Crownsville Nursery [P]
P.O. Box 797
Crownsville, MD 21032
301 923-2212
Variety of perennials
Catalog: $2
MO

Homestead Gardens, Inc. [P,S]
P.O. Box 189
Central Ave.
Davidsonville, MD 21035
301 261-4550
Nursery and garden center
Nu, Gdn

Kurt Bluemel, Inc. [P,S]
2740 Greene La.
Baldwin, MD 21013
301 557-7229
Ornamental grasses and other plants
Catalog: $2
MO

Lilypons Water Gardens [P]
P.O. Box 10
6800 Lilypons Rd.
Buckeystown, MD 21717-0010
301 874-5133
Water-garden plants and supplies
Catalog: $5
MO, Nu, Gdn

Meyer Seed Co. [P,S]
600 S. Caroline St.
Baltimore, MD 21231
301 342-4224
Plants that do well in the Baltimore/Washington area
Catalog: free
MO, Nu

Valley View Farms [P,S]
11035 York Rd.
Cockeysville, MD 21030

301 527-0700
Full-service garden center
Nu

Wicklein's Aquatic Farm and Nursery [P,S]
1820 Cromwell Bridge Rd.
Baltimore, MD 21234
301 823-1335
Aquatic plants and hard goods
Catalog: $4
MO, Nu (appt), Gdn (appt)

Mississippi

Flower Place Plant Farm [P]
P.O. Box 4865
Meridian, MS 39304
601 482-5686
Broad range, some old-fashioned Mississippi plants
Catalog: $2
MO

North Carolina

Camellia Forest Nursery [P]
125 Carolina Forest Rd.
Chapel Hill, NC 27516
919 967-5529
Shrubs and trees; camellias, other Asian plants
Catalog: $1
MO, Nu (appt)

Holbrook Farm & Nursery [P]
P.O. Box 368
115 Lance Rd.
Fletcher, NC 28732
704 891-7790
Variety of perennials and native wildflowers
Catalog: $2
MO, Nu, Gdn

Montrose Nursery [P]
P.O. Box 957
Hillsborough, NC 27278
919 732-7787
Perennials suited to the Southeast, specializing in cyclamen
species

Catalog: $2
MO, Gdn (appt)

Niche Gardens [P]
1111 Dawson Rd.
Chapel Hill, NC 27516
919 967-0078
Southeastern wildflowers, native plants, and others
Catalog: $3
MO, Nu (appt), Gdn (appt)

Sandy Mush Herb Nursery [P,S]
Rte. 2, Surrett Cove Rd.
Leicester, NC 28748
704 683-2014
Herbs and variety of other plants
Catalog: $4
MO, Nu (appt), Gdn (appt)

We-Du Nurseries [P]
Rte. 5, Box 724
Marion, NC 28752-9338
704 738-8300
Rock garden, rare and woodland plants, wildflowers
Catalog: $2
MO, Nu (appt), Gdn (appt)

South Carolina

Coastal Gardens & Nursery [P]
4611 Socastee Blvd.
Myrtle Beach, SC 29575
803 293-2000
Variety of perennials
Catalog: $2
MO, Nu (appt), Gdn (appt)

The Greenery [P,S]
P.O. Box 6569
960 William Hilton Parkway
Hilton Head, SC 29938
Full-service garden center
803 785-3848
Nu

Martin Nursery [P]
198 Martin Rd.
Greenville, SC 29607

803 277-1818
Full-service garden center
Nu

Park Seed Co. [P,S]
Cokesbury Rd.
Greenwood, SC 29647-0001
803 223-7333
Wide selection
Catalog: free
MO, Nu, Gdn

Wayside Gardens [P]
Hodges, SC 29695-0001
800 845-1124
Variety of plants
Catalog: free with phone call
MO

Woodlanders, Inc. [P]
1128 Colleton Ave.
Aiken, SC 29801
803 648-7522
Southeastern native and adapted plants
Catalog: $1
MO, Nu (appt), Gdn (appt)

Tennessee

Mouse Creek Nursery [P]
Rte. 2, Bell Springs Rd.
Riceville, TN 37370
615 462-2666
Perennials for the Southeast
Nu, Gdn

Native Gardens [P,S]
5737 Fisher La.
Greenback, TN 37742
615 856-3350
Nursery-propagated native plants
Catalog: $2
MO, Nu (appt), Gdn (appt)

Owen Farms [P]
Rte. 3, Box 158-A
Curve-Nankipoo Rd.
Ripley, TN 38063
901 635-1588 (6–9 p.m. CST)

Trees, shrubs, perennials
Catalog: $2
MO, Nu (appt), Gdn (appt)

Sunlight Gardens [P]
Rte. 1, Box 600-A
Andersonville, TN 37705
615 494-8237
Perennials, native shrubs, nursery-propagated southeastern wildflowers
Catalog: $2
MO, Nu (appt)

Texas

Antique Rose Emporium [P]
Rte. 5, Box 143
Brenham, TX 77833
409 836-9051
Old garden roses, companion perennials
Catalog: $5
MO, Nu, Gdn

Wildseed, Inc. [S]
P.O. Box 308
Eagle Lake, TX 77434
409 234-7353 or 800 848-0078
Seeds of native grasses and wildflowers
Catalog: free
MO, Nu (appt), Gdn (appt)

Yucca Do Nursery [P]
P.O. Box 655
Waller, TX 77484
409 826-6363
Native Texas plants and their Mexican and Asian counterparts
Catalog: $3
MO

Virginia

Andre Viette Farm and Nursery [P]
Rte. 1, Box 16
Fishersville, VA 22939
703 943-2315
Wide variety of perennials
Catalog: $2
MO, Nu, Gdn

Thomas Jefferson Center for Historic Plants [S]
Monticello
P.O. Box 316
Charlottesville, VA 22902
804 979-5283
Historic flowers, fruit trees, heirloom vegetables
Catalog: free
MO, Nu, Gdn

West Virginia

Wrenwood of Berkeley Springs [P]
Rte. 4, Box 361
Berkeley Springs, WV 25411
304 258-3071
Herbs and perennials
Catalog: $2
MO, Nu, Gdn

Public Gardens

One of the best ways to learn about plants and garden design is to see superb examples firsthand. Here is a selection from the many excellent possibilities the region has to offer. Be sure to phone or write ahead for opening times, admission fees, and travel directions.

Alabama

Auburn University Arboretum
Garden St.
Auburn, AL
205 844-5770
13 acres, native Alabama trees and shrubs

Birmingham Botanical Garden
2612 Lane Park Rd.
Birmingham, AL 35223
205 879-1227
67 acres, many displays

Huntsville-Madison County Botanical Garden
4747 Bob Wallace Rd.
Huntsville, AL 35805
205 830-4447
112 acres, variety of displays

Jasmine Hill
P.O. Box 6001
Jasmine Hill Rd. off Highway 231
Montgomery, AL 36106
205 263-1440
17 acres, was private garden

Delaware

Hagley Museum and Library
298 Buck Rd.
Box 3630
Wilmington, DE 19807

302 658-2400
Includes restored early-19th-century French-style garden
on 2 acres

Nemours Mansion and Gardens
P.O. Box 109
Wilmington, DE 19899
302 651-6912
300 acres: Versailles in America

Winterthur Museum and Gardens
Kennet Pike, Rte. 52
Winterthur, DE 19735
302 888-4600
200 acres of naturalized gardens

District of Columbia

Dumbarton Oaks
1703 32nd St. N.W.
Washington, D.C. 20007
202 338-8278
16 acres of garden "rooms"

Old Stone House
3051 M St. N.W.
Washington, D.C.
202 426-6851
Beautiful perennial borders, English-style garden

United States Botanic Garden
Maryland Ave. and First St. S.W.
Washington, D.C.
202 225-7099
Many displays

United States National Arboretum
3501 New York Ave. N.E.
Washington, D.C. 20002
202 475-4815
444 acres; over 100 gardens and collections

Florida

Maclay State Gardens
3540 Thomasville Rd.
Tallahassee, FL 32308
904 487-4556
28 acres of azaleas, camellias, other gardens

Georgia

Atlanta Botanical Garden
P.O. Box 77246
Piedmont Park
Atlanta, GA 30357
404 876-5858
60 acres, many displays

Callaway Gardens
U.S. Highway 27 S.
P.O. Box 2000
Pine Mountain, GA 31822
404 663-2281
2,500 acres, azaleas and much else

Founders Memorial Garden
325 S. Lumpkin St.
Athens, GA 30602
No phone
2½ acres, various gardens

State Botanical Garden of Georgia
2450 S. Milledge Ave.
Athens, GA 30605
404 542-1244
313 acres at University of Georgia, many gardens

Kentucky

Bernheim Forest Arboretum
Highway 245
Clermont, KY 40110
502 543-2451
10,000 acres; landscape arboretum has 1,800 labeled varieties
of trees and shrubs

Lexington Cemetery
833 W. Main St.
Lexington, KY 40508
606 255-5522
170 acres, various gardens, 200 species of trees

Louisiana

American Rose Center
8877 Jefferson Paige Rd.
P.O. Box 30,000

Shreveport, LA 71130
318 938-5402
118 acres, 20,000 rosebushes, 500 camellias

Hodges Garden
P.O. Box 900
Many, LA 71449
318 586-3523
60 acres of formal gardens

Longue View Gardens
7 Bamboo Rd.
New Orleans, LA 70124
504 488-5488
8 acres, formal and small gardens

Maryland

Brookside Gardens
1500 Glenallan Ave.
Wheaton, MD 20902
301 949-8230
50 acres, many gardens

Cylburn Arboretum and Park
4915 Greenspring Ave.
Baltimore, MD 21209
301 396-0180
176 acres, including wildflower garden

Ladew Topiary Gardens
3535 Jarrettsville Pike
Monkton, MD 21111
301 557-9466
22 acres, topiary and other gardens

William Paca Garden
1 Martin St.
Annapolis, MD 21401
301 267-6656
Recreated 18th-century urban garden

Mississippi

Crosby Arboretum
3702 Hardy St.
Hattiesburg, MS 39402
601 261-3137
64 acres, native plants and trees

Mynelle Gardens
4736 Clinton Blvd.
Jackson, MS 39209
601 960-1812
6 acres, many gardens

Wister Gardens
Highway 7 N.
P.O. Box 237
Belzoni, MS 39038
601 247-3025
14 acres, many displays

North Carolina

Biltmore House and Gardens
1 N. Pack Sq.
Asheville, NC 28801
704 274-1776
Large estate, formal gardens

Botanical Gardens at Asheville
151 W. T. Weaver Blvd.
Asheville, NC 28802
704 252-5190
10 acres, native plants in natural setting

North Carolina Botanical Garden
Old Mason Farm Rd.
P.O. Box 3375
Totten Center—UNC
Chapel Hill, NC 27599
919 962-0522
300 acres of native southeastern plants

North Carolina State University Arboretum
4301 Beryl Rd.
Raleigh, NC 27607
919 737-3133
8 acres, woody ornamentals, large perennial border and other
gardens

Reynolda Gardens of Wake Forest University
100 Reynolda Village
Winston-Salem, NC 27106
919 759-5593
130 acres, natural and formal plantings

Tryon Palace
610 Pollock
P.O. Box 1007
New Bern, NC 28563
919 638-5109
Recreated colonial English garden

Oklahoma

Tulsa Municipal Rose Garden
21st St. and S. Peoria Ave.
Tulsa, OK
918 749-6401
4½ acres of roses

U.S. Southern Great Plains Field Station
2000 18th St.
Woodward, OK 73801
405 256-7449
Trees, shrubs, wildflowers

South Carolina

Brookgreen Gardens
1931 Brookgreen Gardens Dr.
Murrells Inlet, SC 29576
803 237-4218
35 acres, botanical garden and wildlife refuge

Clemson University Botanical Garden
Perimeter Rd.
Clemson University
Clemson, SC 29634
803 656-4964
250 acres, many gardens

Middleton Place
Ashley River Rd.
Charleston, SC 29407
803 556-6020
100 acres; oldest landscaped garden in America

Tennessee

Memphis Botanic Garden
750 Cherry Rd.
Memphis, TN 38117
901 685-1566
88 acres, many gardens

Tennessee Botanical Gardens and Fine Arts Center
1200 Forrest Park Dr.
Nashville, TN 37205
615 356-8000
55 acres, many gardens

Texas

Dallas Arboretum and Botanical Garden
8525 Garland Rd.
Dallas, TX 75218
214 327-8263
22 acres, Texas and southeastern natives

Dallas Civic Garden Center
Martin Luther King Blvd.
P.O. Box 152537
Dallas, TX 75315
214 428-7476
7½ acres, formal and other gardens

Fort Worth Botanic Garden
3220 Botanic Garden Blvd.
Fort Worth, TX 76107
817 870-7686
114 acres, formal and informal gardens

Houston Civic Garden Center
1500 Hermann Dr.
Houston, TX 77004
713 529-5371
Various gardens

Mercer Arboretum and Botanic Gardens
22306 Aldine-Westfield Rd.
Humble, TX 77338
713 443-8731
12 developed acres, native plants, irises, daylilies

San Antonio Botanical Center
555 Funston Pl.
San Antonio, TX 78209
512 821-5115
33 acres, formal gardens, native plantings

Tyler Municipal Rose Garden
P.O. Box 2039
West Front and Rose Park

Tyler, TX 75710
903 531-1377
22 acres, roses galore

Virginia

Agecroft Hall
4305 Sulgrave Rd.
Richmond, VA 23221
804 353-4241
17th-century gardens

American Horticultural Society
River Farm
7931 East Blvd. Dr.
Alexandria, VA 22308
703 768-5700
25 acres, All-America Selections Display Gardens

Colonial Williamsburg
P.O. Box C
Williamsburg, VA 23187
804 229-1000
90 acres, many recreated gardens of the 1700s

Gunston Hall
10709 Gunston Rd.
Lorton, VA 22079
703 550-9220
1-acre plantation garden, 1750 restoration

Maymont
1700 Hampton St.
Richmond, VA 23220
804 358-7166
100 acres, many gardens

Monticello
P.O. Box 316
Public Affairs Dept.
Charlottesville, VA 22902
804 295-2657
Jefferson's gardens recreated

Norfolk Botanical Garden
Airport Rd.
Norfolk, VA 23518
804 441-5830
175 acres, native plants and other displays

Oatlands
U.S. Rte. 15 S.
Rte. 2, Box 352
Leesburg, VA 22075
703 777-3174
4 acres, formal English garden

West Virginia

Core Arboretum
Monongahela Blvd.
West Virginia University, Evansdale Campus
Curator
Dept. of Biology
P.O. Box 6057
Morgantown, WV 26506-6057
304 293-4794
50 acres, mostly natural woodland, some specimen plantings

The Greenbrier
White Sulphur Springs, WV 24986
800 624-6070, 304 536-1110
12 acres of gardens at famous resort

References

Happily, the number of books about regional gardening has increased in recent years. The advantage of a regional approach, of course, is that you share with the author climate and conditions as well as the gardening bug. The following books are, with a few exceptions, all regional in scope. Available in bookstores, through mail-order catalogs, or at the library, they will make a valuable addition to your basic gardening texts. Contact your state extension service for a list of the many informative books and pamphlets they publish.

Barton, Barbara J. *Gardening by Mail III: A Source Book.* Boston: Houghton Mifflin, 1990.

Foote, Leonard E., and Samuel B. Jones, Jr. *Native Shrubs and Woody Vines of the Southeast: Landscaping Uses and Identification.* Portland, Ore.: Timber Press, 1989.

Halfacre, R. G., and A. R. Shawcroft. *Landscape Plants of the Southeast.* Raleigh, N.C.: Sparks Press, 1988.

Harper, Pamela, and Fred McGourty. *Perennials: How to Select, Grow and Enjoy.* Los Angeles: HP Books, 1985.

Heutte, F. *Gardening in the Temperate Zone.* Norfolk, Va.: Donning Co.

Hunt, William L. *Southern Gardens, Southern Gardening.* Durham: Duke University Press, 1982.

Jones, Samuel B., Jr., and Leonard E. Foote. *Gardening with Native Wildflowers.* Portland, Ore.: Timber Press, 1990.

Ladendorf, Sandra F. *Successful Southern Gardening: A Practical Guide for Year-Round Beauty.* Chapel Hill: University of North Carolina Press, 1989.

Lawrence, Elizabeth. *A Southern Garden: A Handbook for the Middle South,* rev. ed. Chapel Hill: University of North Carolina Press, 1984.

Sperry, Neil. *Neil Sperry's Complete Guide to Texas Gardening*. Dallas: Taylor Publishing, 1982.

Odenwald, Neil, and James Turner. *Identification, Selection and Use of Southern Plants for Landscape Design*. Baton Rouge, La.: Claitor's Publishing Division (P.O. Box 3333, Baton Rouge 70821), 1987.

Wasowski, Sally, and Julie Ryan. *Landscaping with Native Texas Plants*. Houston: Texas Monthly Press, 1985.

Wasowski, Sally, and Andy Wasowski. *Native Texas Plants: Landscaping Region by Region*. Houston: Pacesetter Press, 1988.

Welch, William C. *Perennial Garden Color for Texas and the South*. Dallas: Taylor Publishing (1550 W. Mockingbird La., Dallas 75235), 1989.

Photo Credits

John E. Bryan, Inc.
86A

Rita Buchanan
83A, 85A, 153B, 166B

Al Bussewitz: Photo/Nats
74B, 104B, 118A, 119B

David Cavagnaro
76A, 82A, 84B, 119A, 165B, 203A, 208, 211B

Michael A. Dirr
80A, 87B, 205A

John E. Elsley
95A, 185B

Thomas E. Eltzroth
96A, 98B, 118A, 127A, 135A, 194B, 201A

Derek Fell
75A, 75B, 78B, 79B, 80B, 84A, 94A, 94B, 97B, 99A, 102B,
106A, 113A, 116B, 121A, 122A, 123A, 129B, 139A, 140A,
141A, 147B, 170A, 170B, 184A, 193A, 195A

Charles Marden Fitch
110B, 128B, 132B, 138A, 200B, 204B

Pamela Harper
72, 81A, 81B, 82B, 83B, 86B, 87A, 89A, 89B, 90A, 90B, 91B,
92A, 93B, 97A, 100, 103B, 105B, 107A, 107B, 108B, 109A,
109B, 110A, 111A, 111B, 112A, 112B, 113B, 114A, 114B,
120A, 120B, 124A, 125A, 125B, 126A, 126B, 128A, 129A,
130A, 130B, 131A, 132A, 133B, 134A, 135A, 135B, 136A,
137A, 137B, 138B, 140B, 141B, 142, 144A, 144B, 145A,
146B, 147A, 148A, 148B, 149A, 150B, 151A, 151B, 152B,
153A, 155A, 156A, 157A, 157B, 158A, 159A, 159B, 160B,

161B, 162B, 163A, 164A, 164B, 167A, 167B, 168A, 169A,
171A, 171B, 172A, 172B, 173B, 174A, 174B, 175A, 175B,
176A, 177B, 178B, 179A, 179B, 181A, 181B, 182, 184B,
186A, 186B, 188A, 188B, 189A, 189B, 190A, 190B, 191A,
192A, 193B, 195B, 196, 198B, 199A, 199B, 202A, 203B,
204A, 206, 209B, 210A, 210B, 213A, 213B, 215A, 215B

Walter H. Hodge
122B, 134B

Saxon Holt
92B, 93A

Horticultural Photography, Corvallis, Oregon
91A

Sam Jones
85B, 103A, 117B, 131B, 155B, 158B, 161A, 162A, 169B,
177A, 180A, 194A, 208A, 209A, 211A, 212A, 216A, 216B

Philip E. Keenan
88A

Robert E. Lyons: Photo/Nats
98A, 185A

Frederick McGourty
191B, 212B

Steven M. Still
74A, 76B, 77A, 77B, 78A, 79A, 88B, 95B, 99B, 102A, 105A,
104A, 106B, 108A, 115A, 115B, 116A, 117A, 121B, 124B,
127B, 136B, 139B, 145B, 146A, 149B, 150B, 152A, 154A,
154B, 156A, 160A, 163B, 165A, 166A, 168B, 173A, 187B,
176B, 178A, 180B, 192B, 198A, 200A, 201B, 202B, 205B,
214A, 214B

George Taloumis
96B, 123B, 187A

Index